INDONESIA
Democracy
and the
Promise of Good
Governance

The **Research School of Pacific and Asian Studies (RSPAS)**, a part of the **ANU College of Asia and the Pacific** at **The Australian National University**, is home to the **Indonesia Project**, a major international centre of research and graduate training on the economy of Indonesia. Established in 1965 in the School's Division of Economics, the Project is well known and respected in Indonesia and in other places where Indonesia attracts serious scholarly and official interest. Funded by the ANU and the Australian Agency for International Development (AusAID), the Indonesia Project monitors and analyses recent economic developments in Indonesia; informs Australian governments, business and the wider community about those developments and about future prospects; stimulates research on the Indonesian economy; and publishes the respected *Bulletin of Indonesian Economic Studies*.

The School's **Department of Political and Social Change** (PSC) focuses on domestic politics, social processes and state–society relationships in Asia and the Pacific, and has a long-established interest in Indonesia.

Together with PSC and RSPAS, the Project holds the annual Indonesia Update conference, which offers an overview of recent economic and political developments and devotes attention to a significant theme in Indonesia's development. The Project's *Bulletin of Indonesian Economic Studies* publishes the economic and political overviews, while the proceedings related to the theme of the conference are published in the Indonesia Update Series.

The **Institute of Southeast Asian Studies (ISEAS)** was established as an autonomous organization in 1968. It is a regional centre dedicated to the study of socio-political, security and economic trends and developments in Southeast Asia and its wider geostrategic and economic environment.

The Institute's research programmes are the Regional Economic Studies (RES, including ASEAN and APEC), Regional Strategic and Political Studies (RSPS), and Regional Social and Cultural Studies (RSCS).

ISEAS Publishing, an established academic press, has issued almost 2,000 books and journals. It is the largest scholarly publisher of research about Southeast Asia from within the region. ISEAS Publishing works with many other academic and trade publishers and distributors to disseminate important research and analyses from and about Southeast Asia to the rest of the world.

Indonesia Update Series

INDONESIA
Democracy and the Promise of Good Governance

EDITED BY

Ross H. McLeod
Andrew MacIntyre

ISEAS

INSTITUTE OF SOUTHEAST ASIAN STUDIES
Singapore

First published in Singapore in 2007 by
ISEAS Publishing
Institute of Southeast Asian Studies
30 Heng Mui Keng Terrace
Pasir Panjang
Singapore 119614

E-mail: publish@iseas.edu.sg
http://bookshop.iseas.edu.sg

ISEAS Library Cataloguing-in-Publication Data

Indonesia : democracy and the promise of good government / edited by Ross H.
    McLeod and Andrew MacIntyre.
    Based on the 24th annual Indonesia Update Conference held at the Australian
    National University in 2006.
    1. Indonesia—Politics and government—1998-—Congresses.
    2. Decentralization of government—Indonesia.
    3. Justice, Administration of—Indonesia.
    4. Civil society—Indonesia—Congresses.
    I. McLeod, Ross H., 1946-
    II. MacIntyre, Andrew J., 1960-
    III. Indonesia Update Conference (2006 : Canberra, Australia)
DS644.4 I41 2006   2007

ISBN 978-981-230-466-7 (soft cover)
ISBN 978-981-230-459-9 (hard cover)
ISBN 978-981-230-467-4 (PDF)

Copy edited and typeset by Beth Thomson, Japan Online, Canberra
Indexed by Angela Grant, Sydney
Printed in Singapore by Utopia Press Pte Ltd

CONTENTS

LIST OF TABLES AND FIGURES

TABLES

FIGURES

LIST OF CONTRIBUTORS

Sharon Bessell
Senior Lecturer, Crawford School of Economics and Government, Australian National University, Canberra

Simon Butt
Associate Director, Asian Law Group Pty Ltd, Melbourne

Ron Duncan
Foundation Executive Director, Pacific Institute of Advanced Studies in Development and Governance, University of the South Pacific, Suva, and Professor Emeritus, Crawford School of Economics and Government, Australian National University, Canberra

Andrew Ellis
Director of Operations, International Institute for Democracy and Electoral Assistance (IDEA), Stockholm

I Ketut Putra Erawan
Lecturer, Department of Government and Graduate Program of Local Politics and Regional Autonomy, Gadjah Mada University, Yogyakarta

Natasha Hamilton-Hart
Associate Professor, Southeast Asian Studies Programme, National University of Singapore, Singapore

Andrew MacIntyre
Director, Crawford School of Economics and Government, Australian National University, Canberra

Ross H. McLeod
Associate Professor, Indonesia Project, Division of Economics, Research School of Pacific and Asian Studies, Australian National University, Canberra, and Editor, *Bulletin of Indonesian Economic Studies*

Benjamin Reilly
Director, Centre for Democratic Institutions, Australian National University, Canberra

Arskal Salim
Senior Lecturer, Faculty of Syariah and Law, Syarif Hidayatullah State Islamic University, Jakarta, and Postdoctoral Fellow, Max Planck Institute for Social Anthropology, Halle/Saale

Staffan Synnerstrom
Governance Advisor, Asian Development Bank, Indonesia Resident Mission, Jakarta

ACKNOWLEDGMENTS

This book is based mainly on papers presented at the annual Indonesia Update conference held on 22–23 September 2006 at the Australian National University (ANU), Canberra. Like the book, the theme of the conference was 'Democracy and the Promise of Good Governance'. The Update conferences always lead off with updates on economics and politics. In 2006, the former was presented by M. Chatib Basri and Arianto Patunru and the latter by Rodd McGibbon. Both papers have been published separately in the December 2006 issue of the *Bulletin of Indonesian Economic Studies*. Two additional papers, one by Sharon Bessell and the other by Benjamin Reilly, were specially commissioned for inclusion in this volume. The conference was very well attended. The speakers, commentators and session chairs, all of them experts in their fields, were from Indonesia, Australia and other countries.

We are grateful for the financial and logistical support provided by the Australian Agency for International Development (AusAID) and the Research School of Pacific and Asian Studies (RSPAS) at the ANU, without which neither the conference nor the publication of this volume would have been possible. We wish to specifically thank Karen Guest, Trish van der Hoek and Liz Drysdale from the Indonesia Project in the Division of Economics, and Anne Looker and Thuy Pham from the Department of Political and Social Change, both in RSPAS, for their involvement in organising the 2006 Indonesia Update. We also thank Traci Smith for her assistance with the media, Yogi Vidyattama for looking after all the visual presentations, and a committed group of other student volunteers for helping with logistics. The Chancellor of the ANU, Dr Alan Hawke, gave us his support and kindly delivered the opening address at the conference. Chris Manning, Head of the Indonesia Project, provided valuable advice and encouragement in assembling the conference program. It goes without saying that we are grateful to the loyal and enthusiastic audience that attends the Indonesia Updates.

In editing the manuscript for the book, we were very fortunate to benefit from the professionalism of Beth Thomson. We also thank Angela Grant for compiling the index. We are grateful to the Institute of Southeast Asian Studies in Singapore for again agreeing to publish the latest volume in the Indonesia Update series.

Finally, we thank the authors of the papers contained in this book for their cooperation in preparing their first drafts within the specified deadline, and for revising these drafts in accordance with comments received at the conference and beyond. But most of all we thank them for providing us all with an intellectually stimulating set of discussions of some of the many problems faced by a country such as Indonesia as it struggles to negotiate the twists and turns along the road to sustainable, effective, democratic government.

Ross H. McLeod and Andrew MacIntyre
Canberra, April 2007

GLOSSARY

ADB	Asian Development Bank
aliran kepercayaan	traditional beliefs
aqidah	articles of faith, belief, theology
aurat	those parts of the body that must be kept covered in public
Bappenas	Badan Perencanaan Pembangunan Nasional (National Development Planning Agency)
BKM	Bantuan Khusus Murid (Special Assistance for Students)
BKN	Badan Kepegawaian Negara (National Civil Service Agency)
BKPM	Badan Koordinasi Penanaman Modal (Investment Coordinating Board)
BOS	Bantuan Operasi Sekolah (School Operation Assistance)
dakwah	preaching, predication, Islamic outreach
Darul Islam	House of Islam; a revolutionary Islamic movement that fought between 1948 and 1963 to make Indonesia an Islamic republic
dinas	specialised government unit
DJBPUPTUN	Direktur Jenderal Badan Peradilan Umum dan Peradilan Tata Usaha Negara (Director General for the General and Administrative Courts)
DPD	Dewan Perwakilan Daerah (Council of Regional Representatives)
DPR	Dewan Perwakilan Rakyat (People's Representative Council), Indonesia's parliament
eksaminasi	examination (to determine judicial competence)

fatwa	Islamic legal opinion on socio-religious matters
formasi	establishment plan (approved allocation of positions within an Indonesian civil-service institution)
Forum Nasional Usaha Kecil Menengah	National Association of Small and Medium-sized Enterprises
FPI	Front Pembela Islam (Islamic Defenders Front)
GBHN	Garis-garis Besar Haluan Negara (Broad Guidelines of State Policy)
Golkar	Golongan Karya (Functional Groups), the state political party under the New Order, and one of the major post-New Order parties
gotong royong	mutual assistance
Hizbut Tahrir	Liberation Party
ibadah	worship, religious observances and rituals
IBRA	Indonesian Bank Restructuring Agency
IDEA	Institute for Democracy and Electoral Assistance
Ikatan Hakim Indonesia	Indonesian Judges' Association
IMF	International Monetary Fund
Inpres	Instruksi Presiden (Presidential Instruction), a program of special grants from the central government)
Jamsostek	Jaminan Sosial Tenaga Kerja (Workers Social Security)
JC	Judicial Commission
kabupaten	district
Kadin	Kamar Dagang dan Industri (Chamber of Commerce and Industry)
khalwat	unlawful proximity between unmarried or unrelated couples
Komisi Yudisial	Judicial Commission
kota	municipality
KPK	Komisi Pemberantasan Korupsi (Anti-Corruption Commission)
KPU	Komisi Pemilihan Umum (General Election Commission)
LAN	Lembaga Administrasi Negara (Institute of National Administration)
LeIP	Lembaga Kajian dan Advokasi untuk Independensi Peradilan (Institute for an Independent Judiciary)

LK3	Lembaga Kajian Keislaman dan Kemasyarakatan (Institute for the Study of Islam and Society)
LPD	*lembaga perkreditan desa* (village credit institution)
Mahkamah Agung	Supreme Court
Mahkamah Konstitusi	Constitutional Court
maksiat	immoral act
MenPAN	Kementerian Negara Pendayagunaan Aparatur Negara (State Ministry for Administrative Reform)
MMI	Majelis Mujahidin Indonesia (Council of Indonesian Mujahideen)
MPR	Majelis Permusyawaratan Rakyat (People's Consultative Assembly)
MTEF	medium-term expenditure framework
Muhammadiyah	modernist Islamic organisation founded in 1912
MUI	Majelis Ulama Indonesia (Indonesian Council of Ulama)
negara hukum	law state
New Order	the Soeharto era, 1966–98
NGO	non-government organisation
NU	Nahdlatul Ulama (traditionalist Islamic organisation founded in 1926)
PAH I	Panitia Ad Hoc I (Ad Hoc Committee I)
pamswakarsa	civilian security force, vigilante group
PAN	Partai Amanat Nasional (National Mandate Party)
Pancasila	the five guiding principles of the Indonesian state (belief in Almighty God, humanitarianism, nationalism, democracy and social justice)
Partai Demokrat	Democratic Party
PBB	Partai Bulan Bintang (Crescent Moon and Star Party)
PDI-P	Partai Demokrasi Indonesia-Perjuangan (Indonesian Democratic Party of Struggle)
PDR	Partai Daulat Rakyat (People's Sovereignty Party)
perda	*peraturan daerah* (regional regulation)
perpu	*peraturan pemerintah pengganti undang-undang* (government regulation in lieu of legislation)

pesantren	Islamic boarding school
petrus	*penembakan misterius* (mysterious shootings)
PKB	Partai Kebangkitan Bangsa (National Awakening Party)
PKS	Partai Keadilan Sejahtera (Justice and Welfare Party)
PPP	Partai Persatuan Pembangunan (United Development Party)
preman	thug, standover man
puskesmas	*pusat kesehatan masyarakat* (community health centre, local public clinic)
reformasi	reform
Repelita	Rencana Pembangunan Lima Tahun (Five-year Development Plan)
satu atap	'one-roof' (reforms)
SBY	Susilo Bambang Yudhoyono
SC	Supreme Court
sharia	Islamic law
Shi'a Islam	the second largest branch of Islam after Sunni
SMERU	Social Monitoring and Early Response Unit
Sunni	the majority branch of Islam
surat edaran	circular
susduk	*susunan dan kedudukan* (composition and status [of elected state bodies])
Susenas	Survei Sosio-Ekonomi Nasional (National Socio-economic Survey)
syiar Islam	Islamic festival, any activity that glorifies Islam (such as the celebration of Islamic holidays)
ulama	Islamic scholar
UN	United Nations
US	United States
USSR	Union of Soviet Socialist Republics
zakat	wealth tax

Currencies

$	US dollar
Rp	Indonesian rupiah

1 INTRODUCTION

Ross H. McLeod and Andrew MacIntyre

Ten years ago the Asian financial crisis devastated the Indonesian economy and unleashed far-reaching political change. In the wake of Soeharto's fall there was great optimism about what democratic governance would bring for Indonesia. As with many other much anticipated and hard-fought political struggles, there was more than a little romanticism about it all, and the results achieved thus far have fallen short of the more optimistic expectations. Indeed, around the world the process of democratisation has been long and messy, and frequently marked by disappointments, setbacks and outright reversals.

In this volume we seek to take stock of both Indonesia's progress in establishing and refining a democratic framework of governance, and the extent to which this is yielding satisfactory outcomes. There will, of course, be a range of opinions on these issues within Indonesia and internationally, but two distinctive contributions that analysts can make are to help establish realistic expectations or bases for comparison, and to highlight areas where governance arrangements are not working well or where there may be scope for further refinement.

Undoubtedly, a large part of mankind's material progress may be attributed to the invention of government: a set of mechanisms for collective decision making and action for the common good. At the same time, however, the coercive power of government has very often been used for the benefit of those who exercise that power, rather than the general public they supposedly represent. Developing countries around the world have often seen *coups d'état*, the purpose of which is either to gain access to the potential spoils of office, or to deprive an existing government of those spoils. The stakes are so high that this is often literally a matter of life and death. In the aftermath of the attempted coup in 1965 in Indonesia, for example, hundreds of thousands of communists and their alleged supporters were murdered in order to ensure that this group would never again be a serious contender for power—and also, arguably, as a warning to others of the fate that threatened if they had any ideas about wresting power from the incoming regime.

During his three decades in power, President Soeharto and his close family amassed a fortune widely estimated to amount to several billion dollars. Given that savings from his official salary could only have been trivially small by comparison, this clearly reflects what is meant by 'the spoils of office'. The challenge for society is to design systems of government that will ensure that the interests of society as a whole are promoted effectively, while the conflicting interests of the individuals charged with implementing government are kept in check. This is the essence of 'good governance'. The management of all large and complex organisations, whether they be universities, corporations or governments, needs to be delegated to a relatively small group of people who are supposed to carry out the wishes of those who entrust them with operational authority, and they, in turn, delegate to a larger number of individuals to implement decisions. But once such people are appointed to positions of authority within the organisation, there is always the possibility—indeed the strong likelihood—that they will be tempted to use these positions to further their own interests, over and above the salaries and other formally specified remuneration they receive by virtue of those positions. No large organisation can expect to be successful in the long term unless mechanisms are set up to deal with the so-called principal–agent problem: how to ensure that those delegated with operational authority do indeed carry out the wishes of those who entrusted and empowered them with this authority.

In 1998, as the Soeharto regime crumbled, few focused on this issue. Understandably, attention was consumed by celebration at the breaking of authoritarian rule and the establishment of something more democratic in its place. Questions of governmental effectiveness seemed unimportant compared with the widespread desire to ensure that Indonesia did not return to a system of unchecked presidential power. Soeharto had held the country in an iron grip for more than 30 years, and a significant part of the population had come to greatly resent the seemingly limitless greed of his family and cronies. While his demise was cause for widespread euphoria at the time, and while there is justifiable pride in the fact that Indonesia has subsequently been able to stage many elections successfully at the national and subnational levels, in many other respects the results of the great democratic reform have failed to live up to popular expectations. Socio-economic conditions have been a source of particular disappointment, and the issue of effective governance has come ever more sharply into focus.

Economic performance suffered greatly during the financial crisis that led to Soeharto's downfall, and has yet to recover to the levels achieved under his rule. The annual rate of economic growth has been closer to 5 per cent than the average 7.4 per cent under the New Order, which has very significant implications for the rate of increase in per capita income. Unemployment is high and poverty no longer declining. Investment relative to the size of the economy is significantly lower than it had been, suggesting that a return to the previous rates of growth is unlikely to occur on a sustained basis in the near future. The high level of corruption under Soeharto still exists, and is arguably even more damaging these days, because it is fragmented, incoherent and no longer under the careful control of a dominant president.

These kinds of observations can be interpreted in different ways. Optimistic observers argue that post-Soeharto Indonesia has done surprisingly well given the magnitude of the challenges it faces, that nearly all of the crisis-affected countries in East Asia have been doing less well than before the crisis and that we should not be too impatient for more impressive results. Others argue that democracy will not survive unless it brings forth significant material progress for the people of Indonesia — and fairly soon. Most people have little interest in politics and government; they are much more concerned about their standard of living, and about their ability to survive when things go wrong. They worry about being able to send their children to school; about their ability to cope with significant illness or injury within the family; about how they may be affected by floods and fires, natural disasters and economic shocks. They worry about their vulnerability to theft, extortion and violence, and to state-sanctioned expropriation of their assets. They worry about the prevalence of catastrophic accidents in the transportation sphere, with trains running off the rails, ferries sinking, planes and buses crashing, and so on.

THE VULNERABILITY OF YOUNG DEMOCRACIES

Once well established, democracy proves to be a remarkably resilient framework of government. This was the essence of Churchill's famous quip about democracy being the worst form of government — apart from all the others that have been tried. Careful work by Przeworski et al. (1996) confirms that democracy is highly durable above a certain economic threshold. This reminds us, however, that democracies in poorer countries, which are typically also young democracies, are vulnerable to all sorts of challenges. The performance of governments in terms of delivering social and economic advancement is critical for legitimacy and political survival. Prolonged failure to meet minimal public expectations invites the possibility of not just the fall of a particular government, or even a series of particular governments, but the breakdown of democracy more broadly. Chronic and severe underperformance not only begets mounting public dissatisfaction, but opens the door to ambitious political actors — often in the security forces — who may seek to take advantage of the situation and seize power themselves. Thus it would be dangerous to be complacent about governance in a young democracy such as Indonesia.

Important progress has been made in reforming Indonesia's framework of government since 1998, but major challenges remain. We cannot simply assume that there will be a steady upward trend of improved governance. A quick survey of the region is enough to demonstrate the fragility of democracy. The Philippines rid itself of the dictator Marcos in 1986, and has elected a series of governments since then, but it has also seen the movie star president Estrada dislodged by the military and replaced by Arroyo-Macapagal. In Thailand, reformers were pleased with the constitutional reforms introduced in 1997. Nevertheless, the excesses of the Thaksin government were such that the Thai military staged a bloodless coup in 2006 to get rid of the fabulously wealthy businessman–prime minister, and was still clinging to power at the time of writing. Further to the east, democratically elected governments in Fiji have been toppled by the country's military on more than one occasion — again notwithstanding redesign of the country's constitution to try to create conditions in which governments can be democratically elected and replaced. And in East Timor, the region's youngest nation, democracy is under serious strain.

In Indonesia itself, the available evidence suggests that while there are concerns about the slow pace of progress, public commitment to democracy remains solid. The clearest indicators of this are that voter turnout for elections continues to be very strong by international standards, and that senior military and police officials with political ambitions continue to play within the constitutional framework. There have been some public rumblings by retired military officers that President Yudhoyono should step down on grounds of inadequate progress, but to date such statements have achieved little wider traction. More broadly, while small groups of religious extremists have sought to impose their policy preferences on society through violent action, Indonesians of all religious denominations have opted overwhelmingly to accept the constraints of democracy and the imperative for compromise. Nevertheless, ongoing commitment to democracy cannot simply be taken for granted. Effective governance is an important pre-condition.

For governments everywhere, a key performance variable is the extent to which they are able to advance the economic welfare of citizens. Without this, discontent rises — particularly in situations where the public has become accustomed to significant economic advancement and expects it to continue. Achieving sustained rapid economic progress is a very difficult task for any type of government, as many of the necessary policies are hard to implement. The politics of policies that advance the public economic good — whether they be stable macroeconomic management, minimising monopolistic and other restrictive trade practices, improving the investment climate, lifting agricultural productivity or achieving better educational outcomes — are inherently difficult. Policies of this sort have widespread benefits, but often face highly focused political opposition from narrowly based groups whose interests will be disadvantaged by them. As the large literature on the political economy of policy reform reminds us, because the costs of adjustment are concentrated and the benefits widely dispersed, narrowly based interests threatened by changes to policy are much more likely to mobilise effectively to oppose those changes than are broadly based public interest groups to mobilise to support them.

DEMOCRACY AND EFFECTIVE GOVERNANCE

In any political system, it is a great challenge to fight off vested interests of one sort or another and maintain a policy environment that is conducive to strong economic growth. In Indonesia today, it is not uncommon to hear people say that for all his faults, unlike his democratically elected successors, Soeharto did at least deliver real economic progress for the overwhelming majority of Indonesians. The 'inconvenient truth' (to borrow Al Gore's clever phrase) is that the Indonesian economy grew rapidly and consistently during the three decades of the New Order. In general, the people prospered under Soeharto, notwithstanding the fact that his family and cronies prospered disproportionately, and that opponents of the regime were subject to severe consequences.

Thus, some point to Singapore and China, wondering whether centralised politics might not be a pre-condition for effective national economic governance. Reference to the record of economic underachievement in more democratic states, such as the Philippines for most of the post-Marcos years and Papua New Guinea for much of the post-independence period, would sharpen the contrast further. However, the notion of a causal connection between authoritarian politics and strong economic growth does not stand up to scrutiny. One need only think on the one hand of India's economic success today or that of, say, Mauritius, and on the other hand of the dismal economic failures of many African dictatorships or, indeed, Indonesia under Soekarno's Guided Democracy, to recognise that the issue is not at all straightforward. Notwithstanding examples to the contrary, systematic studies provide little support for the notion that authoritarian politics begets economic success.[1]

The fact that the rich countries of the world (oil-rich nations aside) are overwhelmingly democracies alerts to us to the fact that democracy certainly has qualities consistent with economic success. The great virtue of democracies is that they guarantee freedom of speech, freedom of movement and freedom of assembly, all of which underpin political contestation and thus the fundamental accountability of governments for their performance. It is this check on managerial incompetence and capricious and arbitrary rule that ultimately favours the implementation of sound economic policies over time.

In wrestling with the topic of good governance, rather than focusing at the level of democracies versus non-democracies, it is more instructive to dig deeper and look at the extent to which a country's political architecture either concentrates or disperses decision-making power (MacIntyre 2003). There is wide variation across the full spectrum of political systems, including very considerable variation among democracies. While there is no generally agreed optimal configuration of power, there are characteristic governance pathologies associated with political frameworks that lie towards either extreme of the continuum. Political frameworks that disperse decision-making power widely tend to suffer from chronic problems of indecisiveness or gridlock: that is, it is very difficult for them to make decisions on major policy questions in a timely fashion, because not all constitutionally empowered actors are in agreement. At the other end of the spectrum, countries whose political architecture severely concentrates power are certainly able to take difficult decisions speedily, but the absence of constitutional checks is associated with a lack of predictability about the future policy environment, since dramatic change is possible at any time. In addition, decisions arrived at quickly are not necessarily sensible; policy issues are often not clear-cut, and the quality of decision making is likely to improve, to some extent, if a wider range of perspectives must be considered.

It is not a coincidence that the political systems of most of the advanced industrial democracies today are located away from the extremes of this continuum, and clustered towards the middle. In contrast, those of developing countries are more likely to be found towards either end of the spectrum. Indonesia has undergone major change in its political architecture since the fall of Soeharto. Where power was radically centralised under the constitutional framework of the New Order,

---

1 See, for example, Bueno de Mesquita et al. (2001), Gerring et al. (2005), Przeworski (2004) and Rodrik and Wacziarg (2005).

with no effective institutional checks on presidential legislative power, this changed dramatically with the first wave of post-Soeharto democratic reforms. Suddenly, not only did the president have to bargain over legislation with a highly fragmented legislature, but his ability to do so was acutely constrained by the fact that the legislature could actually dismiss the president. Indonesia thus swung from a situation in which the president had virtually unlimited power to one in which—during the Habibie and Wahid administrations—the president could do very little. Subsequent rounds of constitutional and electoral reform have led to further change, with the president now enjoying a strengthened position *vis-à-vis* the legislature by virtue of having more secure tenure, and a likely trend towards fewer and larger political parties. In the immediate post-Soeharto years, Indonesia's national political architecture was almost unworkable, but subsequent rounds of constitutional refinement have opened up at least the possibility of tolerably effective government. Nevertheless, whether effective government is in fact forthcoming depends on a range of other factors, including the attributes of those in leadership positions and the policy preferences of those supporting them. Weak, lazy or inept leaders are likely to produce disappointing results, whatever the institutional framework.

Indonesia has been experiencing an ongoing process of institutional reform since 1998 in its search for effective governance within a democratic framework, at both the national and subnational levels. Important though the progress has been, there is still much that needs to be done. Indeed, one only has to think about the continuing evolution of basic institutions of governance in older democracies, such as the United Kingdom, the United States or even Australia or Japan, to be reminded that there is in fact no ultimate 'end-point'. Societies seek continuously to adapt their institutions in response to changing circumstances and changing needs, and Indonesia is no exception.

TOWARDS CONSOLIDATING INDONESIA'S DEMOCRACY

Indonesia has resolved—at least for now—some of the primary institutional choices pertaining to the structure of government, most notably the relationship between the executive branch and the legislature; the way elections are organised and the type of party system that will result; and the division of labour between national and subnational levels of government. But there is unfinished business here, as well as a range of important issues that have not yet been addressed. For instance, the status and role of the second parliamentary chamber, the Council of Regional Representatives (DPD), is still the subject of debate; reform of the civil service has hardly begun; and judicial reform has a very long way to go.

What should be the status of the DPD? Members of the House of Representatives (DPR) jealously guarded their own power when they insisted that the DPD's mandate be limited to regional matters and, even there, that the DPD be given only consultative rights rather than full veto rights over legislation. Is this appropriate? Should the DPD have full legislative powers like the Senate in the United States, and thereby provide a further institutional check on legislation? Or, given the existing challenges of forging agreement between the executive and the multi-party DPR, would this be a recipe for legislative gridlock more severe even than in the Philippines? This goes directly to the question of the extent of dispersal or concentration of power in a country's political architecture. Where countries such as the United States, Australia and the Philippines have powerful second chambers, others, such as the United Kingdom, Canada, Malaysia and Thailand, have weak second chambers with no real legislative veto power. The DPR is likely to resist having to share its legislative prerogatives with the second chamber, but members of the DPD are unlikely to let the matter rest.

Arguably even more important than further refinement of the political architecture is far-reaching reform of Indonesia's civil service. The bureaucracy was crucial to the Soeharto system of government, but with a few exceptions, such as broad macroeconomic management, it did far too little to devise policies that would serve the public interest. Rather, its function was to implement policies that would benefit companies owned by Soeharto's cronies and family members, together with a relatively small number of large foreign firms. Beyond this, the main role played by the bureaucracy was to extort rents from smaller domestic and foreign firms and the general population, rather than to serve them by providing such things as sound physical and legal infrastructure. The bureaucracy left behind by Soeharto is clearly incapable of performing the role required of it in a new democracy.

The second institution of crucial importance to democracy (outside the electoral system and the structure of government itself) is the judiciary. The judiciary is an essential element for the enforcement of laws, the enactment of which is a very important part of why societies create governments. As well as this, it serves to protect the general public against abuse of government power. Individuals need to be able to have recourse to the courts when they feel that their rights have been infringed by the state itself. Under Soeharto, however, the judiciary was more the instrument of the regime than a constraint on it. It was used to deflect any legal challenge to the regime, and to emasculate its opponents by putting them in jail. Outside the realm of affairs of state, judges were more or less free to sell favourable decisions to contending parties, such that firms and individuals went to considerable lengths to avoid ever finding themselves dependent on the courts. In such a system, judges had little incentive to hone their legal skills and their understanding of complex legal issues. As a consequence, the entire legal system became increasingly atrophied over the long years of the New Order. This is another part of the Soeharto legacy that is in dire need of reform, yet this need has been largely overlooked, notwithstanding the creation of a new Constitutional Court and an independent Judicial Commission.

Both the judiciary and the legislature are now largely independent of the executive; to a not inconsiderable extent, they can control what the executive does. But this is a two-edged sword. Ideally, the checks and balances provided by the judicial and legislative branches of government are exercised on behalf of the people, but in practice they can also be exercised on behalf of the incumbents themselves, just as Soeharto exercised executive power in his own interest. Indeed, members of both these branches moved quickly after Soeharto left office to cash in on opportunities for self-aggrandisement that had previously been much more limited. Stories soon began to appear in the media of legislators in well-tailored suits being driven to parliament in expensive cars. And when the Indonesian Bank Restructuring Agency (IBRA) attempted to seize assets from the owners of conglomerates whose banks had failed, leaving the government to bail out their depositors, the judges who heard these cases found themselves sitting on a gold mine—which they exploited with such vigour that IBRA simply gave up on the courts as a means of asset recovery. Corruption aside, competence is the major issue. It will take years to make good the steady decline in competence of the judiciary that occurred during the New Order, so the grounds for optimism in relation to the new Constitutional Court and the new independence of the judiciary do not seem particularly strong.

OUTLINE OF THE VOLUME

The financial turmoil that struck Indonesia in 1997 dislodged Soeharto from his position of near absolute power, ushering in an era of democracy in that country. But to the extent that democracy requires not only fair systems for electing the people's representatives, but also a legislature, a bureaucracy and a judiciary characterised by both competence and integrity, Indonesia's democratic reform still appears to have a long way to go. The intention of this book is not to call into question the objective of creating a genuinely democratic system of government in Indonesia. Rather, our purpose is to look more deeply into what is required if those efforts are to be successful and sustainable, drawing to some extent on comparisons with other countries in the region and elsewhere.

The chapters that follow discuss the architecture of government at both the national and regional levels, bearing in mind the dramatic changes in the overall system of government that have occurred since the fall of Soeharto — including decentralisation from the beginning of 2001. They also discuss various aspects of the actual and desirable roles of government: the extent of intervention in the workings of markets; the role of the state in managing natural resources and the environment, and in protecting disadvantaged members of society; and the interactions of government with private business and organised religion. Finally, they focus on the functioning of two of the most important institutions of democracy — the bureaucracy and the legal system — and the clearly evident need for far-reaching reform.

Part I: Forming and Reforming the Architecture of Governance

The first section of the book focuses on the design and operation of Indonesia's new democracy, giving particular emphasis to national and regional political architecture. The ongoing process of refining Indonesia's political institutions is of fundamental importance, since these institutions set the framework in which all the day-to-day battles over policy at the national and regional levels are fought out. In short, the institutional design of a country's political architecture sets the rules for the political game and thereby exerts an important — even if often invisible — influence on politics and policy.

In Chapter 2, Andrew Ellis presents an overview of the major changes to Indonesia's constitution between 1999 and 2002, in the context of experience elsewhere in the developing world. He assesses the preparations for and implementation of the 2004 elections, including such elements of the electoral legislation as the electoral system and the encouragement of the representation of women. He discusses the performance of key elements of the new institutional framework since 2004, including relations between the executive and the legislature, the DPD, the Constitutional Court and the judicial system, and makes some initial comparisons with reference to existing writing on the fundamental issues of whether and how presidential democracies can succeed. Finally, he compares the broadly elite-driven, negotiated constitution-building process in Indonesia with other approaches to constitution building worldwide, noting that the lack of a widely participative process can have advantages as well as drawbacks.

In a short period, Indonesia underwent dramatic constitutional change, but the political window of opportunity for further major institutional reform has been narrowing since 2004. Increasingly, the emphasis has been on making the agreed new frameworks function satisfactorily rather than tinkering with them further. Ellis concludes by highlighting an element of ambiguity in Indonesia's new constitutional framework: the shared nature of legislative power. Will either the presidency or the DPR seek to challenge this, and tilt the balance more decisively in its own favour? He judges that the DPR would face greater obstacles than the presidency in attempting such a change.

In Chapter 3, Benjamin Reilly focuses on the crucial role of political parties in democratic political systems. With democratisation, the operational controls on Indonesia's political parties and the ban on the establishment of new political parties – both essential features of Soeharto's monopoly on power – were lifted, resulting in a rapid proliferation of parties. Subsequent electoral reform has been designed to reshape the party system by encouraging fewer, larger parties. Reilly looks at this process from a comparative perspective, situating the Indonesian reforms in a broader Asian context. He finds that what has been happening with Indonesia's political parties and electoral system post-Soeharto is part of a broader trend towards overt political engineering evident across the Asia-Pacific region as a whole. In his analysis, the design of legislation on political parties has been greatly concerned to diminish the impact of ethnic and regional cleavages in Indonesian society, to which end parties intending to contest elections, even at the regional level, are required not only to have secured a certain minimum percentage of votes or seats in parliament at the previous election, but also to have widespread branch representation throughout the country. As Reilly puts it, 'political reformers in Indonesia have attempted to engineer the development of a few large parties with a national reach' (p. 52). But there is a trade-off here. 'If ethnic or religious groups are unable to mobilise and compete for political power by democratic means, they may seek to achieve their objectives in other ways. A balance therefore needs to be struck between encouraging national parties … and restricting regional ones …' (p. 53). Clearly, the reformulation of the rules governing political parties is still a work in progress, and it will be a while yet before firm judgments can be made about the success or otherwise of what has been done so far. But it does appear that the underlying objective of attempting to promote national cohesion through careful design of the party system parallels trends elsewhere in Asia.

In many parts of the developing world, there have been recent moves to devolve power from national to subnational units of government. In Indonesia, this was an early part of the political reform process; decentralisation was seen as essential both to promoting democracy and preserving national integrity. In Chapter 4, I Ketut Putra Erawan takes a critical look at the gains and losses associated with decentralisation so far. Since it was launched in 2001, decentralisation has become one of the most important state reform programs, and has changed drastically the landscape of central–local government political relationships.

Recent studies of the impact of decentralisation reveal a wide range of perceptions, however. Some highlight the consequences of local government capture and rampant corruption; others focus on the deepening of democracy and emergence of effective government. Research efforts to date have produced findings of governance innovation ranging from best practice to worst case scenarios. Erawan uses several case studies to highlight the range of political factors affecting the ability of local leaders to deliver policy reforms designed to tackle local problems. After noting the way in which initial conditions constrain the options available to leaders, he goes on to show how the extent to which they are able to build workable legislative majorities as well as wider networks of support within society for their policy priorities has a big bearing upon their prospects for implementing reform.

Part II: The Roles of Government

The second section of the book is concerned mainly with what governments do. It looks at changes that have occurred since 1998, questions some aspects of current practice and makes suggestions about what might be more appropriate.

Drawing on the literature on new institutional economics, in Chapter 5 Ron Duncan and Ross McLeod provide an explanation of how the highly corrupt Soeharto regime was able to generate high-level economic performance. They argue that the informal rules in existence in that era more than adequately satisfied the needs of the privileged firms in the modern sector that were driving economic growth. At the same time, the more traditional sectors of the economy, which were much less involved in innovative activity, had very little need of the formal institutions whose responsibility it was to ensure security of property and enforcement of contracts. The consequences of Soeharto's demise have been more severe for the 'insider' firms that had prospered under his protection, but now found themselves vulnerable to a corrupt and incompetent bureaucracy and judiciary. They responded by shifting assets overseas, which, for the most part, they have yet to repatriate—hence the failure of investment to recover, and the consequent relatively slow rates of economic growth achieved following the initial recovery from the crisis of the late 1990s.

The authors argue that the main focus of *reformasi* has been redesigning the political architecture so as to facilitate the public's participation in political processes, while attention to reforming other main parts of the public sector—particularly the bureaucracy, the judiciary and the state-owned enterprises—has been inadequate thus far. They go on to delineate the appropriate scope of government activity, asking, in effect: what *should* governments do, as distinct from they what do they *actually* do? They argue for a change in the predominant belief system that drives much economic policy making in Indonesia and, in particular, for a more sophisticated understanding of the need for the public sector to complement the private sector, rather than competing with it, holding it back with red tape, or telling it how to go about its business. The discussion extends to the provision of public goods and physical infrastructure, the exploitation of natural resources and the environment, income redistribution, and the general requirement that government remain neutral between firms, industries and sectors of the economy.

The business sector has two main ways of seeking to influence government policy to its benefit: individual businesses may seek to cultivate close, mutually beneficial ties with politicians and bureaucrats, or groups of businesses may form associations of some kind in order to undertake lobbying on behalf of them all. In Chapter 6, Natasha Hamilton-Hart discusses these alternatives. She argues that although both forms of activity often benefit the owners of businesses at public expense, it is also possible—and more likely in the second case—that business interests will coincide with those of the general public. Business associations had very little real influence on policy while Soeharto was in power, and non-transparent, close relationships of a limited number of big businesses with government were of key importance in determining policy towards the private sector. Indeed, as Hamilton-Hart says, 'some business owners (or their families) simultaneously held public positions and were thus able to influence policy from inside the government for personal gain' (p. 95). In subsequent years, business associations—particularly the Chamber of Commerce and Industry (Kadin)—have been playing a much more active role, yet they have still to become as influential as might be desirable.

One explanation for this is that although business now speaks with a stronger voice in the new democratic environment, it is also obliged to compete with various other interest groups, including newly influential labour organisations and many NGOs with strongly anti-business inclinations. Moreover, the old way of doing things, in which individual businesses cultivated close relationships with government officials, persists. Hamilton-Hart argues in favour of encouraging the role of business associations as vehicles for the collective, transparent representation of business interests, since this is likely to limit the extent to which government policy panders to individual firm interests. But, recognising that the behaviour of the business community reflects the environment in which it finds itself, she believes that reducing corruption in the bureaucracy and judiciary is likely to be more important. In turn, the political mechanisms through which government is held accountable for its own behaviour by the wider public will be crucial in determining the extent to which government–business relations are malign or beneficial to society at large. In this respect, Indonesia still has a long way to go: the DPR has yet to demonstrate any great capacity to distinguish between privately and socially beneficial demands for policy change, and remains unresponsive to very real concerns about the business environment.

In Chapter 7, Arskal Salim focuses squarely on the tyranny of the majority aspect of democracy, exemplified by the attempts of some aggressive Islamic groups in Indonesia to reinforce the position of Muslims as the dominant religious majority. Drawing on three case studies, Salim provides a detailed discussion of 'Muslim politics', a form of populist politics that involves mobilisation of widespread emotional commitment to Islam for political purposes, providing a powerful means for religious actors and politicians to gain the support of Muslims across numerous political and ethnic divides in furtherance of their own particular interests. He argues that Muslim politics is advocated not only by Muslim groups and Islamic institutions, parties and publishers, but also by regional bureaucracies and even secular political parties. In his view, the willingness of the religious majority to impose its own religious views and values on others places the future of the Indonesian nation state in jeopardy, because of the risk that religious minorities will be pushed to the margins of the polity and have their participation in the political process reduced.

Salim points out the irony that, during the New Order, Muslims actually saw themselves as a minority, because they perceived themselves as being badly treated by the state. In the sham democracy that existed at that time, their votes counted for very little. And yet, despite the fact that no single religion is officially acknowledged in the constitution—which 'guarantees the freedom of all residents to embrace their own religion and to worship according to their own religion and beliefs'—in practice Islam has always enjoyed a privileged position through its dominance of the Ministry of Religious Affairs. In the author's view, the key issue is not whether the state will adopt constitutional secularity (by making the separation of religion from politics more explicit) but whether it will take seriously its constitutional responsibility to enforce religious freedom and equality. If the government fails to act decisively on emerging problems affecting religious minorities, the best hope for maintaining a pluralistic society in Indonesia will lie, paradoxically, with a number of influential figures representative of the great diversity of Islamic legal opinion and culture.

Two interesting but largely unremarked aspects of democracy are the position of particularly disadvantaged citizens (most obviously, orphaned or otherwise neglected children, and adults who are mentally or physically disabled) and that of those not eligible to vote (specifically, children in general). In Chapter 8, Sharon Bessell focuses on the changes that have been occurring in legislation in child-related fields. Child welfare was covered by legislation during the Soeharto era, even if implementation was extremely weak. With the enactment of a new child protection law in 2002, the period since then has seen a shift to an emphasis on children's human rights. Bessell argues that under the earlier approach, children were seen merely as future citizens — human 'becomings' — and the responsibility of government was to help to prepare them for this. In contrast, the new approach sees children as human beings — as citizens in their own right. The government now has a responsibility to ensure the conditions necessary for a fulfilling childhood, and to listen to the voice of children even though they do not vote. The new approach commits governments to following policies that are generally beneficial to children, especially in the fields of education and health.

Many will share Bessell's view that the change in emphasis gives government a more appropriate role in relation to children, although some might also argue that using the term 'rights' to refer to entitlements it is felt children should have is somewhat misleading, on the grounds that rights are meaningful only if some entity can be held to account if those rights are violated. For example, our right to life and liberty is made concrete by laws that impose criminal sanctions for killing and abduction; in contrast, even though the new law stipulates that all Indonesian children have the right to an education, the cost of which is to be borne by the government, 'the vexed question of how to implement the promises of the new framework remains' (p. 154). The law begs the question as to the consequences for the government if children do not actually receive education of a specified quality and extent. In this case, the only sanction would be that delivered by the democratic process through the ballot box. Ultimately, then, actual policy towards children may be determined not so much by the new legislation as by the votes of children's parents.

Part III: Institutions of Government

The final section of the book focuses on two of the most important institutions of democracy (other than the electoral system and the legislature): the civil service and the legal system. It discusses the largely parallel needs for reform in both, and what has been achieved so far.

In relation to the civil service, the New Order legacy can be characterised as non-transparent processes, underfunded institutions, an inadequately skilled public sector workforce and institutionalised corruption. In Chapter 9, Staffan Synnerstrom discusses the immense challenge of reforming the bureaucracy, highlighting in particular the fundamental importance of transparency and accountability. Such reform 'must target features of the civil service that preserve old behaviour in defiance of new legislation and the new democratic system of government' (p. 160). The author emphasises that reform will need to be driven from the top, with the help of democratic forces in society, because the bureaucracy itself will not change in the absence of such pressure. Considerable emphasis is given to the fact that institutional budgets are determined by fixed formulae that result in underfunding for most institutions, and that decisions implying budget impositions and financial liabilities are taken administratively, separate from the budget process. Some progress towards reform has been achieved, but the newly enacted laws on state finance and state treasury still await elaboration of matters of detail, and their implementation has sometimes been obstructed by those who understand how crucial they are for improved governance – and, accordingly, how they threaten their own interests.

Synnerstrom argues that the present government's attempts to detect and punish corrupt officials do not address the roots of corruption or do away with the prevailing 'corruption culture'. He emphasises the militaristic style of civil service structure introduced by Soeharto very early in the New Order, and advocates a return to the kind of position-based system adopted elsewhere, where civil servants are recruited to professionally classified positions in open competition, where selection is based on specific professional requirements and where entry into the civil service from outside is possible at all levels. The current system is incapable of providing institutions with adequate numbers of sufficiently skilled staff, or of making sure that the right people are in the right places. In the absence of this kind of reform, young people with professional ambitions and high motivation are unlikely to want to join the civil service, so that it will continue to be filled mainly by those who are attracted by job security, a pension guarantee and the possibility of taking part in lucrative corrupt activity. Synnerstrom also emphasises the problems that arise from having a large part of take-home pay made up of non-transparent, discretionary and arbitrarily distributed components, and recommends the adoption of a set of single, transparent payments, funded from the budget.

The final chapter, by Simon Butt, clearly illustrates the basic principal–agent problem referred to earlier, in the particular context of the judiciary. It is essential that the government, on behalf of society, appoint individuals to adjudicate and enforce the laws that it has passed. On the one hand, there is a need for judicial independence, so that judges can be relied upon to interpret the law correctly and impartially—especially when there is a legal conflict involving the government itself. On the other hand, there is a need to try to ensure that those individuals are indeed acting competently in society's best interests, and not abusing the trust placed in them; that is, there is also a need for judicial accountability. The inevitable trade-off between these two objectives provides the basic focus for Butt's discussion.

Achieving an optimal balance between judicial independence and judicial accountability is especially difficult given that part of the Soeharto legacy is a judiciary lacking in essential legal skills, unused to having its performance monitored—much less being held accountable for it—and highly resistant to going along with change in this direction. Thus, although it has been argued that accountability should be prioritised until judicial competence and prestige are sufficiently high and corruption less prevalent, the judiciary seems to have managed to ensure that independence has won out, at least for now. The wheels of reform are turning—as can be seen in the establishment of a Judicial Commission and a Constitutional Court, and the relocation of court system administration from the Justice Ministry to the Supreme Court—but as yet those wheels lack traction. Ironically, the fact that the new law on the Judicial Commission was inexpertly drafted has created significant obstacles to its work. At the same time, the Supreme Court's four-volume blueprint for judicial reform—directed particularly towards its own reform—has yet to show any significant results. With corruption endemic in the judiciary, it is perhaps hardly surprising that (at the time of writing) the Supreme Court had failed to act against any of the many judges referred to it by the Judicial Commission. Butt's sobering assessment is that 'the Supreme Court and the courts below it continue to suffer from a raft of significant problems that have brought the judicial system to the brink of complete dysfunction' (p. 184).

REFERENCES

Bueno de Mesquita, B. et al. (2001), 'Political Competition and Economic Growth', *Journal of Democracy*, 12(1): 58–72.

Gerring, J. et al. (2005), 'Democracy and Economic Growth: A Historical Perspective', *World Politics*, 57: 323–64.

MacIntyre, A. (2003), *The Power of Institutions: Political Architecture and Governance*, Cornell University Press, Ithaca NY.

Przeworski, A. (2004), 'Institutions Matter?', *Government and Opposition*, 39(4): 527–40.

Przeworski, A., M. Alvarez, J.A. Cheibub and F. Limongi (1996), 'What Makes Democracies Endure?', *Journal of Democracy*, 7(1): 39–55.

Rodrik, D. and R. Wacziarg (2005), 'Do Democratic Transitions Produce Bad Economic Outcomes?', *AEA Papers and Proceedings*, 95(2): 50–5.

PART I

Forming and Reforming the Architecture of Governance

2　INDONESIA'S CONSTITUTIONAL CHANGE REVIEWED

Andrew Ellis

THE PROCESS OF CONSTITUTIONAL CHANGE

The constitution of any country defines both the institutions by which the country governs itself and the relationship between its citizens and its institutional framework. A constitution is a fundamentally political document, establishing the rights and duties of citizens and state institutions, and reflecting also the way in which society wishes to be governed. It may therefore be expected to be the result of wide-ranging political debate. As with any process of political debate, there will be some with interests to promote or protect. It is legitimate and indeed desirable that constitutional debate should centre on long-term vision. However, it is also inevitable that particular short-term, sectoral or even venal interests will affect the course of that debate, and that a constitution will be the product of its time and environment.

The story of the constitutional amendment process undertaken by Indonesia between 1999 and 2002, and the implementation of the amended constitution, exemplifies this. Although some may have believed that there was some kind of ideal constitution which could be devised or discovered by independent technical experts, in practice that was never going to be the case. Institutional history, narrow political interests and vision on the part of some of the key players were all significant in the progress that was made and the failures and setbacks that took place. It is now over two years since the 2004 general and presidential elections — the first to take place within the framework of the amended constitution. Sufficient time has therefore elapsed to attempt an assessment of the new institutions.

THE 1945 CONSTITUTION OF INDONESIA

In its original form, the 1945 Constitution of Indonesia contained only 37 articles. It was written as a temporary text. Its pattern of state institutions was substituted in practice within three months of its promulgation, and no other nation has since copied it. Yet the 1945 Constitution has enduring emotional significance for most Indonesians as a symbol of the struggle for independence and as a founding pillar of the unitary state of the Republic of Indonesia. In the transition after 1998, not only the substance but also the symbol of 'the 1945 Constitution' was at stake.

The 1945 Constitution was based on the doctrine of an integralistic state, defined by drafting committee chair Soepomo as 'the principles of unity between leaders and people and unity in the entire nation' (Yamin 1959: 111–13). The sovereignty of the people was to be exercised 'in full through the People's Consultative Assembly' (MPR),[1] which was to be established as the highest institution of state and 'the manifestation of all the people of Indonesia', and was to 'determine both the Constitution and the Broad Guidelines of State Policy' (GBHN).[2]

The MPR was to consist of directly elected legislators, regional representatives and representatives of functional groups, the latter being 'cooperatives, labour unions and other collective organisations'.[3] It was to meet once every five years 'to decide the policy of the state to be pursued in the future'[4] and to give its mandate to the president. The five high institutions of state—the President, the People's Representative Assembly (DPR), the Supreme Advisory Council, the State Audit Board and the Supreme Court—would submit reports to the MPR at the end of each five-year electoral term. This structure rejected both the principle of separation between the individual and the state and the principle of separation of powers between the institutions of the state, and thus also rejected any concept of 'checks and balances'.

A 'Presidential System'?

The president was to be 'the chief executive of the state' and 'the true leader of the state', and would 'hold the power of government in accordance with the Constitution'; but presidential power was 'not unlimited'.[5]

---

1   Article 1(2) of the 1945 Constitution.
2   Section 6(III) of the elucidation to the 1945 Constitution.
3   Elucidation to article 2(1) of the 1945 Constitution
4   Elucidation to article 3 of the 1945 Constitution.
5   Title of section 6(VII) of the elucidation to the 1945 Constitution.

The president would be 'subordinate and accountable' to the MPR, and 'the highest administrator of state below the MPR'.[6]

The conventional definition of a presidential system requires three specific characteristics: a one-person rather than collegiate executive; an executive directly elected by the voters; and a fixed-term chief executive not subject to legislative confidence (Lijphart 1999: 117–18). The 1945 Constitution was thus not conventionally presidential, although Indonesians described it as such. The president was elected indirectly by the MPR, not directly by the voters. The MPR set state policy through the GBHN without presidential involvement. The president was specifically tasked with implementation of policy in line with the GBHN. The MPR had the right to dismiss the president before the end of his or her term in the event of clear violation of national policy—which included not only the 1945 Constitution itself but also the contents of the GBHN. The removal from office of President Abdurrahman Wahid in 2001 showed that the design of these procedures could have real teeth. By contrast, in a conventional presidential system, the grounds for impeachment are normally restricted to breach of the constitution or criminal acts, with moral turpitude sometimes added.

It was a long time before the concepts of the 1945 Constitution were tested under conditions that could be described as democratic or even transitional. It was not possible to establish the institutions envisaged in the 1945 Constitution while Indonesia was still fighting to realise its independence from the Netherlands. In October 1945, institutions that were more parliamentary in nature were put in place. Although their consistency with the 1945 Constitution is debatable, they were generally accepted, and lasted until the Round Table agreement with the Netherlands in 1949, under which the Dutch formally accepted the independence of the 'United States of Indonesia'. The federal constitution of the Round Table settlement was rapidly replaced by the 1950 temporary constitution, which established a unitary state and a substantially parliamentary form of government. However, the 1950s did not see a consolidation of democratic institutions, leading to the persisting belief that a parliamentary institutional framework is inappropriate for Indonesia. In the same way, the legacy of the Dutch attempt to divide and rule in the Round Table settlement is that both the word and the concept of federalism are non-starters in Indonesian constitutional debate.

On 5 July 1959 President Soekarno reintroduced the 1945 Constitution by decree, characterising it as a historic document; a symbol of the basis of the revolution; and not amenable to amendment, addition or improvement. President Soeharto also promoted the doctrine that the

---

6   Section 6(IV) of the elucidation to the 1945 Constitution.

1945 Constitution was a fixed text which was not capable of amendment or improvement. He took iron control of the various nomination processes leading to MPR membership to ensure that the MPR remained a pliant body, enabling real power to lie with himself and the executive. The MPR merely met every five years as required. It acted by agreement reached through deliberation and consensus rather than the mechanism of voting.

Constitutional change was a key demand of those who demonstrated for Soeharto's removal in 1998. Legislation and preparations for the general election of June 1999 soon swamped the agenda, however. Radical students demanding immediate constitutional reform were rapidly sidelined. Although the need for institutional change was a consistent undertow of discussion, most parties fighting the 1999 election reaffirmed their commitment to the symbol of the 1945 Constitution and avoided raising the subject of its substance. Substantive change was put on the public agenda only after the election.

THE CONSTITUTIONAL REVIEW PROCESS

This was a time of great political change and ferment. The explosion of media free from government control, the deregulation of political party formation, the successful holding of the 1999 elections and the passage of 'big bang' regional autonomy legislation were just some of the major components of that change. Many established politicians recognised the need for institutional change and rode this wave.

At the general session of the MPR that followed the 1999 general election, the agenda had already moved far enough for members to agree by consensus on a review of the constitution during the following year. The importance of the 1945 Constitution as symbol was clear; it was therefore proposed to make amendments to the existing constitution rather than writing an entirely new constitution. With the momentum of the euphoria of change still strong, the first priority was a significant transfer of power from the executive to the legislature. A new law-making process was immediately agreed upon—although the real transfer of power was not as significant as many imagined. Under the new procedure, the legislature and the president would jointly discuss and approve bills; that is, a representative of the government would attend the meetings of the DPR committee dealing with the bill and present the position of the government during the debate. When the bill returned to plenary session from committee, assent to the text would have been signified both by the elected members of the committee and by the government representative. The jointly approved bill would then be signed into law by the

president. These changes collectively formed the first amendment to the
1945 Constitution.

At the same time, the MPR introduced annual sessions from 2000
onwards. The subsequent annual public discussion by the MPR of a performance report from the president moved the balance of power substantially away from the presidency during the transitional period. In
addition, the new MPR introduced term limits, agreeing that the president and vice-president could 'be re-elected to the same office for one
further term only'.

Most of the members of the MPR were new. Their capabilities and
current political positions were not necessarily well known, and political knowhow and experience were thus valuable. The membership of
the committee formed to handle the review of the constitution — Ad Hoc
Committee No. I (PAH I) — reflected the political balance of the MPR. Its
leadership positions, chosen by the committee itself, went in order of
seniority to the four largest political groups. Its chair, Jakob Tobing of
the Indonesian Democratic Party of Struggle (PDI-P), the largest single
party in the MPR and the embodiment of Indonesian secular nationalism, did not look or sound like a radical firebrand. As a result, opponents
of constitutional change continually misunderstood his direction and
underestimated his determination. The four PAH I leaders were committed to major amendment of the 1945 Constitution. They managed for
over three years to maintain their vision of a presidential constitution
with full separation of powers, while also maintaining a broad unity
across political party lines within PAH I. They recognised that following
the rules was an important factor in ensuring legitimacy. They learnt as
they went along, especially in the context of constitutional amendment
requiring agreement by deliberation and consensus in the MPR, with the
consequent question of how to overcome the veto that this appeared to
give to diehard opponents of change.

While most PAH I members had a broad commitment to fundamental
constitutional change, they held lively differences of opinion on a substantial number of key issues. Importantly, the committee rapidly developed a collective identity and loyalty. Its leaders encouraged and fostered
this, recognising that reform would only be successful if it enjoyed wide
support and understanding across all groups. They managed committee proceedings in a quiet, open and consensual style which gained and
retained members' trust.

PAH I's first act was to reaffirm its support for the existing preamble
to the constitution, for the unitary state of Indonesia and for the presidential system — without saying what a 'presidential system' actually
meant. Where no consensus to amend existed, the original constitutional
text was to be retained. Amid the excitement of transition, the commit-

tee's proceedings attracted little attention, although it met two or three times most weeks, consistently in public, and set up a series of consultation and witness hearings in both Jakarta and the provinces. In July 2000, it presented a comprehensive report containing new, carefully negotiated drafting relating to almost all articles of the 1945 Constitution. Disagreements were reflected by alternatives at 24 points. Inevitably, some chapters were well drafted and others rather less so.

Political Problems and Procedural Delays

While most PAH I members had become knowledgeable about constitutional issues during the course of their work, many other MPR members focused on them for the first time only at the 2000 annual session. For some, especially traditional nationalists, Soekarno loyalists and the more conservative military members, the PAH I report was much more wide ranging and fundamental in scope than they had envisaged. The compromises in the report began to unravel. Existing procedural conventions were inadequate to enable the discussion of a significant volume of complex material. Only about a third of the tabled amendments were even discussed — and those were the easy ones. As MacIntyre (2003: 147) observed, much less progress was made at this time in implementing reform than during the earlier period of ferment. Indeed, he wondered whether the failure of central control had resulted in 'overshooting' amendment, creating a system whose excessive fragmentation could lead to policy rigidity and a future strong recentralising reaction (MacIntyre 2003: 148).

The failure to address most of the constitutional amendment agenda led to division between the MPR itself and many in Jakarta elite circles outside. The latter were vocal in their disappointment, and increasingly sought to develop a new concept of the state and a new constitution. The MPR's legitimacy to conduct the constitutional debate, taken as read following the 1999 election, would henceforth be under steady external attack.

The MPR had, however, reached consensus on issues relating to regional government, the DPR, citizenship, defence and security, and human rights; collectively these formed the second amendment to the 1945 Constitution. The DPR would become a fully elected body at the next general election in 2004, with an end to military and police representation in the legislature. Its powers were specified: to legislate, to exercise oversight and to approve the national budget. The presidential 'pocket veto' was abolished; if the DPR and the president jointly agreed to legislation and the president failed to sign it within 30 days, the legislation would take effect regardless. (This, again, was widely misinterpreted, with many people thinking for some time afterwards that the DPR had the power to sign into law any bill that it alone had agreed if presidential approval was not forthcoming.)

In 1945, proposals to include human rights provisions in the constitution had been specifically rejected; in the first explicit change to 1945 principles, they were now added through the second amendment. The new human rights chapter proved controversial, however. Human rights and NGO activists attacked the provision against trial under retrospective legislation as the outcome of a hidden agreement with the military designed to block calls for justice for Soeharto-era human rights violations. Most MPR members appeared taken by surprise that this reaction was generated by a provision inspired by the Universal Declaration on Human Rights.

Core Unresolved Issues

After the 2000 annual session of the MPR, both PAH I and democracy and governance NGOs attempted to widen the constitutional debate. However, hearings in the regions did not generate much active response or discussion. At a consultation meeting in Central Java in late 2000, at which the author was present, amendments to the constitution were not the major concern of the 300 or so local government officers and community leaders who attended. Rather, they wanted to express their concerns about the failure of the government to issue key implementing provisions for the regional autonomy legislation due to take effect on the ground a few weeks later, the universal perception being that while different groups locally were cooperating to get things done, politics and government in Jakarta were characterised by confusion and deadlock. While the consultation team from PAH I gamely tried to pursue the constitutional agenda, they and their audience mostly talked past each other.

Constitutional debate was effectively suspended in 2001 while the drama surrounding the removal from office of President Wahid was played out. A special session of the MPR in July removed the president from office, replacing him with Vice-President Megawati Soekarnoputri. These events demonstrated vividly how the relationship between the MPR and the president under the existing provisions of the 1945 Constitution had changed in practice in the new era of legislative assertiveness.

Fundamental Change Enacted

The 2001 annual session of the MPR was delayed until November. By then, the political tension of much of the preceding year had largely dissipated. During the session the two largest parties, PDI-P and Golkar, reached a deal on many of the core issues under discussion, but it could not be completed by consensus because the other parties were not prepared to accede to a provision allowing the MPR to conduct the second round of a presidential election if no clear result emerged from the first round. When it finally became evident that full agreement would not be reached, a quick decision was made to enact everything that had already been agreed, and to use the options identified on the remaining issues as source material for a further year's debate. This decision was a major tactical success for the PAH I leadership and faction leaders, especially Jakob Tobing and the PDI-P constitutional reformers, who had thereby managed to outflank their internal opposition.

The third amendment to the 1945 Constitution put in place the principle that the sovereignty of the people was to be exercised directly, not through the MPR. It established the fundamental structure of a presidential system based on the principles of separation of powers, direct presidential election, and impeachment of the president and vice-president for constitutional breaches, not on policy or confidence grounds. It provided for an independent judiciary, a constitutional court and a second legislative chamber made up of regional representatives (albeit with limited powers) — the Council of Regional Representatives (DPD). The result added up to a fundamental change in the institutions of Indonesia — even though almost nobody noticed it happen. In political circles, and even more so among media and other commentators, the full implications of the third amendment did not sink in until well into 2002.

When reality dawned, debate was particularly fierce within PDI-P. Even though the third amendment was to take effect immediately, a number of significant figures argued that the rejection of a fourth, final amendment would result in a return to the original 1945 Constitution, and promoted this course of action. The constitutional reformers within PDI-P had to fight another internal battle, while ensuring that Megawati remained onside despite her view of the original 1945 Constitution as constituting her father's legacy. The internal argument in the party abated only after Megawati herself chaired a key central party meeting in May 2002.

The Proposal for a Constitutional Commission

The proposal to establish an independent constitutional commission to draw up a new (rather than amended) constitution was first promoted by a large coalition of NGOs after the disappointments of the 2000 annual session, and gained considerable momentum after being mentioned favourably by President Megawati in August 2001. The NGOs drew parallels with the constitutional reform experiences of Thailand, the Philippines and South Africa. But the previous Thai constitution had originated with the military, that of the Philippines with former President Marcos and that of South Africa with the apartheid regime. All three were thus discredited documents. The 1945 Constitution as a symbol of Indonesia's independence was very different. By conflating the idea of a constitutional commission with that of a new rather than amended constitution, the proponents of this course of action became marginalised from much of the later constitutional discussion.

The proposal for a constitutional commission gained new support in 2002 for very different reasons. Retired generals brought strong pressure to bear to roll back the whole amendment process and return to the integralistic concept of the 1945 Constitution. Given the momentum behind the final amendment at this stage, their idea was to use the constitutional commission to reverse the changes made up to that point.

Amendment Completed

The question of whether the second round of a presidential election should be conducted directly or indirectly appeared to be the most difficult issue outstanding in advance of the 2002 annual session of the MPR. Opponents of direct second-round elections cited their cost and security implications. Equally, indirect second-round election by the MPR was questioned on the ground that the final decision would be taken by a relatively small (and thus potentially corruptible) group, and because of the legitimacy questions that would arise if the MPR overturned a first-round popular plurality.

By July 2002, PDI-P had come round to the idea of a direct second-round presidential election — Megawati probably perceiving the desirability of maximum legitimacy for the second term that she, and most others, then expected would result from a direct election. This was thus agreed without argument at the 2002 annual session. The military representatives announced that they would withdraw from all representative institutions in 2004, saying that their role lay in defence and security, not politics. This signalled a recognition that the powers of the new MPR would be limited, and that a small group of military members would merely be a focus for unpopularity.

The constitutional review had enabled political parties based on Islam to reopen the debate on the addition to article 29 of the constitution of seven key words of the Jakarta Charter of 1945: (in English) 'with the obligation for adherents of Islam to carry out sharia law'. This phrase had been contained in the original 1945 Constitution until its penultimate draft and had remained the subject of deep divisions during the constitutional debates of the 1950s. It was controversial not only among more secular nationalists and followers of other religions, but within Indonesian Islam itself. Its inclusion was never going to command a simple majority in the MPR—let alone the two-thirds required if the issue had gone to a vote.

The Islamic parties finally indicated that they would not oppose the decision of the MPR to retain the original wording of article 29, although they 'regretted' the rejection of their amendments. They had, however, demonstrated their position to the public and been formally recognised, while their opponents had retained article 29 unamended—the elements of a win–win situation. In contrast, the abolition of functional group representation was finally agreed by a vote. This marked a unique exception to the principle that constitutional amendment required deliberation and consensus, reflecting the eventual isolation of the functional group representatives.

With everything seemingly settled, the military submitted a last-minute proposal that the amendments should apply only to enable the 2004 elections to take place, and that a constitutional commission should then be set up. Most politicians saw this as simply another attempt to overturn the new structure, and regarded it as an unacceptable breach of a previous consensus. The military finally recognised that it had insufficient support for its proposal and withdrew it. The fourth amendment to the 1945 Constitution was adopted, and MPR members marked the completion of the amendment process by singing the national anthem.

THE AMENDED CONSTITUTION

Indonesia is no longer an integralistic state with a single highest state institution. It has become a state with constitutional checks and balances and with separation of powers between the legislature, executive and judiciary. The major changes made to the 1945 Constitution through the series of four amendments include the following.

- The sovereignty of the people is no longer exercised in full through the MPR but is implemented in accordance with the constitution itself.
- The MPR has limited specific functions only. These include considering constitutional amendments, swearing in the elected president and vice-president, and deciding what action is to be taken if the Constitutional Court rules that an impeachment charge is well grounded. The presidential/vice-presidential impeachment process excludes removal from office on policy grounds.
- The MPR consists entirely of elected representatives: the members of the DPR and the members of the new regional chamber, the DPD.

- The DPD participates in debate on legislation related to regional autonomy, centre–region relations and natural resource management. It exercises oversight on these issues, as well as on budget management, tax, education and religion.[7]
- The president and vice-president are elected as one ticket in a direct election, with two rounds if no ticket achieves 50 per cent of the vote +1, and at least 20 per cent in half the provinces in the first round.
- The independence of the General Election Commission (KPU) is specified. Political parties are the participants in DPR elections, and individual candidates in DPD elections.
- A Constitutional Court separate from the Supreme Court has been established with the power to conduct judicial reviews of legislation, resolve disputes between state institutions, hear claims for the dissolution of political parties and disputes relating to election results, and rule on motions to impeach.
- An independent Judicial Commission has been established to deal with judicial ethics issues and proposals for Supreme Court appointments.
- Constitutional backing is given for the principles of regional autonomy.
- Constitutional provision is made for a central bank whose independence and accountability is to be determined by law.
- Human rights provisions have been added, for the most part in line with the Universal Declaration of Human Rights.
- Future constitutional amendments can be introduced by at least one-third of the members of the MPR and will require the support of over half its total membership with two-thirds of the members present. The preamble to the constitution is not amendable. The form of the unitary state is also unamendable, although the article containing this provision can itself be amended.

THE 2004 ELECTIONS AND AFTER

With the new constitutional framework agreed, five major pieces of legislation were necessary before elections could be held: a general election law; a political party law; a law regulating presidential elections; a *susduk*

---

7 In practice, under the consequent 2003 law on the composition and status of elected state bodies (*susduk*), 'participation in debate' has been defined as taking place prior to the formal joint discussion and debate of bills by the DPR and president — in effect limiting the power of the DPD, because it has no formal input into either the principle or the detail of this later stage of debate.

law; and a law to fill in the necessary details to establish the Constitutional Court.

The DPR continues to use a party list, proportional representation system, but the average number of members per district has been reduced to about eight. Voters are given a very limited (and in practice ineffective) form of open choice between candidates. In practice, there continues to be a firm tendency for political parties to exercise tight control, with nominations of candidates submitted by central party organisations.

While a vigorous campaign by women for gender quotas did not result in the adoption of mandatory quotas, parties were encouraged to 'seriously take account of' the desirability of 30 per cent of their candidates being women. Although this was not fully achieved in 2004, this provision did lead to the parties feeling some degree of obligation. The proportion of women elected to the DPR has risen to 12 per cent. In addition, 21 per cent of DPD members are women.

A recall provision has been put in place, under which political parties may under some circumstances remove elected members from the DPR and replace them with other party members. This provision has in practice enabled parties to sanction dissident members, as for example when Golkar replaced two newly elected DPR members who had campaigned for President Susilo Bambang Yudhoyono (SBY) against party instructions.

The electoral system for the DPD is the single non-transferable vote, a system whose effects vary wildly with context. Each province elects four representatives, and each voter has one vote only.

Three elections were held successfully in 2004: legislative elections in April, a first-round presidential election in July and a second-round presidential election in September. Incumbent president Megawati was challenged by SBY, her former coordinating minister for politics and security, who led after the first round and secured a clear victory in the second round. Voters appeared to be seeking a convincing alternative to a government perceived as being complacent and unwilling to act on issues of corruption. Despite Megawati's initial lack of willingness to accept defeat, the successful and peaceful transfer of power was an early positive sign of robustness in the new institutions.

The 2004 election results initially suggested looming deadlock or conflict between the executive and the legislature. Megawati's PDI-P was clearly not expected to support SBY's government, and Golkar had endorsed Megawati's candidacy in the second round. Between them, these two parties held well over 40 per cent of the seats in the DPR, and their initial move was to form an alliance. Tussles immediately followed, with the sharing out of DPR committee chairs and SBY's decision to review Megawati's attempt to appoint a new military commander in chief shortly before leaving office both proving highly controversial.

However, the political landscape changed in December 2004. SBY's choice of Jusuf Kalla as his vice-presidential candidate bore fruit when Kalla, a prominent former Golkar figure from Sulawesi, succeeded where many others had failed in ousting Golkar chair Akbar Tanjung. Golkar thus moved from a predominantly oppositional stance to one broadly supportive of the government. This was confirmed in early 2005 when an attempt in the DPR to reject SBY's decision to reduce fuel price subsidies failed, even though the decision had appeared initially not to command majority DPR support.

The SBY–Kalla administration has chalked up some significant successes in its first two years in office. The Aceh peace agreement has held better than many expected. The anti-corruption stance that contributed to the success of SBY's election campaign has led to some successful high-profile prosecutions, notably of members of the General Election Commission (KPU) — although the view remains that bigger fish have retained their immunity. While the president and vice-president have often complemented each other, there have also been visible tensions between them. The question is now being asked as to how well government will function during the run-up to the 2009 elections if SBY and Kalla emerge at the head of opposing tickets.

The relationship between the executive and the DPR is very different from the one that existed before 1999. A senior official of the Ministry of Home Affairs remarked to the author in 2003 that 'unlike the old days, we can never get any work done because of the amount of time we have to spend in DPR committee sessions'. However, the effectiveness of the DPR is limited by the lack of commitment of a substantial number of its members, with legislation often delayed or stalled.

THE PROCESS OF CONSTITUTIONAL CHANGE: REPRESENTATIVE OR PARTICIPATORY?

Jakob Tobing commented shortly after the passage of the final amendment to the constitution that 'most people did not realise what was happening until it was too late'. While the implications of the amendments were understood by the constitutional reformers within PAH I, they were not realised more widely until the major principles of change were agreed and the final amendment already under discussion. Nonetheless the process was not secret: plenary meetings were open to the press and public throughout, and many meetings for socialisation or consultation took place. The entire amendment process appears to have followed the constitution, MPR standing orders and other legal instruments in force at the time. But given the principle of constitutional amendment by deliberation and consensus, it is doubtful that these far-reaching changes would have been agreed if all MPR members had been fully aware throughout of what was going on.

Although relatively open, the Indonesian constitutional reform process was less participatory than in some other parts of the world. The South African constitution, for example, was a result of wide-ranging participation and has gained widespread acceptance and legitimacy. In other countries, the outcome of the participation process has been less clear-cut. The 1997 Constitution of Thailand appears to be an excellent document, yet, as Ghai and Galli (2006: 14–15) have observed, many of its provisions are ignored, and a politician who regularly criticised the constitution and violated its spirit was elected prime minister on two successive occasions with impressive majorities. Despite its pluralist provisions, it was not able to prevent the centralisation of power under Prime Minister Thaksin Shinawatra, and was subsequently suspended in September 2006 following a military coup. A participatory process in itself thus does not appear to be sufficient to ensure that a constitution is robust and can be put into practice.

A further criticism of the amendment process has been that it contrasts unfavourably with the clear-cut achievements of the founding fathers of Indonesia or the progenitors of the US Constitution. What is forgotten is not so much that history is written by winners (although that is relevant) but that it is by definition condensed. The result is often a story of grand purpose and achievement, which inevitably does not reflect the experience of a contemporaneous participant or observer. The day-to-day problems or histrionics of the Indonesian constitutional review process should not hide the scale of change that has taken place.

As part of the work of the International Institute for Democracy and Electoral Assistance (IDEA), Samuels (2006) has compared constitution-building processes in 12 countries worldwide, including Indonesia. She classifies these according to four criteria: whether they are incremental or follow a grand design; whether they are inclusive; whether they are representative; and whether they are participatory.

Samuels observes that while participatory and inclusive processes broaden the constitutional agenda, they tend to threaten established power structures, which react by undermining, amending or preventing the adoption or enforcement of a new constitution. She cites Kenya, Colombia and Guatemala as illustrations of this tendency. In Kenya, the final approval of the new constitution was in the hands of the political elite, who sought to delay and undermine its adoption. In Colombia, sitting members of Congress were excluded from the 1991 Constitutional Assembly, and politicians and traditional elites sought to undermine the enforcement of the new constitution that it developed. In Guatemala, the new constitution was defeated in the 1999 referendum by a strong 'no' campaign mounted by the conservative elite.

Ghai and Galli (2006) note that the most participatory processes have often taken place in countries where the paucity or absence of effective intermediary institutions means that there is no alternative to the direct engagement of the people. But since such a process does not readily lead to institutionalisation, the situation easily reverts to 'politics as usual' after the participation process comes to an end and its structures are dismantled. Ghai and Galli cite Thailand, Ethiopia and Uganda as examples.

The case for participatory constitution-building processes emphasises the achievement, acceptance and anchoring of positive change through wide and inclusive debate. At one level, the limited nature of such debate across Indonesia was not for want of trying to kindle it. At another, the absence of debate in some circles in Jakarta assisted the acceptance of the key amendments.

The Success (and Limitations) of Elite-driven Transitions

Samuels (2006) concludes that representative, negotiated processes appear to be a minimum requirement for a sustainable transition to democracy, and provide a forum for a negotiated transition from an authoritarian regime. She puts Indonesia in this category, alongside Chile, Fiji and Hungary.

Of these, the constitutional transitions of Chile and Hungary may be described as at least partially successful. In the constitutional and legislative package put together to reach agreement over transition in Chile, several provisions protected the position of the outgoing military rulers and froze the system against change. These included a provision that further change would require a 60 per cent majority to pass an organic law; an electoral system that made this a steep hurdle; and the inclusion of appointed and *ex officio* seats in the Senate to try to ensure that this chamber would resist any change that was unwanted by the outgoing power. At the same time, the constitution provided that the legislature could not increase the budget above that proposed by the president, and that if no agreement was reached on the budget within 60 days, the president's budget would take effect; a law was also enacted guaranteeing a minimum level of military spending (Baldez and Carey 2001). The return of democracy was thus accompanied by constraints on both the composition and powers of the legislature. It took more than 15 years for changes to these negotiated provisions to become politically feasible.

Only in 2005 were amendments put in place eliminating the remaining political role of the military, removing appointed and lifetime senators, and giving the legislature additional powers of control and accountability over the executive.

The political cycle in Chile has been characterised by periods of significant or even massive change interspersed with periods in which existing political dispensations are, if not fossilised, certainly not subject to effective political challenge. Even in 2006, when the possibility of electoral system reform existed seriously for the first time since 1989, the interests of those elected under the existing system continued to restrict the chance of radical change.

In Hungary, it can be said that constitutional change followed rather than accompanied the negotiated process of political change that took place in 1989. Although the 1990 constitutional referendum on the election of the presidency was closely fought and has had far-reaching consequences for the subsequent direction of Hungarian democracy, there was never any serious suggestion that democratisation itself was in doubt, that violence or disorder would break out, or that the USSR would intervene. Nonetheless, what took place can still best be described as an accommodation between elite groups.

We may view the Indonesian transition as following this pattern, with Chile the closest parallel. Between the middle of 1998 and about the end of 1999, huge institutional changes proved possible, although even at that time some institutions — such as the single nationwide civil service system — could not be changed or substantially reformed. From 2000 to 2003, the process of institutional change became more difficult, with the completion of the constitutional amendment process in 2002 a substantial achievement. In 2004, the focus shifted from institutional change to making the new institutions work. Further constitutional amendment appears highly unlikely in the near future. But despite the controversy surrounding the process of change, the amended 1945 Constitution has rapidly become an accepted fact.

Whether or not the amended constitution eventually leads to stability, economic success and established democratic institutions, the MPR set a rare precedent by agreeing peacefully and voluntarily to vote away its own all-powerful status. The system that has been created is still in the process of establishing its traditions, and its robustness has not yet been tested by real political conflict. Such a test may come sooner or later, a realisation faced by Mexico in and following the summer of 2006, when well-resourced institutions for electoral management and electoral dispute resolution established over a 20-year period of transition found themselves at the centre of deep divisions. The high regard that these institutions had established for themselves was put to the test by the closeness of the 2006 presidential election. Their robustness in resolving and gaining legitimacy for the result that finally emerged from that close and bitterly fought contest is not yet clear, but their reputation has certainly been bruised.

HOW INDONESIA'S NEW INSTITUTIONS ARE FARING

The DPD and the Constitutional Court are new and visible institutions created by the amendment process. The DPD has faced an uphill task in carving out a role for itself, facing opposition not only from those traditional nationalists who do not believe it should exist, but also from those whose freedom of action might be affected by an effective DPD. In its early months, some of its members were more concerned about how to acquire more powers for the DPD than about exercising its existing powers to any effect. During 2006, the DPD gave greater priority to developing its oversight role, by holding public hearings in various regions, for example. It has perhaps more scope to establish a reputation in this role than in the legislative field. The acceptance of important DPD recommendations in the 2006 annual statement of the presidential program as well as the role given to oversight in the 2006 DPD strategic plan suggest that the DPD will be able to establish a real, if limited, role for itself.

The 2003 Law on the Constitutional Court enabled the rapid establishment of this new institution. The court's justices have shown a willingness to make controversial judgments if the facts so indicate, tempered by a recognition of political realities. Its 2006 judgment on the powers of the Judicial Commission in relation to complaints against existing Supreme Court judges is analysed elsewhere in this volume (see Chapter 12). In its judgment on the division of the province of Papua and the creation of the new province of West Irian Jaya, its view that the process was flawed was nullified in practice by its effective recognition of West Irian Jaya as a fact on the ground.

It should be remembered that, from the US Supreme Court onwards, courts established to rule on constitutional issues have faced political pressures. It was no accident that while *Marbury v. Madison* (1803) is now enshrined as the landmark case on which the power of judicial review over legislation is founded, it did not in fact give Marbury the remedy he sought: the handing over of his commission as a justice of the peace. The subsequent judgment in *Stuart v. Laird* (also 1803), which upheld legislation requiring Supreme Court justices to exercise their original jurisdiction as circuit judges, confirmed that the justices were judiciously accepting that political realities had changed from the federalist climate of 1787 to the Jeffersonian republican climate of 1802 (Ackerman 2005:

172–98). While some of the decisions of the Indonesian Constitutional Court may be questioned in legal argument, it is not realistic in a real-world process of change to expect that all its judgments will stand well on pure legal grounds.

WILL PRESIDENTIALISM SUCCEED IN INDONESIA – OR ELSEWHERE?

While presidentialism is well established as a theoretical form of demo-cratic government, considerable doubt has been expressed outside the unique context of the United States as to whether it can work effectively in practice. Experiences in Latin America, where presidential constitu-tions are the common form, have sometimes suggested a bumpy ride (Mainwaring 1992). Many Latin American democracies face problems both of corruption and, in an even more acute form than in Indonesia, of the implications for democracy of huge disparities in wealth. In fran-cophone Africa, presidential regimes do not appear to have led to demo-cratic consolidation, with the single exception of Benin. The question to be asked is thus how to design institutions to improve the chance of suc-cess and stability of presidential systems.

Cheibub (2002) identifies the relative rarity of the electoral defeat of incumbents in presidential systems as potentially problematic. He sug-gests that limitations on re-election may be necessary, while regarding term limits as perhaps too blunt an instrument. Indonesia has adopted presidential term limits, however – and has already seen the first defeat of an incumbent in a presidential election.

Mainwaring and Shugart (1997: 436) have suggested three factors that may be helpful in making presidential systems work: an electoral system likely to give the president a substantial block (not necessarily a majority) of reliable supporters within the legislature; the absence of wide-ranging, independent presidential legislative powers (governing by decree); and political party control over elected members that is neither too tightly disciplined nor loose and chaotic. Under Indonesia's amended constitu-tion and political laws, the first is more likely than not to be true – and illustrates the importance of Jusuf Kalla's victory within Golkar. The sec-ond is substantially true; the most important form of direct presidential legislation, the government regulation in lieu of legislation (*perpu*), is limited to cases of urgency and in any event requires early subsequent ratification by the legislature. The third, however, is not so likely, with the central leadership of political parties seeking to maintain strong con-trol over elected members and the candidate selection process. While it is possible that the direct election of heads of the executive at the provincial and district levels will, over time, create an alternative route to political recognition and national power, it is too early to tell whether this will be the case. Early signs are mixed, with some regional success stories balanced by some heavy-handed interventions by central party organisations in candidate selection for the direct elections.

Indonesia now provides a case study in elite-driven constitutional transition. This approach has been successful in enabling the adoption of a recognised democratic institutional framework, a peaceful transfer of power, and a presidential government able to make at least some progress in addressing daunting governance challenges. It has also demonstrated limitations, in that power is still concentrated in restricted, predominantly Jakarta-based, circles, if less so than before. The need for some of the existing holders of power and influence to accept the legitimacy of the new framework still inhibits or prevents action on significant aspects of the good governance agenda.

It is interesting to speculate how the new constitutional settlement would hold up if challenged by either a president or a legislature set on accumulating power. The inclusive nature of the legislature under the current electoral system perhaps makes the latter less likely. A president who wished to take on the legislature would face the twin hurdles of overcoming the joint approval process for legislation and the requirement for early ratification of emergency legislation by the DPR—and in addition the operation of the new impeachment process has not yet been tested in practice. Perhaps immobilism may be the bigger danger arising from the new settlement.

As its political patterns consolidate, Indonesia looks set to contribute to understanding of a second major practical question of debate about constitutions and institutional frameworks: how to make a real presidential system succeed—or why such a system may fail. In 2007, Indonesia's experience with presidentialism still requires time and development before it can be assessed fully and properly.

REFERENCES

Ackerman, B. (2005), *The Failure of the Founding Fathers*, Cambridge MA: Harvard University Press.

Baldez, L. and J. Carey (2001), 'Budget Procedure and Fiscal Restraint in Post-transition Chile', pp. 105–48 in S. Haggard and M. McCubbins (eds), *Presidents, Parliaments and Policy*, Cambridge: Cambridge University Press.

Cheibub, J.A. (2002), *Presidentialism and Democracy*, pp. 104–40 in A. Reynolds (ed.), *The Architecture of Democracy*, Oxford: Oxford University Press.

Ghai, Y. and G. Galli (2006), *Constitution Building Processes and Democratisation*, Stockholm: International Institute for Democracy and Electoral Assistance (IDEA).

Lijphart, A. (1999), *Patterns of Democracy*, New Haven CT and London: Yale University Press.

MacIntyre, A. (2003), *The Power of Institutions*, Ithaca NY and London: Cornell University Press.

Mainwaring, S. (1992), 'Presidential Systems in Latin America', pp. 111–17 in A. Lijphart, *Parliamentary versus Presidential Government*, Oxford: Oxford University Press.

Mainwaring, S. and M. Shugart (1997), *Presidentialism and Democracy in Latin America*, Cambridge: Cambridge University Press.

Samuels, K. (2006), 'Constitution Building Processes and Democratisation: A Discussion of Twelve Case Studies', second draft, <www.idea.int/conflict/cbp/index.cfm>, accessed 15 August 2006.

Yamin, M. (1959), *Naskah Persiapan Undang-undang Dasar 1945* [Texts on the Preparation of the 1945 Constitution], Volume I, Jakarta: Yayasan Prapanca.

3 ELECTORAL AND POLITICAL PARTY REFORM

Benjamin Reilly

Political parties are a crucial part of democratic political systems. With Indonesia's return to democracy in 1999, operational controls on political parties and the ban on the establishment of new parties were lifted. Subsequent electoral reform was designed to reshape the party system by encouraging fewer, larger, parties. This chapter looks at this process from a comparative perspective, situating the Indonesian reforms in a broader Asian context. It also attempts to answer some basic questions about institutional reform. What are the trade-offs inherent in different electoral rules and party system configurations? Where does the Indonesian party system sit within the spectrum of party systems around the world? And how do trends in Indonesia compare with those elsewhere in the Asia-Pacific region?

DEMOCRATISATION AND POLITICAL REFORM

The number of East Asian regimes that can be considered to meet the basic Schumpeterian definition of democracy — governments chosen through open and competitive elections — has snowballed over the past 20 years (Schumpeter 1947: 269). While at the end of the Cold War only Japan could lay claim to being an 'established' East Asian democracy, the years since then have ushered in a new era of liberalisation and democratisation across the region (Lijphart 1999). Major transitions from authoritarian rule to democracy began with the popular uprising against the Marcos regime in the Philippines in 1986 and the negotiated transitions from autocratic governments in South Korea and Taiwan in 1987. They continued with the resumption of civilian rule in Thailand in 1992; the

UN intervention in Cambodia in 1993; the fall of Indonesia's Soeharto regime in 1998; and the international rehabilitation of East Timor which culminated in 2001. While the 2006 coup in Thailand was a clear step backwards, today more East Asian governments are chosen through democratic processes than ever before.

Indonesia, the largest of these new democracies, has now experienced several peaceful transitions of power since the end of the Soeharto era. Using Samuel Huntington's 'two-turnover test' of democratic consolidation — that consolidation may be said to occur when the party or group that takes power in an initial election loses a subsequent election and turns over power, and those election winners then peacefully turn over power to the winners of a later election — then Indonesia (along with South Korea, the Philippines, Taiwan and Thailand) clearly passes this minimal test of democracy (Huntington 1991: 266–7). But while Indonesia has had four turnovers of power since the fall of the Soeharto regime, only one of these — the election of President Susilo Bambang Yudhoyono in 2004 — has come as a direct result of the electoral process.[1] A more sober assessment of democratic consolidation thus suggests that Indonesia should probably be viewed as an emerging democracy. Despite rapid progress, Indonesian democracy cannot yet be said to be truly consolidated, in the sense of democracy being considered the 'only game in town' and any reversion from it unthinkable.[2] Nonetheless Indonesia has clearly made great strides in a relatively short period of time, especially if a minimalist, Schumpeterian definition of electoral democracy is used.

In this chapter, I argue that democratisation in much of East Asia, including Indonesia, has opened up opportunities for political elites to engage in overt 'political engineering' — that is, the conscious design or redesign of political institutions to achieve specific objectives. In East Asia in general and Indonesia in particular, incumbent politicians have sought to engineer more consolidated, aggregative and stable democratic systems while simultaneously limiting potential challengers to the established political order. The emergence of this distinctive regional model of institutional design has been facilitated by deliberate reform strategies whereby the region's electoral democracies have sought to transform the way their political systems operate in order to achieve certain specified outcomes — more stable government, for instance, or stronger political parties.

1 Indonesia's first democratically chosen president, Abdurrahman Wahid, was elected by the members of parliament, not through a mass suffrage election. His successor, Megawati Soekarnoputri, inherited the position when Abdurrahaman was forced from office in 2001.
2 This is the definition suggested by Przeworski (1991).

This chapter examines the impact of these changes of political architecture—'the complex of rules that make up the constitutional structure and party system' (MacIntyre 2003: 4)—across the new democracies of East Asia. Drawing on a book-length study (Reilly 2006), I examine the way in which Indonesia's new political arrangements are part of a region-wide reform process. In Indonesia, for example, political reformers have introduced majority-favouring electoral systems and political party laws that encourage nationally focused political competition and that restrict parties which base their appeals upon regional or ethnic ties. While Indonesia has taken this process further than most, it is part of a broader trend towards overt political engineering evident across the Asia-Pacific region as a whole.

BACKGROUND

The Asian approach to political engineering illustrates one of the recurring themes animating the choice of political institutions: the trade-off between efficiency and representation. Classically, 'representational' institutions are considered to facilitate the direct translation of popular preferences and cleavages into the political sphere with as little interference as possible, by means of parties representing distinct social groups, elections based on proportional representation, and low barriers to minority enfranchisement. Together, these institutions should ideally lead to the development of a diverse multi-party system in which all significant groups and interests are separately represented. In contrast, 'efficient' institutions that can deliver clear parliamentary majorities offering distinct policy alternatives are more often associated with majoritarian elections and 'catch-all' political parties that command electoral support across social cleavages. In theory, these make it more likely that minority and majority interests alike will be aggregated into a few large parties which alternate in power over time.

By the terms of this long-running debate, most of the political reforms in the Asia-Pacific region over the past decade have clearly come down on the side of efficiency and against representation. The move away from proportional representation systems (in which each party receives seats in close proportion to its overall share of the vote, thus advantaging smaller parties and minorities) towards majoritarian ones (which tend to advantage large parties through their 'winner-takes-all' outcomes) has been one of the Asia-Pacific region's more striking reform trends. Major changes to the electoral systems in Japan, South Korea, Indonesia, Taiwan, Thailand and the Philippines, as well as reforms to existing systems in Cambodia, Indonesia, Malaysia and Singapore, have all promoted the interests of incumbent parties by making it more difficult for smaller parties or minority movements to gain representation.

The interplay between competitive electoral politics and social cleavages—such as the multiple cultural, linguistic, religious and regional schisms at play in Indonesia—is thus an important piece of the reform picture. Many Asian and Pacific states have long experience with the problems caused by the inter-relationship between democratic government and ethnic diversity. At the end of World War II, independent and nominally democratic regimes were installed in post-colonial Burma, Indonesia, Malaysia, the Philippines and Singapore, as well as in Japan. With the exception of Japan, all of these new states were ethnically diverse; again with the exception of Japan, by 1972 all had fallen under some form of non-democratic rule. In each case, the interaction of social diversity and competitive politics provides part of the explanation for the failure of democracy.

Thus, Indonesia's first chaotic experience with democracy, between 1950 and 1957, was characterised by 'ethnic conflict of two kinds, religious-based and cultural/regional-based, [which] threatened to tear apart the infant republic' (Liddle 1997: 311). The failure of this abortive initial period of democratic government was at least in part a problem of competitive representative politics in a polity marked by major communal cleavages. Weak party systems, fragmented legislatures and an inability to maintain stable government led to the acute political gridlock and polarisation that is often blamed for the failure of Indonesia's initial attempt at democracy (see, for example, Feith 1962).

Similarly, the quasi-authoritarian political systems of both Malaysia and Singapore evolved partly as a result of a perceived need to control the political expression of ethnicity; as a result, the management of communal relations has remained a cornerstone of politics in both states (Crouch 1996; Rodan 1996). In the Philippines, where family, clan and regional identities are key political commodities, democracy remains fragile and 'candidates for national office have tended to be elected in large part on the basis of their ethnolinguistic and regional ties' (Montinola 1999: 67). Even in Thailand, where an assimilative, civic Thai identity has long been present, democratic politics retains a marked ethno-regional dimension (Maisrikrod 2002: 192). This growing rural–urban cleavage between the affluent middle-class population of Bangkok and the poorer rural regions was highlighted by the September 2006 coup that removed Prime Minister Thaksin Shinawatra from power.

The interplay between social cleavages and processes of democratisation can unleash powerful political pressures for segmental politics, presenting aspiring political entrepreneurs with the temptation to exploit ethno-political divisions in their quest for electoral success. In recent years, increasing elite awareness of these problems, combined with the inevitable calculations of self-interested actors seeking to advance their own political prospects, has stimulated a search for appropriate ameliorative responses through changes to the rules of the democratic game. Across the region, these attempts to engineer political outcomes have typically sought to improve government stability, encourage party aggregation, restrict the enfranchisement of regional or ethnic minorities, and foster majoritarian political outcomes. Indonesia has taken these measures the furthest, introducing a range of reforms to voting rules, electoral arrangements and political party regulations that are all aimed at producing a more consolidated party system. These will now be examined in more detail.

ELECTORAL REFORM

One particularly striking trend in recent years has been reform in the area of electoral system design. Because electoral systems determine how votes cast in an election translate into seats won in parliament, they are the central 'rule of the game' determining who governs. The constituent elements of any electoral system — such as the formula for translating votes into seats, the way electoral boundaries are drawn, the structure of the ballot and the extent to which voting is candidate or party centred — all exert an independent influence on the behavioural incentives facing political actors, and hence on the development of political parties and the kinds of campaign strategies and policy appeals they employ.

Despite the considerable differences in forms of government, political culture and democratic consolidation across the Asia-Pacific, increasingly convergent reform patterns are evident in the region, with Japan, South Korea, Taiwan, the Philippines and Thailand all enacting similar electoral reforms over the last decade.[3] A clear trend has been the increasing adoption of 'mixed-member' electoral systems, in which both proportional and district-based elections are run side by side, in parallel. Under such systems part of the legislature is elected, usually at a national level, by proportional representation, and the rest at the district level, usually by plurality rules. While mixed systems have become common around the world in the past decade, they have been a particularly popular choice in Asia's new democracies, perhaps because they appear to

---

3 For excellent recent surveys of Asian electoral systems, see Croissant, Bruns and John (2002) and Hicken and Kasuya (2003). The most comprehensive collection on the subject is Nohlen, Grotz and Hartmann (2001).

combine the benefits of proportional outcomes with the accountability of district representation.[4]

In Indonesia, the seven-member team of government officials and academics set up in 1998 to examine alternative electoral models (Tim Tujuh) also favoured a mixed-member model.[5] Under their proposed 'district plus' system, 76 per cent of seats would have been allocated to single-member districts, with the remaining 24 per cent elected by proportional representation. While popular with reform-minded activists, this proposal was rejected by Indonesia's main political parties, who instead pushed through an unusual hybrid system for the 1999 elections. They devised a party list, proportional representation system with 'personal vote' characteristics, whereby the vote spread in particular districts/municipalities (*kabupaten/kota*) within each multi-member electorate would determine which individual candidates would be elected. In theory, locally popular candidates who attracted a significant personal vote would thus increase their chances of gaining a seat from their party list. In practice, however, this provision proved almost impossible to administer, and was widely ignored by the electoral authorities.

For the 2004 elections, a more conventional model of 'open list' proportional representation was adopted. This time all candidates were chosen from party lists, but voters were able to influence the composition of the lists by voting directly for a chosen candidate. Again, the motivation for this reform – common in Europe but unique in the Asia-Pacific – was to give voters more influence over which candidates from a given party list would be elected, thus in theory strengthening the link between voters and politicians. As in 1999, however, this provision had a negligible influence on election outcomes: in 2004 only two of the Indonesian parliament's 550 seats were chosen in this way, as an exceptionally large number of personal votes was needed to alter a candidate's position on the party list. This may have been fortunate, given that the broader thrust of electoral reform in Indonesia was to encourage party cohesion by centralising control of party organisations – an objective incompatible with open list voting, which 'allows entrants to free-ride on the party label while simultaneously encouraging them to curry a personal reputation for the provision of particularistic goods' (Haggard 1997: 140).

Nonetheless, demand for some form of district-based system remains strong, fuelled in part by the expectation that Indonesia's democratic prospects would be enhanced if the power of party elites was reduced and politics brought closer to the people (Ellis 2000). In response to these widely expressed sentiments, one reform that did get implemented was a

---

4 For more on mixed-member systems, see Reynolds, Reilly and Ellis (2005).
5 For a good account of Tim Tujuh's work, see McBeth (1998).

drastic reduction in 'district magnitude': the number of members elected from each electoral district. In contrast to previous years, when provincial units delineated constituency boundaries, the 2004 elections were conducted using much smaller constituencies, capped at a maximum of 12 members per district. This raised the threshold for electoral victory considerably, and made it much more difficult for smaller parties to win seats than at previous elections, when districts were based on entire provinces (Sherlock 2004: 4). The overall effect, as in other Asian cases, was to make Indonesia's electoral arrangements considerably more advantageous to the large, well-organised, established parties than previously.

Indonesia also held its first direct elections for president and vice-president in 2004. Like the new party laws, the presidential voting system contained several measures designed to ensure that only broadly supported, nationally oriented candidates would be elected to office. First, only parties that had gained at least 5 per cent of the vote or 3 per cent of seats in the parliamentary elections were able to nominate candidates for the presidency, thereby sidelining smaller parties. Second, presidential and vice-presidential candidates had to run together as a team; as a result, it was assumed that major parties would choose a combination of a Javanese and an outer island candidate in order to maximise their appeal. Third, the election was conducted over two rounds of voting; to avoid a second round, first-round winners had to gain an absolute majority of votes nationwide, as well as at least 20 per cent in half of all provinces.[6] This latter provision—known in the scholarly literature as a 'distribution requirement'—was borrowed from Nigeria, another large and ethnically diverse country. Again the aim was to ensure that the winning candidate not only commanded support from a majority of voters, but also from different parts of the country. This made it difficult for candidates with strong regional support but limited nationwide appeal to win. In this respect, the presidential electoral system shares with the party formation laws a common centripetal logic, in that it aims to promote nationally focused politics by advantaging parties with a cross-regional support base.

How did these provisions work in practice? No candidate gained a majority of votes in the first round of the July 2004 presidential elections, necessitating a run-off in October. The second round was won convincingly by Susilo Bambang Yudhoyono, a secular and relatively progressive Javanese ex-general from the new Democratic Party (Partai Demokrat); his vice-presidential running mate was Jusuf Kalla, a Golkar stalwart from Sulawesi. Yudhoyono swept the field, carrying 28 of Indonesia's 32

---

6   The second round of voting entailed a straight run-off between the two leading teams of candidates, with no distribution requirements.

provinces. His opponent, incumbent president Megawati Soekarnoputri of the Indonesian Democratic Party of Struggle (PDI-P), won only the predominantly Hindu island of Bali (a traditional stronghold) and a few smaller provinces in eastern Indonesia. Thus, while not put directly to the test, the overall outcome of Indonesia's first direct presidential election did result in the election of a candidate with broad cross-regional support, in line with the aspirations inherent in the presidential electoral provisions.

POLITICAL PARTY REFORMS

Scholars of democracy have long considered political parties to play a crucial role not just in representing interests, aggregating preferences and forming governments, but also in managing conflict and promoting stable politics. However, the extent to which parties are able to play these roles varies significantly depending on the nature of the party system. In two-party systems, for instance, parties must cultivate and maintain support across a range of social groups to win elections, and therefore need to provide broad public goods — goods that benefit everyone without exclusion, such as property rights, the rule of law, public education, health care, roads and other basic infrastructure — in order to maximise their chances of success. In fragmented multi-party systems, in contrast, parties may need only a small plurality of votes to win office, and so can focus on providing sectoral benefits to their own supporters rather than to the broader electorate (Haggard 1997: 140). This is a particular problem in culturally diverse societies such as Indonesia, where political parties often form around distinct social cleavages based on ethnic, religious or regional identities.

The historical experience shows that democracy in Indonesia has been hampered recurrently by the consequences of social cleavages and party fragmentation — both in recent years, following the collapse of the Soeharto regime, and earlier, during the country's initial democratic interlude in the 1950s. Then, shifting coalitions of secular, Islamic, nationalist, communal and regional parties led to six changes of government in seven years, providing a ready pretext for the overthrow of democracy and the declaration of martial law by President Soekarno in 1957. In Indonesia — one of the most ethnically complex states in the contemporary world — various social and religious cleavages, as well as the longstanding regional division between Java and the outer islands, have strongly influenced the development of the party system. For instance, the influence of more modernist and secular parties tends to be higher within Java, while stricter Islamist parties often have strong bases in the outer islands.

The result has been a highly fragmented political party system during the periods of competitive democracy — that is, during the 1950s and again today. This is far from being an optimal form of party system for democratic consolidation and stable government. A range of comparative studies have emphasised the pitfalls of a highly fragmented party system for the survival of new democracies. Powell's work on democratic durability suggests that the most favourable system comprises a limited number of cohesive and broad-based parties, rather than many small, fragmented, personalised or ethnically based parties (Powell 1982: 99–108). Diamond, Linz and Lipset's multi-volume comparison of democracy in developing countries concludes that 'a system of two or a few parties, with broad social and ideological bases, may be conducive to stable democracy' (Diamond, Linz and Lipset 1995: 35). In the same vein, Weiner and Özbudun (1987) find that the one common factor among the small number of stable Third World democracies is the presence of a broad-based party system with no strong links to the cleavage structure of society.

The flip side of having a system of aggregative political parties is that minorities tend to be assimilated into the political majority rather than having their own independent voice. Indonesia's recent political party reforms, which have sought to remodel parties and party systems through a variety of institutional incentives and constraints, highlight these risks. While only three officially sanctioned and controlled 'national' parties were allowed under Soeharto's New Order, the collapse of the regime in 1998 saw over 100 new parties emerge in a matter of months, many with extremely limited support bases. This mushrooming of new parties provoked widespread fears that Indonesia's emerging party system would be too fragmented, with too many parties, for democracy to function effectively (Tan 2002). With Indonesian politics in flux, a widely held view was that the country needed nationally focused parties that could gain the support of voters across the archipelago and form legitimate, stable governments. Indeed, the development of such a national party system was seen as an essential step in countering secessionist sentiment and building a viable democracy.

To achieve these twin goals — promoting broad-based parties while resisting the emergence of separatist ones — Indonesia's political reformers introduced a complex collection of incentives and restraints to guide party system development. On the one hand, all parties were required to demonstrate a national support base as a pre-condition for them to compete in the transitional 1999 elections. Under the new rules, each party had to establish branches in at least one-third of Indonesia's (then) 27 provinces, as well as offices in more than half the districts or municipalities within those provinces, before they could contest the election. As King (2003: 51) notes:

where previously the number of election contestants was stipulated by law, permitting only three, now they were limited on the basis of insufficient geographical coverage and depth of penetration of their organisations.

The bias in favour of national parties was so strong that regional parties were even banned from competing in elections for the *regional* assemblies. This took the national bias in the electoral system to an extreme: instead of allowing regional governments to be representative of their own constituent populations, the law forced them to be comprised of the same parties that were competing at the national level.

These new rules had an immediate effect on party numbers: of 141 parties that applied to contest the national elections in 1999, only 48 gained approval to run, and of these only five gained significant representation at the election itself. These were PDI-P led by then president Megawati Soekarnoputri; Golkar, the party machine created by Soeharto; and three Islamic parties – the National Mandate Party (PAN), the United Development Party (PPP) and the National Awakening Party (PKB) of Megawati's predecessor, Abdurrahman Wahid (Suryadinata 2002: 90–2). For the next elections in 2004, the party laws went even further. Before being permitted to compete in the elections, new parties had to establish branches in two-thirds of all provinces and in two-thirds of the districts within those provinces, while each local party unit had to demonstrate that it had at least 1,000 members (or at least one-thousandth of the population in smaller regions). This led to a further drop in party numbers, with only 24 qualifying for the 2004 elections: the six top parties from 1999 plus 18 new parties that met the organisational and membership requirements.

At the April 2004 parliamentary elections, most of the major parties were able to attract a significant spread of votes across western, central and eastern Indonesia. While there were clear regional strongholds – the Islamic parties dominated in Sumatra, PDI-P did best in Java and Bali, and Golkar remained strong in eastern Indonesia – all major parties gained seats across the archipelago. Whereas the 1999 assembly was dominated by the 'big five', Indonesia's 2004 parliament featured a 'big seven': the five main parties from 1999 plus two new entrants, the Justice and Welfare Party (PKS) and Yudhoyono's Democratic Party (Sherlock 2004). Of these, PDI-P and Golkar together controlled around 40 per cent of seats, while the five other parties each controlled 8–10 per cent. Although King (2003: Ch. 7) argues that Indonesia's post-Soeharto elections broadly replicated the societal and religious cleavages present in 1955, the fact that the major parties were able to command such cross-regional support is actually a significant difference.

As well as restricting regional parties, Indonesia's new party laws attempted to limit the number of parties by introducing systemic pressures for smaller parties to amalgamate. Following the 1999 elections, parties that had failed to gain more than 2 per cent of seats in the lower house of parliament or 3 per cent of seats in regional assemblies had to merge with other parties to surmount these thresholds and contest future elections — a provision that resulted in a number of smaller parties merging before the 2004 elections. Pressure for this kind of party amalgamation is likely to increase in the future, given the new laws now in place.

How did these provisions work in practice? As stated above, the absolute number of parties dropped from 48 contesting the 1999 elections to 24 contesting the 2004 poll — a 50 per cent decline over one parliamentary term. There was a similar but less extreme decline in the number of parties in parliament, from 21 in 1999 to 17 in 2004, as votes that went to smaller parties in 1999 were spread more evenly across the larger, established parties in 2004. As a result, although the total number of parties decreased, the fragmentation of the Indonesian parliament became even more pronounced. Over time, however, it is likely that the new rules of the game will encourage greater consolidation in the party system.

But party engineering has costs as well as benefits. As evidenced by the 50 per cent reduction in the number of parties between 1999 and 2004, Indonesia's electoral laws favour incumbent parties by restricting the level of political competition and placing barriers in the way of potential new entrants into the political marketplace. As a result, there is a real danger of overkill inherent in the new party provisions, especially given that plans for future elections include raising the barriers to smaller parties and new entrants even higher. Under existing legislation, parties that failed to win more than 3 per cent of seats in the 2004 elections will be barred from competing at the next elections in 2009 unless they amalgamate with other parties to reach this support marker. Even more severe restrictions will be placed on future candidates for the presidency; under current plans, only parties that win at least 20 per cent of the vote at the 2009 parliamentary elections, or at least 15 per cent of seats, will be entitled to enter candidates for the presidential and vice-presidential race. All of this not only discriminates against smaller parties, but tilts the electoral playing field markedly in favour of incumbents and established parties more generally.

CONCLUSION

As Diamond (1990: 55) has noted, one paradox of democracy is that in some circumstances 'a political system can be made *more* stably democratic by making it somewhat *less* representative' (emphasis in original). This clearly has been the strategy pursued by many Asia-Pacific reformers, including those in Indonesia, as they seek to encourage more programmatic party politics and stable executive governments. Harking back to the success of the East Asian 'Tigers' and their unorthodox but successful interventions in the economic arena, an increasing number of East Asian democracies are seeking to manage political change by institutional innovations aimed at changing the way their political systems function. These reforms typically have multiple objectives: protecting incumbents, limiting ethnic or regional movements, and promoting more centrist and stable politics by encouraging broad-based parties.[7]

Indonesia has been at the forefront of this region-wide movement. Through a combination of spatial registration for political parties, pressures for smaller parties to amalgamate into larger ones, reductions in the electoral system's proportionality requirement, and regional vote-distribution requirements for presidential elections, political reformers in Indonesia have attempted to engineer the development of a few large parties with a national reach. The interests of incumbent politicians are a key part of the reform story, as restrictions on new entrants to the political arena and on the multiplication of smaller parties inevitably work in favour of established political elites and the larger, better-resourced political parties. But it would be a mistake to see these reforms as purely self-serving. Opinion surveys, for instance, find a strong popular preference for a system of moderate multi-partism, rather than party fragmentation, in Indonesia (Tan 2002: 501–2).

To date, the results of these ambitious exercises in political engineering have proven somewhat ambiguous. Despite all the institutional incentives promoting greater consolidation, Indonesia experienced an increase in party fragmentation between 1999 and 2004. Measures to promote nationally focused parties and limit the enfranchisement of minorities have had some modest successes, but have not fundamentally changed the nature of electoral politics. On the other hand, Indonesia's new electoral laws do appear to have played a modest but important role in curbing the fragmentation of electoral support, by encouraging parties and candidates to compete for votes across the archipelago rather than relying on regional support pockets.

Whether political engineering will be enough to change the way the Indonesian political system works and forge more durable and stable party politics thus remains to be seen. Current trends are somewhat contradictory: while the number of parties has declined by half, parliamentary fragmentation has increased. Indonesia's new laws have also been criticised for locking minorities out of power, and for placing unreasonably high hurdles in front of new parties. As one observer has noted,

---

7 For more on this, see Reilly (2006).

if the laws requiring parties to prove minimum membership numbers all the way down to the district level are enforced strictly, 'parties may, instead of collecting dues from members, be paying them to sign up in future' (Tan 2002: 488).

A major impetus behind the new laws was the desire to reduce the overall number of parties, consolidate the party system and make mono-ethnic, regionalist or separatist parties unviable. As a result, it is now virtually impossible for a party to get its name on the ballot in Indonesia unless it can demonstrate a level of national support that is likely to be beyond the reach of even the most well-organised regional movement (although at the time of writing an exception appeared to have been made for Acehnese parties as part of the peace deal). The new presidential electoral laws only strengthen this approach.[8]

While improving the prospects for a nationally consolidated party system, the new rules may also undercut the ability of all but a few established parties to form and mobilise support. If ethnic or religious groups are unable to mobilise and compete for political power by democratic means, they may seek to achieve their objectives in other ways. A balance therefore needs to be struck between encouraging national parties, which is generally a positive strategy, and restricting regional ones, which can have clear downsides. The danger of overkill — weighting incentives so much in favour of party aggregation and against regional or ethnic parties that they form a pattern of systemic discrimination and disempowerment — is clearly present.

REFERENCES

Croissant, A., G. Bruns and M. John (eds) (2002), *Electoral Politics in Southeast and East Asia*, Singapore: Friedrich Ebert Stiftung.

Crouch, H. (1996), *Government and Society in Malaysia*, Ithaca NY: Cornell University Press.

Diamond, L. (1990), 'Three Paradoxes of Democracy', *Journal of Democracy*, 1: 48–60.

Diamond, L., J. Linz and S.M. Lipset (1995), 'Introduction: What Makes for Democracy?', pp. 1–33 in L. Diamond, J. Linz and S.M. Lipset (eds), *Politics in Developing Countries: Comparing Experiences with Democracy*, Boulder CO: Lynne Rienner Publishers.

Ellis, A. (2000), 'The Politics of Electoral Systems in Transition: The 1999 Elections in Indonesia and Beyond', *Representation*, 37: 241–8.

---

8   The relevant laws are Law No. 31/2002 on Political Parties; Law No. 12/2003 on General Elections; and Law No. 23/2003 on the Election of the President and Vice-President.

Feith, H. (1962), *The Decline of Constitutional Democracy in Indonesia*, Ithaca NY: Cornell University Press.

Haggard, S. (1997), 'Democratic Institutions, Economic Policy, and Development', pp. 121–52 in C. Clague (ed.), *Institutions and Economic Development*, Baltimore MD and London: Johns Hopkins University Press.

Hicken, A. and Y. Kasuya (2003), 'A Guide to the Constitutional Structures and Electoral Systems of East, South and Southeast Asia', *Electoral Studies*, 22: 121–51.

Huntington, S.P. (1991), *The Third Wave: Democratization in the Late Twentieth Century*, Norman OK: University of Oklahoma Press.

King, D.Y. (2003), *Half-hearted Reform: Electoral Institutions and the Struggle for Democracy in Indonesia*, Westport CT and London: Praeger.

Liddle, R.W. (1997), 'Coercion, Co-optation, and the Management of Ethnic Relations in Indonesia' pp. 273–320 in M.E. Brown and S. Ganguly (eds), *Government Policies and Ethnic Relations in the Asia-Pacific*, Cambridge MA and London: MIT Press.

Lijphart, A. (1999), *Patterns of Democracy: Government Forms and Performance in Thirty-six Countries*, New Haven CT and London: Yale University Press.

MacIntyre, A. (2003), *The Power of Institutions: Political Architecture and Governance*, Ithaca NY: Cornell University Press.

Maisrikrod, S. (2002), 'Political Reform and the New Thai Electoral System: Old Habits Die Hard?', pp. 187–209 in J.F. Hsieh and D. Newman (eds), *How Asia Votes*, New York NY: Chatham House.

McBeth, J. (1998), 'Dawn of a New Age', *Far Eastern Economic Review*, 12 September.

Montinola, G.R. (1999), 'The Philippines in 1998: Opportunities amid Crisis', *Asian Survey*, 39(1): 64–71.

Nohlen, D., F. Grotz and C. Hartmann (eds) (2001), *Elections in Asia and the Pacific: A Data Handbook*, 2 volumes, Oxford: Oxford University Press.

Powell, G.B. (1982), *Contemporary Democracies: Participation, Stability, and Violence*, Cambridge MA: Harvard University Press.

Przeworski, A. (1991), *Democracy and the Market: Political and Economic Reforms in Eastern Europe and Latin America*, Cambridge: Cambridge University Press.

Reilly, B. (2006), *Democracy and Diversity: Political Engineering in the Asia-Pacific*, Oxford: Oxford University Press.

Reynolds, A., B. Reilly and A. Ellis (2005), *Electoral System Design: The New International IDEA Handbook*, Stockholm: International Institute for Democracy and Electoral Assistance (IDEA).

Rodan, G. (1996), 'Elections without Representation: The Singapore Experience under the PAP', pp. 61–89 in R.H. Taylor (ed.), *The Politics of Elections in Southeast Asia*, Washington DC: Woodrow Wilson Center Press, and Cambridge: Cambridge University Press.

Schumpeter, J.A. (1947), *Capitalism, Socialism and Democracy*, New York NY: Harper.

Sherlock, S. (2004), 'Consolidation and Change: The Indonesian Parliament after the 2004 Elections', Canberra: Centre for Democratic Institutions.

Suryadinata, L. (2002), *Elections and Politics in Indonesia*, Singapore: Institute of Southeast Asian Studies.

Tan, P.J. (2002), 'Anti-party Reaction in Indonesia: Causes and Implications', *Contemporary Southeast Asia*, 24(3): 484–508.

Weiner, M. and E. Özbudun (eds) (1987), *Competitive Elections in Developing Countries*, Durham NC: Duke University Press.

4   TRACING THE PROGRESS OF LOCAL GOVERNMENTS SINCE DECENTRALISATION

I Ketut Putra Erawan

Formally launched in 2001, the decentralisation of governmental authority is one of the most important reform programs in Indonesia. Both supporters and critics of the program acknowledge that decentralisation has changed the landscape of the central–local political relationship. However, a closer examination of the effects of decentralisation reveals significant variations across the country. Recent research indicates local state capture and rampant corruption in some jurisdictions, but deepening democracy and the emergence of effective government in others. What explains these variations in outcomes across Indonesia? What conditions are shaping the experiences of local governments with decentralisation? And, at this early stage, what conclusions can we draw about the gains and losses associated with decentralisation?

In this chapter I investigate some of the factors determining decentralisation outcomes at the local level. I identify some of the gains and losses associated with decentralisation and explain the conditions shaping these. Based on an examination of how decentralisation has actually been implemented in four localities, I argue: (1) that decentralisation should be viewed as an extended process; (2) that the power and interaction of state and societal actors at the local level, as well as the penetration of national and international actors, are salient factors determining the trajectory and outcome of decentralisation in particular localities; and (3) that these interactions happen iteratively and are shaped by the local political–economic context. I focus on three districts and one municipality: the district of Bangka in the recently created province of Banka-Belitung, the district of Bantul in Yogyakarta, the district of Jembrana in Bali, and the city of Mataram (the capital of West Nusa Tenggara) in Lombok. They were chosen to highlight the wide variations that exist in the extent to which local governments have adapted to the new political framework.

Viewing decentralisation as a process that takes time to evolve — rather than as a condition that exists fully formed from the outset — allows us to explore the impact of both local actors and contextual factors in shaping the experience and outcome of decentralisation at the local level. It will be argued here that the same national decentralisation program has generated widely varying experiences across Indonesia. These variations are mainly explained by differences in the capacity of local actors to respond to political, societal and institutional conditions in their localities. It is important to assess the role of local actors, not only because they are significant in creating the strategic programs for the implementation of decentralisation, but, more importantly, because they play a pivotal role in shaping the political environment that determines the extent of possible innovation and reform.

If they are to succeed in shaping the political environment, local leaders must take control of the policy-making process by creating effective coalitions among political parties. But this is not enough; they must also enhance their engagement with the electorate and society, to build community support for their policies and programs. Unless they can meet these conditions, they are unlikely to be able to protect their reform initiatives from partisan interests in and around government. According to Geddes (1994: 46–7), these include 'political activists accustomed to distributing jobs in return for political support and employees who got their jobs that way, and whose status is threatened by the change to a merit-based system'. She continues:

> Members of Congress may use funds for pet projects from which they derive electoral benefits, or officials in the finance ministry may informally reallocate funds to serve more pressing political needs. The separation of the funding process from the traditional political game may be necessary in order to prevent funds allocated for development projects from being used for other purposes ... If bureaucrats form part of the political exchange network, their own success will be linked to that of particular politicians, and they will have compelling reasons to make decisions that maximize support for their patrons rather than furthering agency goals (Geddes 1994: 47).

To minimise the risk of capture, rent seeking and free riding, Geddes advises local leaders to insulate their programs from the demands of 'the individuals most capable of undermining state efforts to initiate change', namely 'politicians, party activists, and bureaucrats intent on "spending" scarce state resources to "buy" political support' (Geddes 1994: 82). She introduces the notion of insulation to refer to the act of responding to such pressures by creating mechanisms to guarantee the emergence of a competent state, saying that:

> an insulated agency is like a cell surrounded by its semipermiable membrane. Information and resources flow through the membrane from the environment into the agency and vice versa, but the agency, like the cell, is able to maintain its organisational integrity and stick to its own goals ... In short, insulated agencies interact with their environments, but they are not overwhelmed by them (Geddes 1994: 50).

To counter the risk of capture, rent seeking and free riding, political leaders need to create democratic mechanisms that are responsive to the interests of the people. These might include:

> meritocratic recruitment to ensure the competence of personnel; sources of funding protected from the depredation of rivals within government; and an incentive structure for bureaucrats that makes *achieving their personal career goals consistent with achieving agency goals* [emphasis added] (Geddes 1994: 78).

Such mechanisms would provide the structure for a new pattern of relationships between political actors and their voters and coalition partners.

In short, there is an obvious connection between the political environment and the mechanisms developed to protect the agency or program from capture. I argue that the capacity of local actors to respond to the political environment and shape institutions is an important factor explaining the outcome of the decentralisation process at the local level.

This chapter is organised as follows. The first section describes the context in which the national decentralisation program emerged. The second examines the extent to which local leaders in four localities have been able to build political coalitions and networks of societal support. The third section traces the policy reform initiatives of these local leaders and the fourth examines the extent to which they have been able to insulate their initiatives from capture by vested interests and rent seekers. The final section summarises the preceding discussion.

THE CONTEXT OF DECENTRALISATION

The New Order Regime

The New Order regime (1966–98) ruled Indonesia through centralism and authoritarianism. Under former president Soeharto, there was little room for any genuine participation by local governments or citizens in public agenda setting, decision making, or the evaluation and implementation of policies. The New Order government exercised tight control over society, ensuring that all decisions were made by and served the interests of the centre (Polokda 2003). It exercised control through three mechanisms: the security apparatus, co-optation of the legislature and corporatist control of interest group activity. Political forces were centralised, with the regime determining which parties would be permitted to participate in general elections. Parties were structured hierarchically, with a strong central leadership exercising tight control over branches down to the local level. Responsibility for decision making lay with party leaders at the centre, not with local branch members. The regime often interfered in the recruitment of party elites and public officials. As well as making all political, economic and security decisions, the central government designed and implemented public services for the entire country, channelling them through a long, hierarchical state apparatus. Consequently, public services were designed, not to meet the needs of the people as defined at the local level, but to accord with the strategic interests of central actors and their cronies.

The Transition to Democracy

Following the fall of Soeharto, wide-ranging reforms were carried out at both the national and local levels. The new government set about designing new structures of state power and implementing a new electoral system. The repercussions at the local level were tremendous. The reforms opened the way for new arenas of political participation, new actors and power constellations, and new forms of political interaction.

One of the most important reforms was the enactment of two new decentralisation laws: Law No. 22/1999 on Local Autonomy and Law No. 25/1999 on Financial Balance between the Central and Local Governments. The formal start of the decentralisation program in 2001 marked a deep-seated change in the landscape of the central–local political relationship.

The new laws brought change in three areas. First, the bureaucracy was restructured to emphasise local delivery of and responsibility for public services. Second, with the introduction of a new, direct electoral system in 2004, governors, district heads and mayors became representatives of their constituents rather than appointees of the central government. Indonesians also voted for their first directly elected president (Susilo Bambang Yudoyono) in 2004. Third, local governments were guaranteed wide authority and discretion in policy innovation. The new laws also guaranteed the allocation of a certain level of finances to the regions, to enable them to fulfil their autonomous functions.

Regions responded in different ways to the opportunities opened up by the historical conjunctures of 1999–2001. Local governments do not work in a historical or political vacuum; differences in their political–economic heritages and societal conditions inevitably affect local trajectories. In shaping local politics, local actors must respond to existing political–economic conditions and forge strong political–economic and societal bases. In shaping local policy, their challenge is to create innovative programs, isolate them from short-term demands, create networks of supporters and institutionalise the process. So far, only a few have succeeded in this difficult task.

POLITICAL COALITIONS AND SOCIETAL SUPPORT NETWORKS

This section focuses on local politics post-decentralisation in four locations: Bangka, Bantul, Jembrana and Mataram. First, I discuss existing political–economic conditions in each of the localities at the time of decentralisation, and show how they influenced the decentralisation strategies adopted by their leaders. I then trace the trajectory of each locality since decentralisation, focusing in particular on the role of political coalitions and societal support networks. I argue that the degree of success of local leaders in building political coalitions and societal support networks has played a crucial role in determining local trajectories, and helps explain why innovations were possible in some localities but not others.

Initial Political–Economic Conditions

I begin by mapping political–economic conditions at the time of decentralisation in each locality.

In Bangka, tin mining has historically been the main driving force of the local economy.[1] Close to 40 per cent of land in the district is used for purposes related to mining industry activity. PT Timah, the dominant state enterprise in the Indonesian tin industry, virtually ruled the locality until 1998. It was the dominant employer and landowner, and the main provider of essential public services such as electricity, water and roads. When the new province of Bangka-Belitung was created in 2000, PT Timah offered to hand over some of its buildings for use as provincial government offices. The company was restructured in the same year because of a continuing decline in international tin prices. The decision to cut 20,000 jobs created significant problems for Bangka. The amount of unauthorised tin mining soared, resulting in widespread environmental damage and creating social tensions. The tin miners encroached on

---

1 According to one source, even the name of the district comes from the word *vanka* meaning 'tin'.

plantation areas (causing conflict with plantation owners and workers) and on the seas (causing conflict with fishermen). The continuing significance of the tin industry to the local economy has easily overshadowed all other political and economic considerations as Bangka has adapted to decentralisation.

In the city of Mataram, socio-cultural factors set the context for decentralisation. Riots broke out just a few days after the election of the new mayor, Muhammad Ruslan. On 17 January 2000, a demonstration in support of Maluku's Muslims erupted into anarchy. Rioters burned several churches, robbed Chinese-owned properties and threatened several minority groups. Refugees fled the town, among them at least 175 teachers, 16 medical specialists and 38 non-medical specialists (*Kompas*, 27 January 2000, 31 January 2000). The ethnic riots cut off educational and health services to the city for several weeks and threatened the future of tourism in the area. It is not surprising, then, that the top priority for Mataram since decentralisation has been to maintain security and rebuild the city's image as a safe place to visit and live.

In both Bantul and Jembrana, local political leaders were confronted with the problem of restructuring the local government after long periods of authoritarian rule. In Bantul, the previous district head, Sri Roso Sudharmo, had governed coercively, and had a reputation for dealing harshly with dissenters and protesters.[2] Since being elected in 1999, the new district head, Idam Samawi, has worked hard to rebuild public confidence in local government, despite having to deal with a relatively fragmented regional assembly in which five parties are represented: the Indonesian Democratic Party of Struggle (PDI-P), Golkar, the National Awakening Party (PKB), the National Mandate Party (PAN) and the United Development Party (PPP). In Jembrana, too, the defining theme of local politics since the start of decentralisation has been to restore public faith in local authority.

Building Political Coalitions

I now consider the extent to which local leaders have succeeded in creating effective political coalitions, enabling them to pass legislation.

In Mataraman, the newly elected mayor, Muhammad Ruslan, was quick to recognise that concerns about safety posed a considerable threat to the city's economy, and so put security at the top of his policy agenda. This focus on security was natural considering the history of ethnic tensions in the region. Mataram has many ethnic groups, including the Sasak, Balinese, Mbojo and Bugis, and has often experienced ethnic tensions in

2   One local journalist who criticised his administration was murdered.

the past.[3] Perhaps surprisingly, these social tensions have not resulted in a fragmentation of local politics; although Ruslan is a member of Golkar, he has governed with strong support from PDI-P and PPP. This is no mean achievement considering that political power in Mataram is almost evenly divided between PDI-P and Golkar, which won 28 per cent and 27 per cent of the vote respectively in the 2004 regional assembly elections; PPP holds the balance of power with 14 per cent. Ruslan's ability to gain the support of other political parties has meant that the relationship between the executive and the regional assembly in Mataram is a solid one. As a result, the mayor has succeeded in gaining the assembly's support even for some quite controversial decisions (Polokda 2003).

The district head of Bangka, Eko Maulana Ali, also enjoys strong support from the dominant political parties in the region: PDI-P and Golkar. He has used this to marshal support for tighter regulation of mining activities in Bangka. As part of this effort, he has worked to build ties with other sections of the local business community, international investors and officials in central government agencies in Jakarta.

The district head of Jembrana, I Gede Winasa, has also been successful in building a strong political support network. Winasa was a relative novice to political life before being elected district head. Upon securing the top position in the dominant party in the region, PDI-P, he moved quickly to build a broader base of support within the legislature. His personal popularity (and the relative unpopularity of his competitors) helped him build an effective legislative coalition which, in turn, enabled him to introduce a range of important policy reforms.

The district head of Bantul, Idam Samawi, inherited a pluralist and relatively fragmented political constellation. In this situation, the support of any one party alone would have been inadequate; he has needed to accommodate the interests of a number of parties to achieve a legislative majority. The key to his ability to do this has been an astute willingness to trade concessions.

Building Societal Support Networks

In addition to building coalitions among parties in the legislature, successful leaders need to reach further to create wider networks of support in the local community. The ability of the four local leaders to build societal support networks is the focus of this subsection.

---

3 In 1998, for example, ethnic riots broke out when Harun Al Rasyid, an ethnic Mbojo, defeated Lalu Mudjitahid, an ethnic Sasak, in the gubernatorial election.

In Bangka, Eko Maulana Ali has striven to cultivate networks of support among the district's NGOs and mass organisations. For a district with a population of less than 1 million, Bangka has a huge number of these—at least 163 according to Polokda (2003), most of them political free riders (*kelompok perkeliruan*).[4] According to local journalists, it was these groups that mobilised demonstrators to reject the accountability speeches of the governor and district head. It has even been claimed that some local politicians have paid these organisations to prevent them from launching protests against them. In Bangka, the role of social critic is the domain of the mass media rather than the universities.[5] This means that, to build societal support for their policies, local politicians must be responsive to the mass media while also managing the demands of the NGOs and mass organisations. Eko Maulana Ali has proven reasonably successful in treading this fine line.

In Mataram, Muhammad Ruslan has had to cope with a fragmented society placing heavy demands on the local government. The frictions among the leaders of competing groups have exacerbated political, ethnic and social tensions in the city. Nahdlatul Wathan, for example, split into two factions, one supporting the People's Sovereignty Party (PDR) and the other supporting Golkar (Polokda 2003). Rivalries among Lombok's multitude of civilian security forces (*pamswakarsa*), the largest of which is Amphibi, have also posed challenges for the local government (Polokda 2003). While often succumbing to pressure from interest groups, the local government has also used the state security agency to quell protests from NGOs that have expressed their dissatisfaction with government policy too loudly and too often (Polokda 2003).

In Bantul, the local government has made great progress in shaping the social base. Since taking power, Idam Samawi has worked hard to win over those alienated by the previous regime. Often describing himself as more of a journalist than a ruler, Samawi communicates local government policies and development programs to the people through his own talk show on television. He has also established good channels of communication with local NGOs, which play a vital role in communicating people's concerns on local issues.

In Jembrana, Winasa has proven skilful in using state resources to develop programs with strong appeal to the electorate, thereby creating a loyal support base among community groups. The government regularly provides financial support to various informal social leaders and groups.

---

4   Bangka has so many lobby groups that one local activist has called the district 'a small river with a lot of crocodiles' (*sungai kecil banyak buayanya*).
5   There are three main newspapers in Bangka: *Bangka Belitung Pos* (affiliated with *Jawa Pos*), *Bangka Pos* (affiliated with *Kompas*) and *Rakyat Pos*.

In September–December 2005, for example, the local government offered Jembrana's 1,516 informal traffic guides (*juru arah*) Rp 200,000 each in financial support (Polokda 2003). It is their job to inform people about local policy, going door to door. Closer to an election, however, they could easily be transformed into tools of vote mobilisation.

INITIATING POLICY REFORM PROGRAMS

This section explores the extent to which local governments have succeeded in developing and implementing new programs. Among the four local governments that are the focus of this chapter, Jembrana has proven to be the most innovative in terms of its bureaucratic, service delivery and social policies. It is followed by Bantul with its emphasis on education and health. The other two districts have been less innovative, because of a preoccupation with security issues in the case of Mataram and because of problems in the mining sector in the case of Bangka.

In Bangka, the local government developed two main strategies to implement decentralisation. The first was to restructure the bureaucracy by creating some new offices, merging several existing ones and getting rid of those that were no longer necessary. Although the aim was to reduce the overall size of the bureaucracy, this was not achieved in practice because of the pressure on the government to maintain existing bureaucratic structures and programs. The second strategy was to regulate strategic sectors such as tin mining. Under Regional Regulation 20/2001, the district of Bangka assumed authority for trade in tin and other strategic goods.[6] This program remains controversial.

The city of Mataram has emphasised public services since decentralisation, focusing its efforts on education and security in particular. In 2002 almost 40 per cent of the city budget was devoted to education; the proportion was even higher in 2003. At first glance these significant allocations of budgetary funds indicate a serious attempt by the government to reduce poverty through education. However, closer scrutiny reveals that almost 70 per cent of the money was spent on the construction of new buildings—including, controversially, three luxurius elementary schools and two high schools—even though significant numbers of existing schools were in poor condition (Polokda 2003). In the area of security, the Mataram government has focused on enforcing strict sanctions against wrongdoers; creating a more secure environment for residents and busi-

---

6 This regulation was preceded by Regional Regulation 6/2001, which gave the local government authority to regulate all mining in the district, particularly tin mining.

nesses; and supporting the *pamswakarsa*. The latter policy of supporting the creation of *pamswakarsa* and embedding them with the formal security forces has proven controversial; many people think that by legitimising the *pamswakarsa*, the local government runs the risk of increasing ethnic tensions and the use of coercion.

In Bantul, the local government proposed two main strategies for implementing decentralisation, the first focusing on education and the second on health. It began by merging several schools to increase their efficiency. It also offered significant numbers of scholarships to students and increased financial support for teachers. The main problem has been to ensure continued funding for the government's educational programs, due to the inadequacy of the local budget. In the area of health, Bantul tackled the restructuring of health care services by increasing the capacity of 17 community health centres (*puskesmas*) to hospitalise patients, by creating six special *puskesmas* and by changing the status of the general hospital to that of an autonomous hospital. But the local government faces problems in this area as well, because of the lack of medical staff and because of Bantul's challenging geographic conditions.

Since 2001, Jembrana has adopted four main strategies to improve development outcomes in the district: a free school tuition program; a public health insurance scheme; a program of soft loans to professional groups; and a bureaucratic restructuring program.

The free school tuition program applies to elementary and high school students attending both public and private schools. In addition, the local government provides subsidies to poor students. These programs were preceded by a rationalisation of schools to cut costs and increase efficiency. Schools that were not performing well or that had poor enrolments were either closed or merged with other schools. The local government also introduced new management procedures and selected some schools with specially trained teachers to lead the way in providing a high-quality education (Polokda 2003). In another local government initiative, new high school graduates were offered the chance to undertake training in Japan for three years.[7]

Rather than continue to subsidise the *puskesmas* and hospitals, in 2003 Winasa set up a public health insurance scheme. This has forced local health-care providers to become autonomous and find alternative sources of revenue, with most increasing their charges for services (Polokda 2003). However, some local residents can still obtain free health

---

7 The local government provides loans to cover the cost of training and internship expenses while the trainees are in Japan. Participants are asked to repay the loans after they obtain jobs.

care and generic medicines through service providers contracted by the local government.

Jembrana has attempted to strengthen the local economy by providing soft loans to selected professional groups, whose monthly repayments are then used to finance loans to other groups. During 2000–04, the local government distributed over Rp 20 billion to 595 groups, cooperatives and village credit institutions (LPDs) across four subdistricts in Jembrana (Polokda 2003).

The local government has also restructured and streamlined its bureaucracy, by merging several offices and closing others. This resulted in 178 positions being lost in 2003 (Polokda 2003). Offices were merged on the basis of synergies in their core activities, in particular economic activities (production, markets, capital), public services, and support activities (planning and evaluation, human resources, finance).

INSULATING PROGRAMS FROM POLITICAL CAPTURE AND RENT SEEKING

In attempting to implement major policy reforms, a critical challenge for all leaders is to protect the new programs from grasping hands in and around government. This section examines the extent to which local leaders in each of the four localities have been able to insulate their policy reforms from capture.

In Bangka, the struggle to insulate programs from capture has focused on Eko Maulana Ali's efforts to regulate strategic sectors like mining. He managed to attract the support of local state and societal actors who wanted the income from mining to be returned to Bangka, but was not able to resist their short-term demands or those of other actors. As mentioned above, the local government tried, but failed, to streamline the bureaucracy. To create support among international businesses and central government bureaucracies, it has offered various concessions that have accelerated the exploitation of the district's natural resources and damaged the environment. Some critics argue that in this respect the local politicians have been no more successful in resisting sectoral interests than their predecessors in PT Timah, the provincial government and the central government ministries.

Mataram has wasted resources on building luxurius new schools while failing to improve the standard of existing ones. This indicates the inability of the local leaders to insulate programs from personalistic and partisan demands, in this case from the city's middle and upper classes. The rest of the community, who form a majority of the population, have not been well served by such policies. Muhammad Ruslan's thrust to support the creation and promotion of the *pamswakarsa* provides another example of the inability of the local leaders to resist sectoral interests, in the latter case those advocating the use of vigilante groups to maintain security.

In Bantul, Idam Samawi has been partially successful in shielding programs from short-term demands. As part of the local government's education reforms, he consulted widely among the community, setting up both an education council to support the bureaucracy and a school council to support schools. Samawi's efforts to include the public in the reform process expanded his support base among families, who appreciated his attempts to improve educational outcomes. Nevertheless, some people questioned the composition of the education council, which was chaired by Notosuwito (Soeharto's younger brother) and heavily stacked with bureaucrats. Since being established in 2001, the contribution of this institution has been uninspiring. Bantul also has a mixed record on security issues. Samawi invited the involvement of all sections of society in a program to reduce crime and counter social ills such as prostitution, gambling, and drug and alcohol abuse. It is not apparent that this has led to a drop in the incidence of crime, drug abuse or other illicit activities, however.

Among the localities studied here, Jembrana appears to have been the most successful in introducing innovative programs and protecting them from short-term demands that might jeopardise their success. Winasa has proven skilful in marshalling networks of supporters from across the political and social spectrums. At the same time, he has proven adept at neutralising his opponents. In the face of opposition to his plans to cut jobs and merge government offices, for instance, Winasa actually managed to increase his level of support among public officials by increasing their salaries and bonuses. Similarly, he managed to ensure the support of certain sections of society by providing financial support to influential groups and leaders (Polokda 2006).

To institutionalise better practices in the bureaucracy, Jembrana introduced new, open mechanisms of public-official recruitment, including job tendering and a 'fit and proper' test for echelon 3 and 4 positions. Candidature is now open to all public officials who fulfil the requirements for a job, and an independent team from Undayana University conducts the fitness for office tests. The local government is also employing new technologies — such as handkey and fingerprint systems and surveillance cameras — to reduce the level of absenteeism in the civil service and ensure that staff work a minimum of 150 hours each month.

To summarise, this comparison of four localities indicates that the fruits of decentralisation have varied widely from one region to another. Some regions stagnated; others introduced innovative programs and did very well indeed. But no matter how strong the political and societal bases of local government leaders, unless they were able to insulate their programs from political capture, their success in bringing about reform was qualified.

LESSONS LEARNED AND CONCLUSIONS

This chapter has compared the experiences since decentralisation of four local governments in Indonesia. The approach taken here has been to highlight variance across districts and try to explain it. The focus has been on how the political and policy strategies of the district head have influenced outcomes. The core of the argument is that variance in success in introducing policy reforms is largely explained by variance in the ability of the district head to secure a political coalition and achieve a legislative majority; to create a wider network of social support; and to insulate or shield initiatives from interests that would seek to subvert them.

In translating decentralisation into actual programs, local governments do not work in a historical or political vacuum; differences in their political–economic heritages and societal conditions inevitably affect local trajectories. In shaping local politics, local actors must respond to existing conditions and forge strong political–economic and societal bases. In shaping local policy, they must be able to create innovative programs, isolate them from short-term demands, create networks of supporters and institutionalise the process. Only a few have been wholly successful in this task.

An examination of the programs introduced by the four local governments that are the focus of this chapter indicates that Jembrana was the most innovative in terms of its bureaucratic, service delivery and societal policies. It was followed by Bantul with its emphasis on education and health. The other two districts were less successful in introducing innovative programs because of their emphasis on just a few strategic sectors, especially security in the case of Mataram and mining in the case of Bangka.

Table 4.1 summarises the main findings of the chapter.[8] Working backwards in the chain of causality, the success of leaders in actually delivering planned policy reforms can be seen to be dependent upon their ability to insulate such initiatives from capture. In Jembrana, the district head shielded the civil service from capture in the personnel arena by

---

8 The author is grateful to Andrew MacIntyre for his incisive suggestions on how to make the comparison theoretically coherent. It was his suggestion to present this information in tabular form.

*Table 4.1   Success of District Head in Introducing Innovations:
Summary of Findings*

Locality	Building a Political Coalition	Building a Societal Support Network	Introducing Policy Reforms	Insulating Programs from Capture
Bangka	Solid (Golkar & PDI-P)	Active, but limited success	Low	Low
Bantul	Weak, fragmented	Active & successful	Medium	Medium
Jembrana	Solid (PDI-P)	Successful but dependent on financial favours	High	High
Mataram	Diverse, but solid (PDI-P & Golkar)	Factionalised, militaristic response, not successful	Low	Low

making recruitment open; in the financial arena by securing sufficient funding for programs; and in the bureaucratic arena by creating an incentive structure for civil servants that made 'achieving their personal career goals consistent with achieving agency goals' (Geddes 1994: 78). Bantul also attempted to streamline the structure of its bureaucracy, but was less successful in isolating the agency from political and economic capture. Neither Bangka nor Mataram was successful in insulating its programs from capture.

Moving further back in the chain of causality, the capacity of local government leaders to insulate their reform initiatives can, in turn, be seen to be dependent upon their ability to secure both a solid political coalition and a wider network of public support. In Jembrana, a combination of a solid political coalition and an effective network of public support (though one fuelled in substantial measure by selective financial incentives) gave the district head the capacity to isolate programs from political capture and minimise rent seeking. Despite relatively fragmented support from the electorate (because of the existence of multiple parties), the district head of Bantul succeeded in building a strong network of supplementary societal support and had at least some success in containing, if not eliminating, the grasping hands of local vested interests. This allowed him to make some headway in implementing his reforms. The district head of Bangka also had a strong political support base. However, he was not as successful in creating a societal base, and was even less successful in minimising capture of the policy agenda. The mayor of Mataram failed to create a strong societal base. He was relatively less successful in creating mechanisms to minimise capture, because of the proliferation of local coercive apparatuses.

The differing trajectories of Bangka, Bantul, Jembrana and Mataram help explain their choice of decentralisation strategy. They also help us understand why innovations were possible in some localities but not others. The four cases discussed above indicate that local trajectories are important in shaping both politics and policies, and in determining the outcome of the decentralisation process in particular localities. The extent to which local governments in Indonesia have been able to introduce innovations since decentralisation was implemented in 2001 has been shaped by the ability of local actors to isolate their programs from personalistic and partisan demands and, at the same time, create networks of supporters. These two factors have in turn been influenced by the existing shape of local political–economic circumstances.

REFERENCES

Geddes, B. (1994), *Politician's Dilemma: Building State Capacity in Latin America*, Berkeley LA: University of California Press.

Polokda (Program S2 Politik Lokal dan Otonomi Daerah) (2003), 'Human Rights and Good Governance in Indonesia', unpublished research report.

PART II

The Roles of Government

5 THE STATE AND THE MARKET IN DEMOCRATIC INDONESIA

Ron Duncan and Ross H. McLeod

> *It must be remembered that there is nothing more difficult to plan, more doubtful of success, nor more dangerous to manage, than the creation of a new system. For the initiator has the enmity of all who would profit by the preservation of the old institutions and merely lukewarm defenders in those who would gain by the new ones. (Machiavelli, 1469–1527)*

INTRODUCTION

Indonesia's economic performance has been significantly less impressive in the democratic (post-Soeharto) era than previously. The key indicator is the average annual rate of output growth, which not only reflects general improvements in living standards but is also by far the most important factor in reducing poverty. The rate of output growth over the three decades of the New Order regime (through 1997) was 7.4 per cent, but since the turn of the century (marking the start of the period of recovery from the economic crisis) it has been more than one-third lower, at 4.7 per cent (Figure 5.1). In terms of growth rates of per capita income, the decline has been even larger. From an economic point of view, it is this decline in economic performance that demands that we speak only of democracy's *promise* of good governance in Indonesia; it is a promise yet to be fulfilled.

We seek explanations for the decline in Indonesia's economic performance in the literature on new institutional economics. Writers in this field suggest that poor public sector governance, resulting in slow or no growth and development in many developing countries, is largely due to the lack of an appropriate set of the institutions critical to economic

Figure 5.1 Growth of GDP (% per annum)

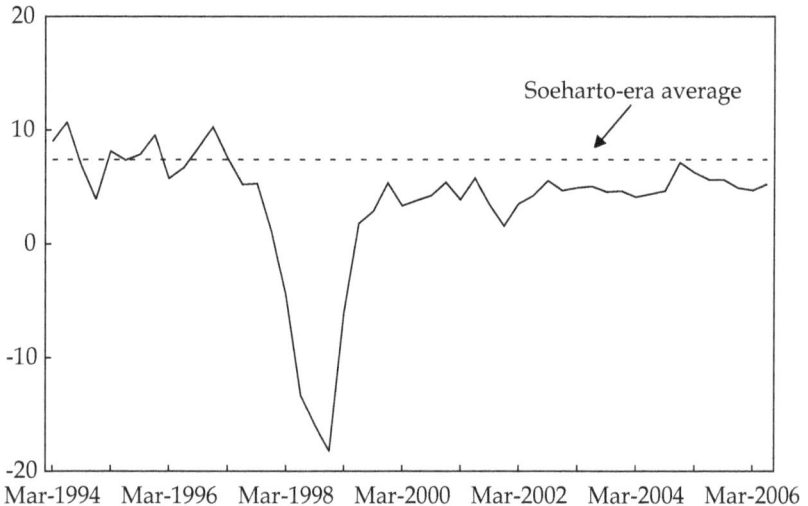

Source: CEIC Asia Database.

growth and development—or to lack of enforcement of those institutions. In this literature, 'institutions' are defined broadly as constraints devised to provide a structure for political, economic and social interactions (North 1991). Since this rather abstract definition differs from everyday use of the term—note, in particular, that *institutions* are distinguished from *organisations*—we begin by elaborating North's concept in more detail.

Institutions may be state or non-state, formal or informal. Non-state institutions are social institutions, values and norms. Formal institutions are constitutions, electoral systems, administrative systems, law and justice systems, and government rules and regulations. Traditional institutions such as customs may be seen as formal or informal, perhaps depending upon the degree of integration with other formal institutions such as constitutions and law and justice systems (Duncan 2003). According to North (1994), institutions are the underlying determinants of economic performance. In this analytical framework it is natural, therefore, to focus on institutional change that has occurred in Indonesia since 1998 if we wish to explain the significant slowdown in economic growth.

According to Sir Winston Churchill: 'It has been said that democracy is the worst form of government, except all those other forms that have been tried from time to time'. The post-Soeharto decline in Indonesia's economic performance calls this view into question. Can we actually say that the institutional changes that constitute Indonesia's recent democratisation are generally for the better? To put it more bluntly: was democratisation the right approach? Or was it a mistake to impose such a system on Indonesia at this stage of its development, simply because it has been highly successful in the West? Certainly, the changes allow wide participation in politics by citizens and their organisations, but what about the impact on economic performance? As noted at the outset, the record does not look good so far, eight years down the track.

Will matters eventually improve of their own accord? Not necessarily. While it is becoming more widely accepted that institutions determine the governmental and economic performance of an economy, it is also being recognised that inefficient institutions can be very difficult to change. In the terminology of the new institutional economics, the 'transaction costs' of moving to a more efficient institution will often be so high as to prevent the change; that is, the economy will remain in a 'second-best' world and, indeed, could be far from the optimum (Coase 1960; McCloskey 1998).

Although there has clearly been a decline in Indonesia's economic performance in the post-Soeharto era, we should stress that it has not been a disastrous one. Indonesia is not about to implode; rather, it seems set to keep on muddling along, reducing poverty rather slowly. Our modest aim in this chapter is to redress the seeming imbalance of attention between political and economic institutional reform, and to make some suggestions for policy changes that would likely lead to better economic outcomes. Institutional change in the post-Soeharto era has focused primarily on facilitating the public's participation in political processes; little of it has been directed to facilitating business activity, on which economic progress depends. There has been much talk but little action in this regard; at the time of writing, the business sector still awaited new legislation needed to create greater certainty in the fields of investment, taxation, mining, forestry and so on. In short, we suggest that the approach until now has been too narrow, and could be self-defeating in the long run if the balance is not redressed. It is not at all uncommon to hear of people pining for 'the good old days under Soeharto', when things seemed much more predictable.

A PUZZLE: EXPLAINING SOEHARTO'S SUCCESS

North (1990), Olson (1996), de Soto (2000) and others have stressed the overriding importance for the effective operation of a market economy of well-defined and secure private property rights, the impartial enforcement of contracts and the absence of discretionary behaviour on the part of civil servants. If individual rights to factors of production (especially land and capital) are ill-defined in legislation, and contracts made between parties to an economic exchange are not impartially enforced by the judicial system — that is, if property rights and contracts are not free from discriminatory intervention by politicians and bureaucrats — the costs of transactions and of production will make economic activity infeasible or highly suboptimal.

Yet both these requirements were lacking under Soeharto. Firms and individuals were highly vulnerable to extortion under the threat of violence by organised crime, thugs (*preman*), the military and the police. They were also victims of 'white collar' extortion by the bureaucracy. And justice was on sale to the highest bidder, so that people simply avoided using the courts as a means of resolving disputes. Thus it is something of a puzzle as to why the economy should grow so rapidly over such a long period in such circumstances.

Our explanation of this puzzle has two main parts. First, we note a very important point of North's argument: that the beliefs and institutions of a society do not necessarily evolve to provide a basis for economic growth. On the contrary:

> most societies throughout history got 'stuck' in an institutional matrix that did not evolve into the impersonal exchange essential to capturing the productivity gains that came from the specialization and division of labor that have produced the Wealth of Nations (North 1994: 364).

We interpret this to imply that security of property and enforceability of contracts are much less important in the informal and traditional sectors of the economy, where there is little emphasis on finding new things to do, or new ways of doing things.[1] Rather, it is the modernising sectors of developing economies that generate the demand for institutional innovation, because of the increasing complexity and scale of economic activity in these sectors. Provided such demands are met, the economy will experience the kind of structural change that results in steady increases in productivity and incomes.

Second, we argue that the dynamic modern sector of Indonesia's economy did in fact benefit from security of property and enforceability of contracts — not by way of the formal legal system, but rather as a result of its symbiotic relationship with Soeharto, his ministers, key bureaucrats and the military. This relationship — the 'Soeharto franchise' — has been described in detail by McLeod (2005), and is illustrated in Figure 5.2.

---

1 We hasten to add that in countries such as China and Vietnam, institutional change in the form of individual leasehold tenure over agricultural land has also had a dramatic effect on more traditional economic activity.

Figure 5.2   The Soeharto Franchise

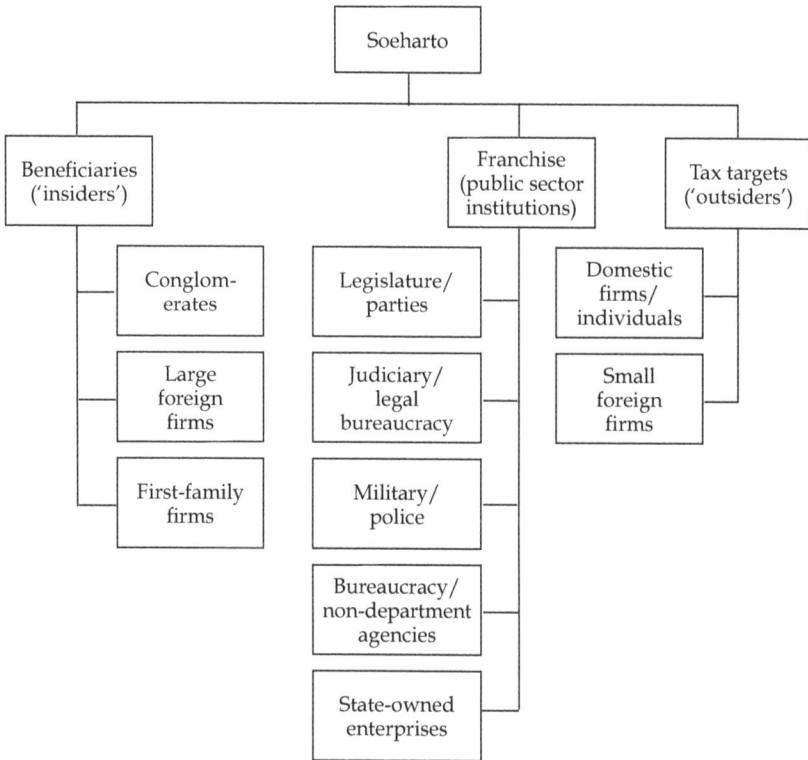

```
                          ┌──────────────┐
                          │   Soeharto   │
                          └──────────────┘

┌──────────────┐      ┌──────────────┐      ┌──────────────┐
│ Beneficiaries│      │  Franchise   │      │ Tax targets  │
│ ('insiders') │      │(public sector│      │('outsiders') │
│              │      │ institutions)│      │              │
└──────────────┘      └──────────────┘      └──────────────┘

      ┌──────────────┐   ┌──────────────┐   ┌──────────────┐
      │  Conglom-    │   │ Legislature/ │   │  Domestic    │
      │  erates      │   │  parties     │   │  firms/      │
      │              │   │              │   │  individuals │
      └──────────────┘   └──────────────┘   └──────────────┘

      ┌──────────────┐   ┌──────────────┐   ┌──────────────┐
      │  Large       │   │  Judiciary/  │   │  Small       │
      │  foreign     │   │  legal       │   │  foreign     │
      │  firms       │   │  bureaucracy │   │  firms       │
      └──────────────┘   └──────────────┘   └──────────────┘

      ┌──────────────┐   ┌──────────────┐
      │  First-family│   │  Military/   │
      │  firms       │   │  police      │
      └──────────────┘   └──────────────┘

                         ┌──────────────┐
                         │  Bureaucracy/│
                         │ non-department│
                         │  agencies    │
                         └──────────────┘

                         ┌──────────────┐
                         │  State-owned │
                         │  enterprises │
                         └──────────────┘
```

Like franchises in the world of business, the (unwritten) rules of the Soeharto franchise were designed to provide strong positive and negative incentives for its success. Key public sector officials could rapidly become wealthy if they lived by these rules, but if they did not abide by them or failed to perform well they would find themselves sidelined. The franchise prospered by means of 'private taxation', that is, various forms of informal taxation of individuals and firms. The 'taxes' imposed by franchisees took two main forms: extortion of 'outsider' firms; and sharing of rents generated by the public sector through its economic policies and harvested by 'insider' firms – cronies of the regime (the 'conglomerates'), members of the first family and large foreign firms.[2] These

---

2 For example, a crony firm might be given a valuable concession to log natural forests or a monopoly on certain kinds of imports. Various rent generation mechanisms are discussed in McLeod (2000: 155–6).

last three groups were the major beneficiaries of the system (aside from the franchisees themselves), since the rents generated for them in various ways by the franchise were shared with the latter, rather than being confiscated. And since the franchise depended on the profitability of these large, modern-sector, insider firms, it had every reason to ensure the security of their assets and to see that contracts to which they were party were enforced.

Treatment of 'outsider' firms and individuals by the franchise was exploitative or predatory, but to a controlled extent. It was in accordance with the 'stationary bandit' thesis developed by Olson (2000). The thesis argues that, unlike 'roving bandits', a stationary bandit—or a dictatorial regime—will have an interest in seeing the economy grow, so it is in the interest of the authoritarian regime to put in place institutions that will allow this to happen. Thus we argue that although the Soeharto franchise imposed net 'private taxes' on the outsider firms, it still provided sufficient in the way of the institutions needed for reasonably good economic performance, because it was in its own interest to do so.[3] On occasion when elements of the franchise became too greedy, Soeharto stepped in to bring them back into line. For example, the notoriously corrupt customs service was replaced by a private international shipments surveillance company, SGS, for several years during the 1980s (Parker and Hutabarat 1996: 29); and there was a wave of extra-judicial killings—'mysterious shootings' (*petrus*)—of petty criminals and thugs at around the same time (Elson 2001: 236–38).

In short, the success of the New Order regime in generating rapid and sustained economic growth over some three decades seems perfectly compatible with North's arguments about the importance of institutions for growth. The Soeharto franchise can be interpreted as a highly effective institution, or set of rules, guiding the behaviour of the entire public sector so as to ensure rapid economic growth, but without relying on a well-functioning formal legal system.

The authoritarian regimes of China and Vietnam have also experienced good economic growth by providing sufficient security of property rights and contract enforcement to give domestic and overseas businesses the confidence to invest. A point of optimism that can be drawn from the common experiences of Indonesia, China and Vietnam is that governance conditions do not have to be ideal in order for good economic growth to be achieved. These experiences reinforce the argument

---

3 McLeod (2000) portrays this as an application of the Laffer curve concept: the idea that when tax (or extortion) rates become too high, revenue declines because the activity in question shrinks.

that secure property rights and contract enforcement are the essential conditions or institutions for rapid growth, but they also confirm Grindle's point about 'good enough governance':

> Among the governance reforms that 'must be done' to encourage development and reduce poverty, there is little guidance about what's essential and what's not, what should come first and what should follow, what can be achieved in the short term and what can only be achieved over the longer term, what is feasible and what is not. If more attention is given to sorting out these kinds of issues, the end point of the good governance imperative might be recast as 'good enough governance', that is, a condition of minimally acceptable government performance and civil society engagement that does not significantly hinder economic and political development and that permits poverty reduction initiatives to go forward (Grindle 2004: 526).

With these thoughts in mind, we hope that this chapter can make a useful contribution to the discussion of the priorities for the reform agenda in Indonesia.

EXPLAINING THE POST-SOEHARTO ECONOMIC DECLINE

The economic crisis that began to unfold in the latter half of 1997 was a godsend for those who had become dismayed with the extent to which Soeharto dominated Indonesia, and the all too obvious greed of his children, grandchildren and other family members. At first it was seen as an opportunity to push for the termination of a wide range of microeconomic policies whose main purpose was to enrich presidential cronies and the first family. But as the crisis deepened, it became apparent that it offered the possibility of achieving something that had previously become almost unthinkable: the removal of the president from office.

The implications of this were all too clear for the large domestic and foreign firms that had hitherto enjoyed the protection of the franchise. Security of property rights and enforcement of contracts could no longer be taken for granted, and the only obvious means of protection was to shift assets out of reach overseas. Of course it was impossible to shift physical assets such as factories and office buildings, but the same purpose was served by borrowing domestically and using the funds to purchase assets offshore. Such transactions were undertaken on a grand scale during late 1997 and early 1998, and the resulting capital outflow had the effect of amplifying greatly the magnitude of the initial shock to confidence of the sudden float of the Thai baht.

The actions of the central bank served only to make things much worse; it provided huge liquidity injections to the very banks whose owners were borrowing heavily in order to rearrange their global portfolios. And eventually the government contributed to the carnage by removing the last vestige of constraints on risky lending by the banks, by providing a blanket guarantee of their liabilities. In hindsight it is hardly surprising that the incipient crisis would be so badly mishandled, since under Soeharto there had never been any serious attempt to steadily upgrade the capacity (as distinct from the size) of the bureaucracy. Macroeconomic policy making had been reasonably competent over the previous three decades, but never more than that.

As the crisis deepened the Indonesian intelligentsia and the international community quite suddenly found themselves pushing, not for policy reform, but for Soeharto's departure. When in May 1998 he stepped down and was replaced by his protégé, Vice-President B.J. Habibie, there ensued a rush to redesign Indonesia's political architecture—in particular to dismantle the monopoly over the electoral mechanism that had allowed Soeharto to remain in office for so long.

In deference to the constitution, Habibie was permitted to take over the presidency, but not to serve out the remainder of Soeharto's five-year term. A new election was held as soon as it became practical to do so. A large number of political parties were permitted to compete for parliamentary representation against the hitherto dominant Golkar party and the only other two parties that had previously been allowed to compete in elections (but never to win). With Golkar's monopoly broken, its candidate, Habibie, was defeated. Before long further changes to the political architecture were introduced, motivated by the objective that Indonesia should never again be dominated by another Soeharto. Future presidents would be restricted to a maximum of two five-year terms; the military (on which Soeharto had relied for support) would no longer have a quota of seats in the People's Representative Council (DPR); and presidents would be elected directly by the people rather than indirectly by the People's Consultative Assembly (MPR). The power of future presidents was further diminished by the devolution of many of the functions of government to the local level, and by the fact that NGOs, organised labour and the media could no longer be repressed so heavily.

In this headlong rush to redesign Indonesia's political architecture, the reformers overlooked the crucially important fact that the Soeharto franchise they sought to destroy consisted not only of the president, Golkar, the parliament and the military, but also the bureaucracy, the judiciary and the state-owned enterprises. Reform of these key institutions seems to have been regarded at best as being of secondary importance. In effect, there seems to have been an assumption that with a freely and fairly elected president and legislature, these parts of the public sector would quickly be turned around and begin effectively to serve the interests of the general public. In other words, with democratisation Indonesia would begin to enjoy 'government by the people, for the people', in Lincoln's famous words.

If there was such an assumption, it was badly mistaken; as we have noted, inefficient institutions can be very difficult to change. This is partly because the institutions adopted by a country tend to be determined by the predominant belief system—which itself may be misguided—and, more importantly in the present context, because existing institutions usually reflect existing political power relationships within a society. As North (1994: 360–1) puts it, 'institutions ... are created to serve the interests of those with the bargaining power to create new rules'. The bureaucracy, the judiciary and the state-owned enterprises were crucially important elements of the Soeharto franchise. By playing by its rules, high-level individuals within these institutions had benefited greatly. They could not be expected to acquiesce meekly in the face of reforms that would deprive them of these benefits.

What has been the consequence of this lopsided reform effort? For outsider firms, it appears that democratisation has had relatively little effect. These firms did not previously rely on the bureaucracy and the judiciary for property security or contract enforcement, and that remains the case. The collapse of the franchise has probably led to some increase in the level of extortion to which they are subject, since there is no longer any central control (Wilson 2006); indeed, businesses now have to contend with predation by newly independent and powerful bureaucracies at the local government level.

For insider firms, on the other hand, as we have already suggested, the demise of the franchise has meant that property is no longer secure and contracts are no longer enforceable. The first manifestation of this was the flight of capital offshore during the crisis; the ongoing manifestation is the reluctance of both domestic and foreign firms to repatriate this capital, and their reluctance to undertake new investment in Indonesia. This is hardly surprising, especially for foreign firms, since they can no longer rely on having well-connected joint venture partners to protect their interests. As a result, they are now extremely sensitive to the inadequacies of the legal system and to the predatory nature of the bureaucracy. Foreign portfolio investment has been running at high levels for some time, indicating that investors are willing to accept some (readily liquidated) financial exposure to Indonesia in their global portfolios, but investment in new capital stock remains at far lower levels (relative to GDP) than had become common before the crisis (Manning and Roesad 2006: 146). In short, new investment in the modernising sectors of the economy, on which structural change and economic growth depends, remains conspicuous by its absence.

WHAT NEEDS TO BE DONE?

The implication of the arguments presented above is that, to return to its previous trajectory of rapid growth, Indonesia will need to reform its formal legal system to provide security of property and enforcement of contracts, and thus restore incentives for investment in the modern sectors of the economy. The latest *Doing Business* report published by the World Bank and the International Finance Corporation again provides clear evidence of the inadequacies of the legal system (World Bank 2006). It ranks countries around the world in relation to various matters that affect the ease or difficulty of doing business. Reflecting the weakness of its court system, Indonesia scores extremely poorly relative to the rest of the world with respect to such basic processes as enforcing a (standardised) contract (145 out of 155 countries) or closing a (standardised) business (116 out of 155 countries) (Table 5.1).

In relation to the difficulty of enforcing a contract, Indonesia's rankings for the time required to complete the process and for the overall cost are 134 and 151 respectively. Indeed, Indonesia is one of only nine countries for which the cost of enforcing a contract – at 126.5 per cent of the debt involved – actually exceeds the debt. The process takes no less than 570 days, that is, over 18 months. Small wonder, then, that those private sector entities that are willing to do business in Indonesia largely avoid using the courts for contract enforcement, relying instead on other means of protecting their interests, such as the use of private debt collectors, or simply being very careful in their choice of people to do business with.

The second subindex of interest here relates to the difficulty of closing a business. This measure focuses on bankruptcy law, and the main procedural and administrative bottlenecks in the bankruptcy process. Here we highlight the recovery rate and the time taken to complete this process. At just 13.1 per cent, Indonesia's recovery rate is far below the world average and less than that for every regional grouping – including Sub-Saharan Africa – resulting in a ranking of 119. In other words, only 36 countries perform worse on this measure. One of the main reasons that Indonesia's recovery rate is so poor is that the bankruptcy process takes far too long – some 5.5 years. Over such a long period, interest foregone on the amount of the unpaid debt becomes quite large, physical assets deteriorate, and there is the possibility that other assets are stolen or otherwise shifted beyond the reach of creditors.

We have no doubt that reform of the bureaucracy should also be given very high priority if Indonesia is to return to rapid economic growth. Again, the *Doing Business* report provides abundant evidence of the deleterious effect of the bureaucracy on private business activity (Table 5.2).

Table 5.1   Indicators of Legal System Inadequacies

Indicator	Measure	Rank (among 155 countries)
Enforcing a contract		145
Time	570 days	134
Cost (% of debt)	126.5%	151
Closing a business		116
Recovery rate (% of amount owed)	13.1%	119
Time	5.5 years	133

Source: World Bank (2006).

Table 5.2   Indicators of Bureaucratic Impediments to Business

Indicator	Measure	Rank (among 155 countries)
Starting a business		144
Time	151 days	149
Hiring and firing workers		120
Difficulty of hiring index (0–100)	61	122
Difficulty of firing index (0–100)	70	131
Firing costs (weeks of wages)	144.8 weeks	150
Paying taxes		118
Time	560 hours	119
Registering property		107
Cost (% of property value)	11.0%	126
Dealing with licences		107
Time	224 days	98
Cost (% of income per capita)	364.9%	104

Source: World Bank (2006).

We begin by looking at the most important component of the starting a business subindex: the time taken to establish a (standardised) new business. In Indonesia this is 151 days. Entrepreneurs wanting to establish a business in the form of a legal entity are obliged to deal with slow-moving bureaucrats in the Department of Justice and Human Rights, the local municipality, the tax office, the Department of Industry, the Department of Manpower, the state-owned social security institution, the police and even the state printing company. In contrast, it is possible in a small number of countries to establish a business within the space of a week, and the average for the entire sample is just 56 days. The Indonesian figure is far higher than that in any of the regional groupings, and compares very poorly with the OECD figure of just 20 days. Indonesia ranks 149 out of 155 countries on this measure.

Another area where bureaucratic intervention makes doing business difficult is the labour market. The World Bank study focuses on several areas of labour market rigidity, and shows that Indonesia is far above average in relation to the difficulty of hiring and firing. Its rankings on these two measures are 122 and 131 respectively. But it is with respect to firing costs that Indonesia looks extremely bad by world standards: these amount to 144.8 weeks of wages, compared with only about 14 on average for all countries in the sample. Indonesia's rank on this measure is only five from the bottom, at 150.

In relation to the time cost of tax compliance, Indonesia again compares very unfavourably with other countries. The time devoted by a (standardised) company to tax compliance is far higher than the world average, and nearly three times as high as in the OECD countries; Indonesia's rank here is 119. A similar finding applies to the subindex for registering property. The cost of registering a (standardised) land and building package is as high as 11 per cent of the value of the property; on this measure Indonesia's rank is 126.

Licences are required for a vast array of purposes, and the *Doing Business* report attempts to allow for this by focusing on the bureaucratic procedures involved in building a (standardised) warehouse in each country. To obtain the necessary licence in Indonesia takes 224 days (that is, more than seven months); Indonesia ranks 98 in this regard. In terms of cost, equivalent to 364.9 per cent of per capita national income, it ranks 104.

The World Bank study is valuable in so far as it clearly documents the negative effect of the bureaucracy on private sector activity. The hard part, however, will be to bring about reform. As noted earlier, the institutions adopted by a country tend to be determined by the predominant belief system, which is very difficult to change. They also reflect existing political power relationships, the resilience of which should not be underestimated.

So far as Indonesia's predominant belief system is concerned, we note that the evident belief in the desirability of free and fair competition within the electoral process is not matched by a corresponding belief in the desirability of competition in markets. This perhaps reflects a failure to differentiate the good and bad aspects of both the Dutch colonial system and the New Order regime when learning the lessons of history. It is not surprising that Indonesians who had to fight for independence from the Dutch would be inclined to reject capitalism, which tended to be equated with Dutch colonialism. Yet in important respects the nature of capitalism as implemented by the Dutch colonials departed markedly from its ideal form, since it was characterised by heavy restrictions on competition and by the significant curtailment of individual freedoms. Disenchantment with the Dutch system led the independence movement to place heavy emphasis on the development of cooperatives — an inferior form of business organisation that has never amounted to anything as important as its special billing in the constitution might suggest.

Likewise, disenchantment with New Order economic policies has helped create a bias against big business and in favour of small and medium-sized enterprises (with a continuation of lip service, at least, to cooperatives). There is also heavy distrust of market forces as the mechanism for deciding the allocation of productive resources among competing uses, reflected, within the bureaucracy, in an astonishing degree of faith in the ability of civil servants to make such decisions. An interesting example of the latter is the confidence with which the central bank is pushing its vision of the future for the banking system (Bank Indonesia 2004) — a vision that sees the disappearance of large numbers of small banks, despite the fact that these performed far better than the large banks during the crisis of the late 1990s (Fane and McLeod 2002: 289). There are, we are told, far too many banks in Indonesia, yet the only foundation for this argument appears to be the concern that more banks make more demands on limited supervisory resources. There is no evidence to support the assertion that the number of banks is in excess of the optimal level, and there is no reason that we can see why it should not be left to market forces to determine the structure of the banking system.

Resistance to institutional reform stemming from existing political power relationships can be seen in the recent surreptitious modification of the draft new investment law so as to prevent the loss of regulatory authority by the Investment Coordination Board (BKPM) (Manning and Roesad 2006: 158). Another example is the success of the judiciary in preventing the Judicial Commission from playing an oversight role in relation to Supreme Court judges (see Chapter 10, this volume). The almost total lack of progress in relation to previous governments' commitments to the IMF to undertake wide-ranging privatisation of banks and other state enterprises provides a third example of the capacity of another large remnant of the Soeharto franchise to stand in the way of reform.

The broad message of this chapter, therefore, is that the idea of *reformasi* needs to be thought of much more broadly, as more than mere democratisation. Soeharto did not control Indonesia so completely merely by virtue of setting up a sham electoral system that guaranteed his repeated re-election. For the new democracy to work effectively, a thorough overhaul of both the bureaucracy and the judiciary is essential. The details of this are beyond the scope of this chapter, but are discussed by Synnerstrom (Chapter 9, this volume). We note in passing, however, that there is a great deal to be gained from application of the fundamental idea that competition is beneficial — so readily accepted in the electoral sphere — to the area of personnel management in these two arms of government.

As for Indonesia's state-owned enterprises, which, for decades, have been used to enrich the strong and powerful at the expense of the general public, our recommendation is simple: they should be privatised, in order that their managers will have the strongest possible incentive to manage them efficiently.

We shall restrict ourselves in the remainder of this chapter to setting out what we see as the basic features of good economic policy, with a view to modifying the predominant belief system that underlies much of policy thinking in today's Indonesia.

WHAT SHOULD THE GOVERNMENT DO, AND WHAT SHOULD IT NOT DO?

Our point of departure is the observation that privately owned enterprises operating under free market conditions are the most efficient means of satisfying most demand for goods and services. In Indonesia, it needs to be recognised that the vast bulk of economic activity requires very little input from government. The key to designing sound economic policy is to identify circumstances in which the private sector either cannot operate, or requires complementary inputs from the public sector in order to do so effectively.

The most obvious case in which the private sector cannot operate is in the production of so-called 'public goods' desired by the community. Since this term is usually interpreted differently by economists and non-economists, let us be clear that what we mean by the term is services, consumption of which, once they have been produced, cannot be denied to anyone. It is this characteristic that makes production of public goods uninteresting to the private sector — it is impossible to charge for their consumption, and therefore impossible to cover the costs of production, let alone make a profit. Pure public goods are actually rather hard to find. The major examples are a country's system for providing national security and its system for providing domestic law and order. Citizens benefit from the services of protection provided by the armed forces and police (and courts and prisons), and they cannot be excluded from consuming these services.[4] Another reason for largely ruling out private sector provision here is that the sector lacks the coercive power of the state.[5] We make no comment on the adequacy or otherwise of Indonesian government spending on national security, but we have no doubt that far too few resources are devoted to the domestic system of law and order.

A second area in which public sector inputs are essential to complement private sector capabilities is in relation to the exploitation of natural resources. We take it to be self-evident that this process should be managed so as to maximise the benefits to the general public. It seems clear that this is the intention of article 33 of Indonesia's constitution (although the recently introduced natural resource revenue-sharing arrangements, which require a disproportionate share of the revenues generated from natural resources to be returned to the districts and provinces where they are located, would appear to conflict with this). As has been pointed out, this in no way requires that the government itself should undertake either exploration or exploitation work. All that is necessary is that it create the conditions in which private sector firms can compete among themselves for the right to do so. If bidding processes are fair, the government should be able to maximise the flow of resource revenues to itself for the benefit of the general public.

It is necessary, too, for the government to manage the environment: the atmosphere, waterways and seas. These have always been treated as free waste-disposal mechanisms, and the result has often been excessive pollution. Policy should not be directed to getting rid of pollution totally, since the costs of doing so would usually vastly exceed the benefits. What is needed is to arrive at the optimal trade-off such that, at the margin, the benefit of a further slight reduction in pollution is just offset by the cost of achieving this. In principle, we can get to this optimum by

---

4 Another pure public good is basic knowledge. The fact that it is not possible to establish intellectual property rights over basic knowledge implies that such research would be underfunded in the absence of government support for research in this area. But this kind of policy would seem to have relatively low priority in a country like Indonesia, with its relatively less educated population.

5 Having said that, we note that there is some scope for private sector participation. To give two examples, privately owned security companies are commonplace around the world, and many countries are already relying on the private sector to manage their prisons.

forcing the polluter to compensate all other parties that are harmed by the pollution — in other words, by 'internalising the externality'. In practice this is no simple matter, however.

A third area in which the private sector needs complementary inputs from the public sector is in the provision of infrastructure. Once again, the scope for the private sector to provide infrastructure on its own is very limited, because it lacks the coercive power of the state to acquire the land needed to support this infrastructure. The main examples are transport infrastructure (roads, railways, harbours, airports, bus and train stations); water infrastructure (dams, irrigation canals, drinking water treatment and distribution facilities, stormwater drainage, sewerage systems); electricity supply (power stations, transmission lines, distribution networks); telecommunications (fixed lines, satellites, radio transmission facilities); and gas pipelines (to transport gas from the field to industrial and population centres).

Many of these involve 'natural monopolies', providing a further rationale for government intervention.[6] But there is considerable scope for 'unbundling' of the non-natural monopoly components, and for private ownership of both these and the core natural monopoly facilities. While only a single pipeline, grid or railway line may be needed, the water, gas or electricity pumped into the conduit does not need to be produced by a single supplier, nor does the distribution and sale of the service need to be in the hands of a monopolist. Activity at both ends of the conduit can be privatised to reap the benefits of competition. Moreover, while the medium of transport of these services remains a natural monopoly, access to the service by the competing producers and distributors can be regulated to ensure that the owner of the infrastructure does not take advantage of its monopoly status. Therefore, our broad policy recommendation is that ownership should generally reside with the private sector, and that the firms involved should be forced to compete to the fullest extent possible, or regulated in the case of natural monopolies. Thus we regard the decision by the Constitutional Court to nullify the Megawati government's new electricity legislation — which was intended precisely to bring about greater private sector participation in the electricity industry — as particularly unfortunate.[7]

---

6 For example, only a single electricity grid, water or gas pipe, or railway line may be needed to provide the service, and duplication would result in higher unit costs.

7 In this regard, perhaps one of the most useful things the present government could do would be to push for an amendment to the wording of article 33 of the constitution to resolve the ambiguity of the term *dikuasai* ('controlled by'), in relation to 'important branches of production'. Control can be by regulation; it does not require ownership or direct involvement.

Another area that cannot be handled by the private sector is income redistribution. Indeed, when the private sector becomes involved in this, it is called theft! Only the state has the right to tax citizens in order to make transfers (in cash or in kind) to others. Economics has nothing to say about the extent to which this should be done; this is a value judgment made by society through the political process. But economics does have something to say about the impact of redistribution activity on the performance of the economy. Redistribution can weaken incentives to work hard and take risks, and may give rise to wastage of resources as the losers try to find ways to avoid being taxed and the gainers try to find ways to increase the handouts they receive.[8] Our general recommendation, therefore, is that redistribution should be kept reasonably limited, and that it should be carefully targeted. Redistribution implemented by providing particular kinds of services offers some advantages. For example, free or highly subsidised education and health care can be targeted fairly carefully to low-income families. As in the case of infrastructure, we again argue here for mechanisms that minimise direct government involvement, such as the issuance to target groups of health care cards and education vouchers that can be 'spent' at private sector providers.

We have already argued for the privatisation of existing state enterprises. The objective is not to obtain additional revenue for the budget, but rather to increase the efficiency of resource use in the economy. The managers of state enterprises do not have their own funds at risk, and the owners—the general public—are much too far removed from management to be able to exercise any meaningful supervision or control. Private sector owners whose wealth rises and falls with their firms' profits and losses have far stronger incentives to manage enterprises effectively. State enterprises in Indonesia collectively have a long and sorry history either of making losses or of frittering away the value of natural resources (such as oil) under their control. Nothing has changed in this respect with the advent of democratisation. The incessant scandals surrounding Bank Mandiri (see Hudiono 2006) clearly illustrate the folly of turning away from previous governments' commitments to privatise the state banks.

For the same kinds of reasons, government bureaucrats should avoid introducing policies that amount to telling private sector owners how to manage their enterprises. The fact that the owners have their own wealth at risk implies that they are much more likely to make sound management decisions. Just as it is unfair to the general public when governments step in to bail out failed private enterprises, so is it unfair

8 It has been argued that the recent change of government in Sweden had a lot to do with precisely this problem of large-scale income redistribution policies.

to business owners when governments step in to force decisions on them without having to bear responsibility for the consequences if their decisions turn out to be unwise. And this is highly likely: only a minuscule proportion of Indonesian civil servants have any personal experience in managing profit-oriented enterprises in the private sector. In short, we believe that the government has little if any role to play in deciding how much should be invested in any particular part of the economy.

Finally, we argue that the government should avoid all forms of intervention that have the effect of favouring one firm over its competitors, one industry over other industries, or one sector over the rest of the economy. There are far more important things for the government to do than waste its limited skill resources in trying to pick winners. In reality, when governments operate in this manner, they are more likely to be doing so in return for some kind of pay-off from the beneficiaries of such distortions, than in response to a genuine expectation that there will be a benefit to the public as a whole. Indeed, we would be very happy to see the abolition, or at least a significant scaling down, of government departments such as industry and agriculture, most of whose activity does nothing more than favour particular firms, industries or sectors at the expense of others and at the expense of either taxpayers or the general public as consumers.

SUMMARY

The performance of the Indonesian economy has declined significantly in the post-Soeharto period. We argue that this is a result of the reform program giving priority to ensuring improved public participation in electoral and parliamentary processes, while ignoring the need to ensure that the modern business sector can operate in an effective manner within a democratic environment. We take on board ideas from the new institutional economics to argue that the good economic performance of the Soeharto regime was due to the fact that the regime ensured security of property rights and contract enforcement for favoured businesses. With the collapse of the regime, these *institutions*, which are fundamental to the operation of the private sector, also collapsed. Establishing new institutions in their place that can operate effectively in the new democratic environment has not been a priority of the reform program.

We argue that improved economic performance will require fundamental reorganisation of the underperforming judicial and bureaucratic systems and the state-owned enterprises. However, we recognise that there will be considerable resistance from vested interests in the existing institutions, so that change will not be easy. Such change will require considerable effort to develop better public understanding of the appropriate role of the government in generating healthy, productive economic sectors.

In the interest of overcoming the widespread, fallacious beliefs about the role of government, we have provided a framework for understanding what it is that the government should do and what it should not do. Generally, the government's role should be to undertake activities that the private sector cannot undertake, or can undertake effectively only with complementary action from the public sector.

REFERENCES

Bank Indonesia (2004), *The Indonesian Banking Architecture*, Jakarta, available at <http://www.bi.go.id/web/en/Info+Penting/Arsitektur+Perbankan+ BI/>, accessed 10 January 2007.

Coase, R.H. (1960), 'The Problem of Social Cost', *Journal of Law and Economics*, 3: 1–44.

de Soto, H. (2000), *The Mystery of Capitalism: Why Capitalism Triumphs in the West and Fails Everywhere Else*, New York NY: Basic Books.

Duncan, R. (2003), 'Governance and Growth: Theory and Empirics – Where Do We Stand?', paper presented to the Governance Symposium, University of the South Pacific, Suva, December.

Elson, R.E. (2001), *Suharto: A Political Biography*, Cambridge: Cambridge University Press.

Fane, G. and R.H. McLeod (2002), 'Banking Collapse and Restructuring in Indonesia, 1997–2001', *Cato Journal*, 22(2): 277–95.

Grindle, M.S. (2004), 'Good Enough Governance: Poverty Reduction and Reform in Developing Countries', *Governance: An International Journal of Policy, Administration, and Institutions*, 17(4): 525–48.

Hudiono, U. (2006), 'Mandiri Hopes to Resolve Bad Debts', *Jakarta Post*, 23 December.

Manning, C. and K. Roesad (2006), 'Survey of Recent Developments', *Bulletin of Indonesian Economic Studies*, 42(2): 143–70.

McCloskey, D.N. (1998), 'The Good Old Coase Theorem and the Good Old Chicago School: A Comment on Zerbe and Medema', pp. 239–48 in S.G. Medema (ed.), *Coasean Economics: Law and Economics and the New Institutional Economics*, Boston MA: Kluwer Academic Publishers.

McLeod, R.H. (2000), 'Government–Business Relations in Soeharto's Indonesia', pp. 146–68 in P. Drysdale (ed.), *Reform and Recovery in East Asia: The Role of the State and Economic Enterprise*, London and New York: Routledge.

McLeod, R.H. (2005), 'The Struggle to Regain Effective Government under Democracy in Indonesia', *Bulletin of Indonesian Economic Studies*, 41(3): 367–86.

North, D.C. (1990), *Institutional Change and Economic Performance*, Cambridge MA: Cambridge University Press.

North, D.C. (1991), 'Institutions', *Journal of Economic Perspectives*, 5(4): 97–112.

North, D.C. (1994), 'Economic Performance through Time', *American Economic Review*, 84(3): 359–68.

Olson, M. Jr (1996), 'Big Bills Left on the Sidewalk: Why Some Nations Are Rich and Others Are Poor', *Journal of Economic Perspectives*, 10: 3–24.

Olson, M. Jr (2000), *Power and Prosperity: Outgrowing Communist and Capitalist Dictatorships*, Oxford: Oxford University Press.

Parker, S. and P. Hutabarat (1996), 'Survey of Recent Developments', *Bulletin of Indonesian Economic Studies*, 32(3): 3–31.

Wilson, I.D. (2006), 'Continuity and Change: The Changing Contours of Organized Violence in Post–New Order Indonesia', *Critical Asian Studies*, 38(2): 265–97.

World Bank (2006), *Doing Business in 2006: Creating Jobs*, Washington DC: World Bank and International Finance Corporation.

6 GOVERNMENT AND PRIVATE BUSINESS: RENTS, REPRESENTATION AND COLLECTIVE ACTION

Natasha Hamilton-Hart

CHANGE AND CONTINUITY IN BUSINESS–GOVERNMENT RELATIONS

An apparent paradox of the business–government relationship in Indonesia is that although business players are often powerful, the collective interests of the business sector are frequently neglected. Is business too influential, or not influential enough? Some voices from the business sector claim that they are at best ignored by the government, and all too commonly preyed upon, subject to burdensome regulation and exposed to illegal extortion by state actors. Yet the government continues to confer privileges on many business people, both in the guise of legally mandated benefits and in the form of informal forbearance and illegal collusion. These privileges almost always come at the expense of public welfare, generating economic inefficiencies and often direct costs to the taxpayer.

The basic features of this chequered relationship date back to the 1950s, and to some extent endure simply because of their self-reinforcing character. But to say that things are bad now because they have been bad for a long time does not capture the underlying conditions that led to this situation, or allow us to identify possible avenues for change. This chapter explores the extent of change in the business–government relationship in recent years. It asks why some legacies from the past have persisted and whether there are other reasons why business–government relations in Indonesia are frequently associated with sub-optimal economic outcomes.

While the focus here is on explaining some enduring problems in the relationship, it is important to put Indonesia's performance in perspective. The tendency for business influence to come at the expense of public welfare, while not fixed, reflects a dynamic that confronts all countries. Some features of the Indonesian context raise the costs associated with the efforts of business to seek influence or protection, but the record in many other countries is worse. The Indonesian state has provided the basic conditions for the development of both the economy and private business (Robison 1986). The rise of private investment, particularly from the 1980s, testifies to a business–government relationship that met some minimum, but important, definitions of effectiveness (Hill 1996). The government was able to provide investors with credible enough guarantees that it would, at least to some extent, limit its predatory behaviour, protect property rights and maintain macroeconomic and political stability.[1]

Nonetheless, there is evidence that the growth of private business in Indonesia came at a price. Before 1998, several studies identified the marginalisation of business under the authoritarian, state-dominated political system as a source of various problems (MacIntyre 1994; Hefner 1997). The political system provided almost no scope for organised business input into policy making.[2] Without guaranteed rights, and in a context where many policy makers were suspicious of or hostile to private business, many business actors invested in speculative, short-term economic activities and frequently hedged against uncertainty by accumulating capital offshore (Yoshihara 1988). Moreover, to cope with the lack of formal representation, private businesses sought out personalised links with players in government, through which they secured both protection from harassment and privileges such as monopoly licences and preferential credit (Crouch 1979; Robison 1986).

These personalised links, often described as patrimonial or clientelistic relationships, meant that some business actors were very far from being marginalised. Their proximity to power meant that they were able to distort government policy to channel benefits to themselves while imposing overall costs on the wider economy. Environmental regulations were

---

1 See Haggard (2004: 56–64) for a review of the ways in which governments in East Asia managed to signal their commitment to business development. His conclusion is that all governments in the region 'reached explicit or implicit political agreements with segments of the private sector; these agreements or coalitions served as the political foundation for rapid growth' (p. 71).

2 With the growth of the private sector in the 1980s, some sectoral associations organised themselves to make formal, collective representation of their interests, but their actual influence on policy through these mechanisms remained very limited (MacIntyre 1991).

flouted with impunity, inefficient producers were protected, and unpaid debts to state banks accumulated, with the costs all ultimately being passed on to Indonesian society (Dauvergne 1997; Hamilton-Hart 2002). As the New Order developed, increasing numbers of government officials acquired their own private business interests (Robison and Hadiz 2004). Hence, not only were 'cronies' able to exercise a malign influence on policy from positions outside the government, but some business owners (or their families) simultaneously held public positions and were thus able to influence policy from inside the government for personal gain.

This pattern of particularistic inclusion combined with formal exclusion has, as discussed below, undergone some real changes as a result of Indonesia's transition to democratic rule since 1998. However, particularistic interests in both government and the private sector have in many cases been able to defend their privileges and block productivity-enhancing reforms that might threaten them. From this vantage point, business still looks powerful and its influence still appears to be pernicious. On the other hand, much of the reform agenda has been strongly endorsed by both local and foreign business actors, who have repeatedly expressed concerns about the burden of regulation, graft, inefficient infrastructure services and the lack of legal certainty. Yet post-1998 governments have in practice done relatively little to allay this type of concern. From this perspective, business can be construed as insufficiently powerful.

Problems in the business–government relationship cannot be reduced to the issue of which side has more power. Rather than seeing business as too influential or too weak, it makes more sense to examine the types of demands business makes of government and the ways in which business actors exercise influence (Haggard, Maxfield and Schneider 1997). The self-interested demands of business sometimes coincide with socially efficient reform agendas; but very often the benefits that business actors succeed in gaining come at public expense. As discussed below, the more business actors press their interests hrough broad, multi-sectoral business associations, the more likely it is that they will demand socially efficient government action.

For this reason, the following section's account of business–government relations since 1988 draws particular attention to the new role of business associations. It is followed by a section explaining why business influence on government often (but not always) produces socially inefficient outcomes. It shows that this tendency is far from unique to Indonesia. The chapter concludes with an assessment of the political and bureaucratic obstacles standing in the way of a more productive relationship between business and government.

BUSINESS AND GOVERNMENT SINCE 1998

Democracy has injected a new pluralism into economic policy making in Indonesia. Under the previous system, reforms were designed by senior officials in the economic agencies. These technocrats and their consultants worked largely without any input from parliament, industry groups or other stakeholders to draft legislation and implementing regulations (see, for example, Heij 2001). The only actor they had to convince was President Soeharto. The changes brought about by democratisation have significantly changed this picture of a select group of technocrats competing with 'nationalist' or self-interested bureaucrats and a few cronies for the president's ear. Parliament now plays a much more active role and business competes with a variety of other interest groups, including newly influential labour organisations (Manning 2004).

Business Group Demands

Since 1998, business groups have become much more vocal in expressing their opinions on government performance, policy and legislation. Business association representatives have frequently and robustly conveyed their concerns to government. Their demands are decidedly mixed. The Indonesian Chamber of Commerce and Industry (Kadin) has frequently pressed for changes that would advance a fairly broad set of business interests and hence arguably be beneficial for the economy as a whole. It has made repeated complaints about corruption and declared the organisation's commitment to fight graft, including its decision to launch a series of national anti-corruption campaigns from 2003 (Kuncoro 2006: 14; *Kompas*, 2 October 2003). Other persistent complaints about the business environment have identified concerns about macroeconomic instability; regulatory and legal uncertainty; problems with the tax system, infrastructure and labour laws; and regulatory obstacles to establishing and conducting business (Sen and Steer 2005: 292–5). These have been formally relayed to the government. For example, Kadin detailed its concerns about customs, labour, tax and infrastructure in its 2003 submission to the government's white paper on post-crisis economic policy (*Kompas*, 30 October 2003). Foreign business associations, particularly the Jakarta Japan Club and the Indonesia Business Club, have also made detailed submissions to the government asking for action to address concerns in these and other areas (Castle 2004).

On some issues, Kadin's member-specific demands coincide with broader considerations. For example, the organisation has been supportive of privatisation, an instance where its declared agenda of promoting market competition and the public interest happily coincides with the narrower interests of some of its members, who are potential investors in privatised state enterprises (Prasetiantono 2004: 153). Kadin may also have legitimate grounds for complaint about the quality of infrastructure services, although its threat that members would refuse to pay their electricity bills if the tariff rose can only be seen as an outright demand for a publicly funded subsidy (*Kompas*, 27 January 2006). Kadin's readiness to represent the general, legitimate interests of the business community may also be constrained by its membership; while Kadin is a multi-industry peak association, it has been dominated by large firms and leaders of conglomerate groups closely aligned with (or identical to) members of the political elite. According to the president of the National Association of Small and Medium-sized Enterprises (Forum Nasional Usaha Kecil Menengah), Kadin does not represent the interests of his association effectively, because it is more occupied with playing politics than seriously taking up the issues of concern to 'ordinary' businesses (*Kompas*, 21 February 2004).

Kadin and other industry associations have also pressed for plainly group-specific privileges and protections. For example, the government introduced new measures to protect local industries, including sugar, steel and textiles, from import competition after complaints from major industry players (*Jakarta Post*, 18 November 2002). Kadin has frequently asked the central bank to lower its interest rates to reduce the cost of credit and stimulate the economy (see, for example, *Kompas*, 7 June 2006, 28 December 2005). It has also asked the government to provide shelter for local businesses against competition from multinational firms, saying that while global competition cannot be avoided, it is the practice in other countries for local industries to be protected, especially in strategic and sensitive areas such as telecommunications. Kadin's chair therefore suggested that the government provide incentives for foreign firms that took on local partners, essentially calling for a return to the arrangements that had provided windfall profits for local partner firms during the Soeharto era (*Kompas*, 28 December 2005).

Government Responsiveness

Business groups are now incorporated into government decision making in a much more institutionalised fashion than they were prior to 1998. Kadin frequently meets with the government's economics ministers, and members have been appointed alongside senior officials to teams tasked with developing economic policy reforms such as new tax legislation. The government's much touted (but unfruitful) infrastructure summit in early 2005, which aimed to kickstart major private investment in infrastructure projects, was designed and launched with significant Kadin input. Members of the business community have also been included on the president's council of economic advisers. Representatives of business groups frequently meet with members of the People's Representative Assembly (DPR) for formal discussions. And in 2004 Kadin reaffirmed its aim of becoming a 'critical and constructive' partner of the government (*Kompas*, 21 February 2004; Basri 2004).

On the other hand, the business–government relationship has not yet developed into a transparent, institutionalised and inclusive partnership. Under the Megawati presidency, a leading member of the business community described business–government relations as characterised by government suspicion of business and business distrust of the government (*Kompas*, 21 February 2004). A foreign business representative accused the government of harbouring persistent hostility towards foreign business, and of clinging to a mindset that sought to fix problems by issuing new regulations rather than dealing with basic problems of implementation. He maintained that a basic orientation of seeking to control rather than promote foreign business produced generally unhelpful responses, and produced a worse business climate than in countries such as China – which also suffered from problems of legal uncertainty and corruption (Castle 2004: 77–8, 81–2). Although the government claimed to have resolved half of the detailed concerns raised by the Jakarta Japan Club (which had been actively lobbying on issues such as high tariffs, arbitrary and non-transparent tax and customs procedures, and increases in minimum wages), its response did not address the basic problem of policy implementation.

Particularly since the cabinet reshuffle at the end of 2005, the new government of Susilo Bambang Yudhoyono (SBY) has claimed to take business concerns very seriously (Kuncoro and Resosudarmo 2006). Its new package for improving the investment climate, issued in February 2006, aimed to address business concerns on issues such as the investment law, customs, tax and labour; it included both a list of deliverables and a timetable for achieving them (Manning and Roesad 2006: 156–7). Although Kadin agreed with the content of the package, saying that it reflected its written submissions to the government in early 2005, business leaders were sceptical about its prospects for implementation (*Kompas*, 4 March 2006). Recent pronouncements by senior officials also convey a mixed message in terms of the government's attitude to the business community. Thus, while the trade minister announced that the government was in the process of setting up a high-level investment committee to respond to foreign investors' concerns and promote investment, the head of the Investment Coordinating Board (BKPM) described this committee as a 'watchdog' (*Bisnis Indonesia*, 10 August 2006). Moreover, the industry minister dismissed Kadin's complaints about the high costs of doing business in Indonesia, claiming that these were not the government's problem (*Kompas*, 11 February 2006).

The government has partially responded to some demands reflecting the collective interests of the business sector. For example, complaints about high costs and other problems at Indonesia's ports led to the formation of a government-sanctioned, independent team to examine the issue. When it submitted its report, the government asked the team to provide more specific recommendations for action and promised to follow up on them—a promise that has yielded at least some concrete changes. Other issues relating to port operations remain outstanding, however, and the government has not addressed the underlying reasons for the high handling charges.[3]

Several groups complain that they are still being left out of the policy process. For example, the chair of the electronics producers association said that his organisation had not been included in the government's trade negotiations. 'If the government says it involved industry players in the process', he said, 'most of them would ask, which ones?' He also claimed that most industry players had not been informed of the government's strategy for the private sector as it faced trade liberalisation, maintaining that they had yet to see a concrete plan (*Jakarta Post*, 21 July 2005). These comments were made just a few weeks after the launch of the government's comprehensive National Manufacturing Sector Development Policy, which outlined the priority sectors for development (*Jakarta Post*, 4 July 2005). This suggests very limited consultation with industry in the formulation of what was supposed to be a major policy statement.

The limits to consultation and responsiveness to business are also evident in the revisions to tax and investment laws under way since 2003. Kadin and other business groups were initially not consulted in the formulation of the draft investment law. The Megawati government's approach was described as aiming at 'stealth legislation' of the kind that characterised the Soeharto era, with no public discussion of the draft law (Castle 2004: 82–3). To address investor concerns, the SBY government went back to the drawing board and rewrote the draft with the declared aim of making it more business friendly. When presented to the business community in August 2005, the bill was described as aiming to provide equal treatment between foreign and local investors, and to shift from a non-transparent, approvals-based business establishment process to a registration-based process with clear criteria. At this stage, the bill would reportedly have eliminated the approval power of BKPM, but when it was finally presented to parliament in March 2006, this provision had

---

3 See, for example, *Jakarta Post*, 9 May 2005, 13 May 2005, 12 October 2005, 11 January 2006.

been withdrawn (Sen and Steer 2005: 295–6). Although the bill does provide a more favourable environment for foreign investment in particular,
it does not shift to a simple registration regime for establishing a business, as requested by the foreign business community, and it continues
to protect the prerogatives and interests of officials in BKPM by retaining
the investment board's regulatory role. Further, the effects of the law will
depend greatly on the implementing regulations and the actual execution of the law — which have always been the major issues of concern to
the business community (Manning and Roesad 2006: 158).

A similarly mixed story has unfolded in the area of tax reform,
although in this case Kadin was included on the team established in
2003 to formulate changes to a number of areas of tax law and administration. Several of the concerns of business had been incorporated into
the bill by 2005, including the unification and reduction of business tax
rates. Strong disagreement remained between the business community
and officials drafting the law on the issue of the powers of the tax office.
According to Kadin and foreign business associations, the new law
would further expand the potential for the tax office to exercise arbitrary
and draconian powers (Sen and Steer 2005: 296–7). Revisions proposed
by the finance minister to address such concerns were rejected, and the
three tax bills were set to be enacted by the end of 2006. Apparently their
merits outweighed their problematic aspects in the view of Kadin's chair,
who said that the business community was hopeful that the new laws
would improve the business climate (*Jakarta Post*, 29 August 2006). Along
with the tax laws, amendments to the customs and excise law were also
making their way through the legislative process. This is another area of
concern to business, particularly the issue of corruption in the customs
service and the lack of a transparent dispute resolution process. While
amendments were made to the law to address such concerns, an external
assessment argued that it still contained several grey areas and would
'almost certainly increase bureaucratic harassment of legitimate business
activity' (Kuncoro and Resosudarmo 2006: 21).

Overall, the government has certainly become more consultative of
business and more responsive to some of its collectively voiced requests —
including requests for rents or special privileges. On the other hand, the
government has either ignored or failed to remedy some of the most serious concerns of business, particularly on issues relating to policy implementation. This unwillingness or inability to respond to collectively
voiced business complaints on issues such as corruption and burdensome regulation is directly related to the government's responsiveness
(or susceptibility) to particularistic interests: those of government officials who gain from obstructive regulations and those of privileged business actors who benefit from discretionary government action.

Individualised Business–Government Interaction

Despite the renewed level of business association organisation and lobbying, informal and firm-specific deal making continues to character-
ise a large part of the government's relationship with private business.
Although this mode of business interaction with government is opaque,
circumstantial evidence suggests that longstanding patterns of accommodation and collusion remain entrenched. The most telling evidence
for this comes from the way in which enormous private debts to the
state sector have been dealt with since the financial crisis. These debts
had accumulated as a result of loans by state banks to the New Order's
major conglomerates and were further massively swollen by the government's crisis-related bail-out of private banks (Soedradjad 2005; McLeod
2004). Although the major debtors were required to surrender some of
their business assets to the government, the lengthy, complex and non-
transparent process surrounding the repayment of debts and the resolution of other issues supports two fairly clear conclusions: first, many
of the major debtors have escaped a large part of their liabilities; and
second, some business actors have been able to use positions of political
influence or proximity to power holders to generate exceptional gains for
themselves (Robison and Hadiz 2004: 187–222).

The degree to which former bank and conglomerate owners have
maintained their privileges is contested and unclear. Some accounts suggest, for example, that the country's largest conglomerate during the
New Order era, the Salim group headed by long-time Soeharto associate
Liem Sioe Liong, has maintained its privileges through secret buy-backs
of its former assets (Brown 2004), but the evidence for this seems weak.
Some of the former president's cronies have in fact exited the scene and
others have seen their opportunities for new wealth acquisition cur-
tailed. According to *Forbes* magazine's listing of the richest Indonesians,
the Liem family ranks tenth, with assets of $800 million, a decline in both
absolute and relative terms from the early 1990s, when it was judged
the wealthiest family in Indonesia (*Business Times*, 6 September 2006).
The *Forbes* list does point to two things, however: first, that Indonesia's
wealthiest individuals are, for the most part, those who acquired their
fortunes during the New Order with the help of significant state privileges; and second, that many of them operate in business sectors that
depend on securing government licences and favourable regulatory
decisions, such as natural resource-based industries, gaming and ciga-
rette manufacture.

Micro-level studies of the fortunes of particular firms and business
players point to the continuing significance of business–government
relationships mediated along collusive, particularistic lines. Some players have lost their former privileges, but in their place a larger number

of new and not so new entrants enjoy special access to government decision makers. For example, two business families that have seen large
increases in their wealth since 1998 have members directly represented
in cabinet (Pepinsky 2006). The businesses of Indonesia's wealthiest family, that of Sukanto Tanoto (with an estimated fortune of $2.8 billion), are
concentrated in the pulp and paper industry, palm oil development and
energy. Not only are these industries that depend on securing government concessions and licences, but in practice both the pulp and paper
industry and palm oil cultivation continue to profit greatly from systematic evasion of environmental laws that, for example, prohibit land clear-
ing through fire and the use of illegally logged timber (Dauvergne 2005).
The escalation of illegal logging since 1998 has been sustained by the
forging of collusive ties among business players, local governments and
members of the security forces (Lang and Chan 2006).

COLLECTIVE ACTION, RENTS AND
GOVERNMENT REGULATION

As we have seen, self-interested business actors in Indonesia sometimes
call for government action that would benefit the business sector in general rather than specific firms or sectors. Such benefits include secure
property rights, reduced bureaucratic red tape and transparent, consistently implemented taxation policies. Since these benefits do not create
rents — opportunities to acquire above-market profits — they are (with a
few exceptions) benign or even beneficial for the economy as a whole.
They also tend to have the public good characteristics of being non-
excludable and non-rival; the consumption of the 'benefit' of transparent
tax administration, for example, does not reduce the enjoyment of this
benefit by any other firm (Buchanan 1968). In contrast, business demands
for benefits that are specific to a particular firm or industry are almost
by definition attempts to secure rents (Krueger 1974). The rents created
by policies that benefit a specific firm or industry, such as tariff protection or subsidised loans, generally create costs for other firms, industries or members of society, although it is arguable that certain types of
rent potentially provide net benefits to society (Khan 2000). This section
reviews some of the reasons why business influence is more often associated with the creation and distribution of rents than with public goods.
    One line of thinking identifies the mode of business influence, in par-
ticular the degree to which businesses use collective associations to represent their interests, as important. Business actors may organise themselves
into formal associations and lobby transparently for their collective interests or they may work out individual bargains with government officials

in order to protect or advance the interests of their particular firm. There are some grounds for thinking that collective organisation and lobbying has some advantages over individual deal making and may sometimes be beneficial in itself.[4] Collective lobbying necessitates a degree of transparency and therefore generally precludes lobbying for illegal privileges. This avoids the corrosive effects on state institutions of normalised corruption. Also, by bringing demands into the public arena, the checks and balances of the formal policy process (including lobbying by adversely affected groups) can at least potentially constrain rent creation.

Collective lobbying also means that benefits for the group as a whole, rather than privileges specific to one firm, are sought. This rules out the pursuit of certain types of rent that benefit a single player, such as monopoly licensing, and ensures a degree of competition among firms in an industry group, even if the industry as a whole is protected. In Malaysia, for example, the economic inefficiency of official forms of protection favouring indigenous business is at least limited to the extent that many of these are offered to all indigenous firms and thus do not eliminate price-based competition among them (Searle 1999). In contrast, favours such as offering a government contract without tender are firm specific, rule out competition and therefore foster greater economic inefficiency.

Collective organisation may also amplify the voice of business players on issues of legitimate concern and provide useful feedback to government. Intensive interaction between government and organised business groups in South Korea and Japan, for example, underpinned the accelerated industrialisation efforts of these countries (Noble 1998). Thus, while there is certainly no guarantee that collective business associations will advance an agenda conducive to the public interest (and clearly South Korean and Japanese business groups have frequently pursued goals contrary to the public interest), it is plausible to argue that the extremely low level of formal organisation by Indonesia's business sector is a reason for government neglect of legitimate business interests, and a factor in the development of more corrosive forms of personalised business–government collusion (MacIntyre 1994).

Limited recourse to collective lobbying explains only part of the ongoing pattern of socially suboptimal government protection of business, however. Even fully transparent collective lobby groups often organise to secure or retain benefits that come at the expense of overall welfare, as argued by analyses of interest groups and rent seeking.[5] The

---

4 For a review of the potential benefits from the collective representation of business interests, see Schneider and Maxfield (1997: 21–5) and Schneider (1998).

5 See Krueger (1974) for an early statement and Khan and Jomo (2000) for a review and application to cases in Asia.

basic dynamic identified by research into why business interest groups often secure special privileges that impose wider costs on society derives from an Olsonian insight into problems of collective action. Simply put, collective representation is costly for those engaging in it and becomes more costly the larger the number of individuals involved.[6] It will only occur if each member of the group (or a sufficient proportion of members) believes that it is worthwhile to invest the resources required, that is, if the expected gain exceeds the expected cost of lobbying for it. It follows that the most active lobby groups will be those that press for relatively narrow benefits that can be appropriated by a restricted membership. This means that business groups will generally lobby most vigorously for benefits specific to their industry or segment of business — such as tariff protection, subsidies or other privileges. The costs of such privileges tend to be dispersed across very large numbers of individuals (often taxpayers or consumers), each of whom pays only a small amount. This reduces the likelihood that they will resist policies that confer privileges on the few at public expense: the cost to the individual of organising an effective protest is likely to outweigh the potential (private) gain of doing so. This may explain why Indonesian consumers, like their counterparts in most other countries, have not been a major force pushing for lower tariffs or other forms of liberalisation, even when given the political space to organise after 1998.

The tendency for interest groups to pursue relatively narrow, group-specific interests has led some scholars to argue that collective business influence on government is more likely to be beneficial if a broad range of business interests are included under the umbrella of a business association (Schneider 1998). The expectation is that more 'encompassing' business associations, such as peak associations, should produce a degree of self-interested mutual restraint and limit their rent seeking, as protection and privileges for one industry segment often generate costs and inefficiencies borne by other business actors. Similarly, the greater the extent to which influential business actors consist of diversified groups with interests across multiple sectors of the economy, the greater their presumed interest in the overall health of the economy (Kang 2002).

The record of Indonesia's multi-sectoral conglomerates does not lend much support to arguments about the benefits of having a concentrated business sector consisting of large firms with diversified interests. How-

---

6 Clearly, this is no more than a rough generalisation. The costs of organising do not rise linearly along with the number of people being organised, and when models of collective action are transferred to the domestic political arena, it becomes more evident that large groups can enjoy advantages, depending on the political system.

ever, the substantive interests of business actors are not fixed, and under some conditions firms' self-interest can lead them to demand government action that would also promote broader welfare. For example, while firms that produce goods or provide services for the domestic market usually have straightforward interests in protection, exporters who are competitive on world markets and would suffer from retaliatory protection abroad can be advocates of trade liberalisation (Milner 1988). More generally, business actors have an interest in supporting economic liberalisation when they are confident that they will benefit not just from the general economy-wide gains in efficiency and welfare these reforms are supposed to produce, but also from gains they can narrowly appropriate (Schamis 1999). Privatisation and financial deregulation, for example, offer benefits that distributional coalitions can seize, at least under some conditions. Although they did not drive Indonesia's selective liberalisation reforms in the 1980s and 1990s, the country's leading business actors did benefit from them; they were able to compensate for the loss of some privileges with opportunities elsewhere, such as in the booming financial sector (Robison and Hadiz 2004: 73–96; Hamilton-Hart 2002).

Although in this instance Indonesia's leading business actors were happy to acquiesce to selective liberalisation, there are significant limits to how much the business sector is able, or willing, to press for liberalisation. Businesses with an interest in liberalisation are those that are competitive without protection and those that are downstream of businesses protected by tariffs or other limits on competition, since the downstream industries pay a direct price for policies that privilege others. However, a legacy of the longstanding protection and favours surrounding the development of big business in Indonesia is that businesses which benefit from state protection tend to be more politically influential, by virtue of size and proximity to power holders, than those with an interest in liberalisation (Robison 1986; Robison and Hadiz 2004). Another factor that encourages business to pursue government-created rents rather than liberalisation is the role resource-based industries play in the economy. When resource rents are large, as they are in Indonesia, they create strong incentives for firms to specialise in seizing them.[7]

Government regulatory policy is another factor encouraging rent seeking by Indonesian business. Government regulations in all countries almost invariably create rents or the potential for rents (that may arise from selective forbearance in enforcing regulations), and this elicits

---

7 This may explain some of the apparent 'resource curse' — the finding that countries endowed with large natural resources often perform less well than countries without such resources. See Ross (1999) for a review of the explanations.

unproductive rent-seeking behaviour on the part of business and other interested parties (Krueger 1974). In this line of thinking, regulatory policy tends to become captured by the rent-seeking groups it creates, meaning that even regulations introduced for impeccable reasons may end up generating costly inefficiencies (Cook et al. 2004: 8–13). It is also quite plausible that some regulations are intentionally designed to generate power and income for officials in regulatory agencies, and selective benefits for their private sector clients. The deregulatory solution, however, has some obvious limits. First, it begs the question of how it might be politically feasible to change a policy if there are vested interests determined to preserve it.[8] Second, complete deregulation is often an undesirable option, as market failures, oligopolistic intrafirm collusion or normative social agendas may mandate regulation (Cook et al. 2004).

While deregulation may not offer a short cut to resolving problems of government capacity, state capture or corruption, it is also the case that the more a government actively intervenes in the market, the more challenging the task of maintaining policy discipline becomes. Industrial policy opens the door to rent seeking, particularly if it depends on close business–government ties and collaboration to overcome problems of information and coordination.[9] Virtually all analyses of industrial policy and state-led developmentalism identify demanding political and institutional conditions for success, generally including meritocratic, internally disciplined bureaucratic agencies and a pressing political imperative for rapid economic growth (Schneider and Maxfield 1997; Doner, Ritchie and Slater 2005). These conditions are mostly lacking in Indonesia (as in many other countries), which may explain why the government's extensive interventions in the market have more often created pockets of privileged inefficiency than dynamic gains in technological capacity or competitiveness.

In sum, we can conclude that Indonesian business actors are not particularly villainous in their rent-seeking behaviour but that some constraints on rent seeking are relatively weak in Indonesia. First, collective representation of business interests through formal business associations has historically not been the major route by which businesses have attempted to influence government, resulting in a particularly perni-

---

8 This question is taken up by work on the political economy of reform. See Haggard (2000) for a review.

9 There are several reasons why the goal of rapid industrialisation is supported more by a two-way business–government relationship, characterised by the exchange of information, trust and some degree of mutual influence, than by a state that is entirely insulated from the business sector. The conditions for such a partnership to be productive are, however, quite restrictive. See in particular Doner (1992) and Evans (1995).

cious distribution of privileges through informal and personal channels. Second, even if mediated by business associations, the dynamics of collective action mean that business lobbies in all countries often pursue relatively narrow benefits for their members. Third, the size of Indonesia's natural resource-based industries and the legacy of previous protective government policies mean that many of the most influential business owners have entrenched interests in government-created rents. Finally, Indonesia's interventionist industrial policies make it inherently difficult to constrain unproductive rent seeking.

POLITICAL INCENTIVES AND THE BUSINESS–GOVERNMENT RELATIONSHIP

The preceding discussion raises two major questions about the business–government relationship. First, why have the old, personalised patterns of business–government interaction persisted despite the new democratic context and the increased activity of collective business associations? Second, why does the government often seem more responsive to the rent-seeking demands of business interests than to demands that would promote a broader set of interests? The previous section identified several reasons why business is often more *motivated* to press for narrow group interests than broad public-interest agendas, but this does not completely explain the factors underlying the decision-making calculus of business actors, or government responses to business demands.

Particularistic, individualised rent seeking is not necessarily the optimal strategy for business, but may arise because of the difficulties of organising collective action. Business actors may wish to lobby as a group but fear that others in the group will defect from cooperative endeavours, and therefore defect first, or they may defect simply because they wish to free-ride on the efforts of others. To the extent that this is true of business behaviour in Indonesia, longer experience with collective representation mechanisms may build sufficient trust among members and institutionalise the mechanisms for representation and mutual discipline, which would reduce incentives to defect. Kadin has only relatively recently taken up the challenge of becoming a truly representative association rather than a club of privileged big business players, and arguably needs time (as well as commitment) to establish new ways of operating (Basri 2004).

But inefficient institutions may endure for reasons other than collective action problems (Bardharn 2005), and much of the difficulty in Indonesia is that particularistic accommodation is often the optimal choice, not the last resort, for those involved. One important reason for this is the nature of state institutions, which at a minimum facilitate, and in many cases induce, patterns of personal collusion between business and government actors. As long as bureaucratic agencies and judicial organisations lack the internal discipline to enforce rule-based mechanisms for policy implementation and dispute resolution, personalised bargains between individual businesses and government players will frequently offer greater rewards than collective lobbying for policy changes, which may or may not be implemented consistently. This obviously weakens collective representation efforts, as 'firms [that] can secure particularistic rents from the government on their own … have no interest in collective action' (Haggard, Maxfield and Schneider 1997: 45). Of course, a rule-based, disciplined bureaucracy might still obstruct or ignore legitimate business interests, even if its officials did not stand to gain personally from corrupt transactions with business partners. Effective state-sector reform would still make a difference, because an organisation that constrained opportunistic rule breaking among its own staff would offer reduced incentives for corruption and individualised collusion.

Ultimately, political conditions underlie the organisational capacity of the bureaucracy and the business–government relationship more generally. Given the right incentives, politicians invest in reforming bureaucratic agencies to make them more coherent, disciplined agents of government policy (Geddes 1994; Doner, Ritchie and Slater 2005). Similarly, political accountability mechanisms determine the degree to which government actors have any *interest* in promoting economy-wide welfare or efficiency. Political structure may also matter. It can be argued that political centralisation in the New Order period gave Soeharto sufficient security of tenure to allow him to take an interest in the performance of the economy, as well as giving him the means to enforce his preferences (MacIntyre 2000; McLeod 2000). This, along with some need to legitimate his rule, put a cap on both predatory extraction of private wealth by government officials and state largesse distributed to privileged private businesses, although clearly it did not preclude extensive rent creation and collusion.

Indonesia's new democratic and decentralised politics creates different opportunities and constraints for those in political power. As the array and volume of business demands has increased with democratisation, it has become more necessary for the government to discriminate actively among contending demands. The capacity of the political system to provide incentives for government to respond to the legitimate concerns of business while limiting responsiveness to more harmful demands is thus crucial. The record of interest group politics in other countries suggests that dealing with the demands of interest groups in positive ways is an enduring challenge even for mature democracies.

One interesting development in this respect is that Indonesia's new, more fragmented, political context may be making it less rewarding to pursue some types of individual deal making between government and business. Before the decentralisation policies had taken full effect, business respondents in at least some surveys did not consider corruption to be among the most serious obstacles to conducting business in Indonesia, despite levels of bribe payment that were moderately high (Khouw 2004: 206). More recent surveys have pointed to a reduction in bribe payments by business actors as uncertainty about their effectiveness has increased (Kuncoro 2006). That is, greater political decentralisation appears to have fragmented the bribe-taking structure, making bribe paying less rewarding. While the immediate consequences of this are adverse for business in the sense of making it more difficult for businesses to circumvent restrictive regulations and other government-imposed burdens, it is also possible that the reduced opportunity to seek individual accommodation may eventually consolidate business pressure for more business-friendly policies — a corollary of sorts to arguments that corruption is less economically damaging in politically centralised systems such as New Order Indonesia (McLeod 2000; MacIntyre 2000).[10] Of course, this incentive for businesses to press for less obstructive and cleaner government does not mean that they will succeed in bringing it about, or that their businesses will not simply be driven underground or abroad. Nonetheless, it does suggest that democracy and decentralisation may be changing business incentives in some fundamental ways.

Overall, however, the dynamics of Indonesia's democracy offer a mixed prognosis for reforming business–government relations. The 2004 legislative and presidential elections showed that voters were somewhat able to translate concerns about corruption and cronyism into electoral losses for the ruling party and gains for parties (such as PKS, the Prosperity and Justice Party) and individuals (notably Susilo Bambang Yudhoyono) who managed to make reasonably credible promises to tackle corruption. On the other hand, the DPR continues to do a relatively poor job of filtering business demands and has not been very responsive to general concerns about the business environment. Most of the initiative for economic legislation continues to come from the government rather than the DPR, which has been more active in blocking or delaying legislation than in drafting it. There has been a problem with what the current economics coordinating minister earlier called 'fuzzy rules' governing the functioning of new institutions, creating delays and uncertainty in the legislative process (Boediono 2005a). The delays caused by the DPR

---

10 These arguments apply a model put forward by Andrew Shleifer and Robert Vishny, building on an earlier observation by Max Weber.

have been due to more than procedural uncertainty, however. Parliamentary commissions have frequently voiced objections to certain government initiatives, particularly asset sales by the bank restructuring agency and the privatisation of other government assets, which have repeatedly been delayed. Despite the infusion of new legislators following the 2004 elections, the new parliament managed to pass only a few of the bills presented to it during its first year. It enacted only 10 of 55 pieces of legislation (*Jakarta Post*, 4 October 2005), a record similar to that of previous post-*reformasi* parliamentary sessions.

Legislative delays have rarely been due to parliamentarians acting to support the broad interests of the business community, although one such instance may have been the support given by Golkar representatives to Kadin's campaign against the broad discretionary powers accorded to the tax office in the draft taxation laws (Sen and Steer 2005: 297). In general, however, the DPR has not been particularly responsive to the economy-wide concerns of business groups. Some senior parliamentary representatives appear to deny any responsibility for improving economic and business conditions. In 2002, for example, the head of the parliamentary commission dealing with economics and finance, Max Moein (who retained a leadership position in this commission in the subsequent parliament), repeatedly protested that he had never heard of any complaints by foreign businesspeople about the much criticised tax system. During the course of an interview with a company specialising in providing advisory services to foreign businesses in Indonesia, his constant refrain was that if foreign investors did not make their problems formally known to his commission, he could not be expected to know about them. He also insisted repeatedly that it was not the commission's responsibility to scrutinise policy implementation, a perennial area of concern to business associations (Harvest International 2002).

Part of the problem may be attitudinal, but the failure of the parliament to play a more constructive role in mediating business interests probably has more to do with rent seeking by parliamentarians themselves. There has been high-level acknowledgement (and condemnation) of the institution's thriving 'envelope culture' (*budaya amplop*), which invites corrupt payments to legislators in exchange for favours or to avoid obstruction (*Kompas*, 27 September 2002, 30 September 2002, 9 October 2002). There have been reports of government agencies making payments to DPR members to secure approval for their initiatives; state-owned enterprises are also vulnerable to extortion by members who threaten to investigate their affairs. Some private businesses have reportedly been summoned by parliamentarians, apparently in an effort to extract payments from them (Sherlock 2003: 19–20, 27). Not until 2006 was there an investigation into parliamentary corruption that resulted in at least some disciplinary action, including against a member of President Yudhoyono's own party; but it is far from clear that this will lead to a significant shift in the practices of the DPR.

CONCLUSION

Since 1998, business groups have become much more vocal and visible in pressing their demands on government, but business actors have also continued to protect their interests in more informal and individualised ways. The task facing Indonesia's political and bureaucratic institutions is to filter the demands of business more productively. Somewhat wistful hopes of insulating the policy-making process from political and interest group pressure as in the past (see, for example, Boediono 2005b) have little prospect of being realised. Closing off political avenues for business and other interest group influence, even if feasible, is risky. Indonesia's earlier experience suggests that denying business a voice in the official policy-making process was a major factor in driving lobbying underground, and along particularly damaging personal lines.

To some extent the mode of business representation has been changing. Further empowerment of business associations as vehicles for the collective, transparent representation of business interests may place some limits on government policy pandering to narrow interests. Securing real progress with state sector reform, including more effective efforts to reduce corruption in the bureaucracy and judiciary, is likely to be even more important. Ultimately, however, the political mechanisms through which government is held accountable by the wider public are crucial to determining whether government responsiveness to business takes a malign or positive form.

REFERENCES

Bardhan, P. (2005), *Scarcity, Conflicts, and Cooperation*, Cambridge MA: MIT Press.

Basri, M.C. (2004), 'Kadin, dari Ekonomi Rente Menuju Aksi Kolektif?' [Kadin, from Rent Seeking to Collective Action?], *Kompas*, 21 February.

Boediono (2005a), 'Stabilization in a Period of Transition: Indonesia 2001–2004', paper presented to a conference on Macroeconomic Policy and Structural Change in East Asia, Sydney, 24–25 February.

Boediono (2005b), 'Managing the Indonesian Economy: Some Lessons from the Past', *Bulletin of Indonesian Economic Studies*, 41(3): 309–24.

Brown, R.A. (2004), 'Conglomerates in Contemporary Indonesia: Concentration, Crisis and Restructuring', *South East Asia Research*, 12(3): 378–407.

Buchanan, J. (1968), *The Demand and Supply of Public Goods*, Chicago IL: Rand McNally.

Castle, J. (2004), 'Investment Prospects: A View from the Private Sector', pp. 72–89 in M.C. Basri and P. van der Eng (eds), *Business in Indonesia: New Challenges, Old Problems*, Singapore: Institute of Southeast Asian Studies.

Cook, P., C. Kirkpatrick, M. Minogue and D. Parker (eds) (2004), *Leading Issues in Competition, Regulation and Development*, Cheltenham: Edward Elgar.

Crouch, H. (1979), 'Patrimonialism and Military Rule in Indonesia', *World Politics*, 31(4): 571–87.

Dauvergne, P. (1997), *Shadows in the Forest: Japan and the Politics of Timber in Southeast Asia*, Cambridge MA: MIT Press.

Dauvergne, P. (2005), 'The Environmental Challenge to Loggers in the Asia-Pacific: Corporate Practices in Informal Regimes of Governance', pp. 169–96 in D. Levy and P. Newell (eds), *The Business of Global Environmental Governance*, Cambridge MA: MIT Press.

Doner, R. (1992), 'The Limits of State Strength: Toward an Institutionalist View of Economic Development', *World Politics*, 44(3): 398–431.

Doner, R., B. Ritchie and D. Slater (2005), 'Systemic Vulnerability and the Origins of Developmental States: Northeast and Southeast Asia in Comparative Perspective', *International Organization*, 59: 327–69.

Evans, P. (1995), *Embedded Autonomy: States and Industrial Transformation*, Princeton NJ: Princeton University Press.

Geddes, B. (1994), *Politician's Dilemma: Building State Capacity in Latin America*, Berkeley CA: University of California Press.

Haggard, S. (2000), 'Interests, Institutions, and Policy Reform', pp. 21–57 in A. Krueger (ed.), *Economic Policy Reform: The Second Stage*, Chicago IL: University of Chicago Press.

Haggard, S. (2004), 'Institutions and Growth in East Asia', *Studies in Comparative International Development*, 38(4): 53–81.

Haggard, S., S. Maxfield and B.R. Schneider (1997), 'Theories of Business and Business–State Relations', pp. 36–60 in S. Maxfield and B.R. Schneider (eds), *Business and the State in Developing Countries*, Ithaca NY: Cornell University Press.

Hamilton-Hart, N. (2002), *Asian States, Asian Bankers: Central Banking in Southeast Asia*, Ithaca NY: Cornell University Press.

Harvest International (2002), 'No Complaints', *Indonesian Business Perspective Online*, 4(9): September.

Hefner, R. (1997), 'Business in Indonesia: A Vulnerable Actor', pp. 154–6 in A. Bernstein and P. Berger (eds), *Business and Democracy: Cohabitation or Contradiction?* London: Pinter.

Heij, G. (2001), 'The 1981–83 Indonesian Tax Reform Process: Who Pulled the Strings?', *Bulletin of Indonesian Economic Studies*, 37(2): 233–51.

Hill, H. (1996), *The Indonesian Economy since 1966: Asia's Emerging Giant*, Cambridge: Cambridge University Press.

Kang, D. (2002), *Crony Capitalism: Corruption and Development in South Korea and the Philippines*, Cambridge: Cambridge University Press.

Khan, M.H. (2000), 'Rents, Efficiency and Growth', pp. 21–69 in M.H. Khan and K.S. Jomo (eds), *Rents, Rent-seeking and Economic Development: Theory and Evidence in Asia*, Cambridge: Cambridge University Press.

Khan, M.H. and K.S. Jomo (eds) (2000), *Rents, Rent-seeking and Economic Development: Theory and Evidence in Asia*, Cambridge: Cambridge University Press.

Khouw, M.M. (2004), 'The Private Sector Response to Public Sector Corruption', pp. 204–20 in M.C. Basri and P. van der Eng (eds), *Business in Indonesia: New Challenges, Old Problems*, Singapore: Institute of Southeast Asian Studies.

Krueger, A. (1974), 'The Political Economy of the Rent-seeking Society', *American Economic Review*, 64(3): 291–303.

Kuncoro, A. (2006), 'Corruption and Business Uncertainty in Indonesia', *ASEAN Economic Bulletin*, 23(1): 11–30.

Kuncoro, A. and B. Resosudarmo (2006), 'Survey of Recent Developments', *Bulletin of Indonesian Economic Studies*, 42(1): 7–31.

Lang, G. and C.H.W. Chan (2006), 'China's Impact on Forests in Southeast Asia', *Journal of Contemporary Asia*, 36(2): 167–94.

MacIntyre, A. (1991), *Business and Politics in Indonesia*, Sydney: Allen & Unwin.

MacIntyre, A. (1994), 'Power, Prosperity and Patrimonialism: Business and Government in Indonesia', pp. 244–67 in *Business and Government in Industrialising Asia*, Ithaca NY: Cornell University Press.

MacIntyre, A. (2000), 'Funny Money: Fiscal Policy, Rent-seeking and Economic Performance in Indonesia', pp. 248–73 in M.H. Khan and K.S. Jomo (eds), *Rents, Rent-seeking and Economic Development: Theory and Evidence in Asia*, Cambridge MA: Cambridge University Press.

Manning, C. (2004), 'Labour Regulation and the Business Environment: Time to Take Stock', pp. 234–49 in M.C. Basri and P. van der Eng (eds), *Business in Indonesia: New Challenges, Old Problems*, Singapore: Institute of Southeast Asian Studies.

Manning, C. and Kurnya Roesad (2006), 'Survey of Recent Developments', *Bulletin of Indonesian Economic Studies*, 42(2): 143–70.

McLeod, R.H. (2000), 'Soeharto's Indonesia: A Better Class of Corruption', *Agenda*, 7(2): 99–112.

McLeod, R.H. (2004), 'Dealing with Bank System Failure: Indonesia, 1997–2003', *Bulletin of Indonesian Economic Studies*, 40(1): 95–116.

Milner, H. (1988), 'Trading Places: Industries for Free Trade', *World Politics*, 40(3): 350–76.

Noble, G. (1998), *Collective Action in East Asia: How Ruling Parties Shape Industrial Policy*, Ithaca NY: Cornell University Press.

Pepinsky, T. (2006), 'Institutions, Economic Recovery, and Macroeconomic Vulnerability in Indonesia and Malaysia', unpublished manuscript, New Haven CO: Yale University.

Prasetiantono, T. (2004), 'Political Economy of Privatisation of State-owned Enterprises in Indonesia', pp. 141–57 in M.C. Basri and P. van der Eng (eds), *Business in Indonesia: New Challenges, Old Problems*, Singapore: Institute of Southeast Asian Studies.

Robison, R. (1986), *Indonesia: The Rise of Capital*, Sydney: Allen & Unwin.

Robison, R. and V. Hadiz (2004), *Reorganising Power in Indonesia: The Politics of Oligarchy in an Age of Markets*, London: RoutledgeCurzon.

Ross, M. (1999), 'The Political Economy of the Resource Curse', *World Politics*, 51(2): 297–322.

Schamis, H. (1999), 'Distributional Coalitions and the Politics of Economic Reform in Latin America', *World Politics*, 51(2): 236–68.

Schneider, B.R. (1998), 'Elusive Synergy: Business–Government Relations and Development', *Comparative Politics*, 31(1): 101–22.

Schneider, B.R. and S. Maxfield (1997), 'Business, the State and Economic Performance in Developing Countries', pp. 3–35 in S. Maxfield and B.R. Schneider (eds), *Business and the State in Developing Countries*, Ithaca NY: Cornell University Press.

Searle, P. (1999), *The Riddle of Malaysian Capitalism: Rent-seekers or Real Capitalists?* Sydney: Allen & Unwin.

Sen, K. and L. Steer (2005), 'Survey of Recent Developments', *Bulletin of Indonesian Economic Studies*, 41(3): 279–304.

Sherlock, S. (2003), 'Struggling to Change: The Indonesian Parliament in an Era of Reformasi', research report, Canberra: Centre for Democratic Institutions.

Soedradjad Djiwandono (2005), *Bank Indonesia and the Crisis: An Insider's View*, Singapore: Institute of Southeast Asian Studies.

Yoshihara Kunio (1988), *The Rise of Ersatz Capitalism in South-east Asia*, Manila: Ateneo de Manila University Press.

7 MUSLIM POLITICS IN INDONESIA'S DEMOCRATISATION: THE RELIGIOUS MAJORITY AND THE RIGHTS OF MINORITIES IN THE POST-NEW ORDER ERA

Arskal Salim

INTRODUCTION

One of the major dangers of democracy is the potential for 'tyranny of the majority': the risk that certain groups may use their majority to promote their special interests at the expense of minorities. For example, a religious majority may seek to have the state impose its religious values on the entire population, resulting in the oppression of religious minorities. Many countries try to avoid this outcome by constitutional separation of religion from the state, such that their governments do not promote one religion over others, but act only to protect religious freedom where it is threatened.

The authors of Indonesia's constitution were well aware of the problem. Accordingly, the constitutional status of religion is set out in article 29 on religion, which stipulates simply that 'The state is based on belief in One God', and that 'The state guarantees the freedom of all residents to embrace their own religion and to worship according to their own religion and beliefs'. Two aspects of these stipulations are worthy of emphasis. First, since no single religion is officially acknowledged in the constitution, Indonesia is certainly not a theocratic state. The government is required to follow a policy of neutrality towards all religions, and to provide a mechanism to afford equal rights to all citizens regardless of their religious persuasion. Second, the constitution confers religious rights on individuals, not on any religious community. Collective religious rights are no more than a natural extension of each individual's personal rights, so that the government should deal with its citizens individually, not as religious groups (Bell 2001: 795; Salim 2006: 100).

The history of religious majority–minority relationships in Indonesia has always been somewhat troubled, as article 29 has not been widely accepted as requiring a clear demarcation between religion and the state. Islam is the majority religion, and the Ministry of Religious Affairs was established in 1946 to provide autonomy for the Muslim community. The minister has always been a Muslim, and the Islamic section of the ministry the largest. At present each religious section has one director-general, except for the Islamic section, which has two—one for Islamic affairs and one for Islamic institutions. For decades the ministry has been the locus of the internal strengthening of Islamic institutions, the Muslim community and the spread of Islam (*dakwah*) (Lev 1972; Boland 1982; van Bruinessen 1995). Despite all this, however, as argued by Wertheim (1986), many Muslim leaders felt they were treated as 'minorities' under President Soekarno (1945–65) and for much of President Soeharto's term in office (1966–98).

An additional departure from the constitutional requirement for government neutrality towards different religions stems from the misinterpretation of a Soekarno-era presidential decree (No. 1/1965 on the Prevention of Abuse and/or Disrespect of Religion). The elucidation to this decree listed the six religions to which most Indonesian people adhere: Islam, Catholicism, Protestantism, Hinduism, Buddhism and Confucianism.[1] This was not meant to imply that these were the only religions that were officially acknowledged, but since 1974, when religion became a decisive factor in validating marriages, the term 'religion' has been interpreted based on previous regulations—and on this decree in particular. For example, the regulations on identity cards have long required their holders to indicate their religion—a requirement that was reconfirmed in a recently passed law on the administration of residents—thus discriminating against citizens who subscribe to traditional beliefs (*aliran kepercayaan*) rather than any of the six major religions (*Suara Pembaruan*, 28 November 2006).

---

1   In 1967, under Presidential Instruction No. 14/1967, President Soeharto dropped Confucianism from the list of recognised religions because of its allegedly strong relationship with communism. In 2001 President Abdurrahman Wahid annulled that instruction, allowing Confucianism to once again become a recognised religion in Indonesia.

This chapter focuses on the attempts of some aggressive Islamic groups to reinforce the position of Muslims as the dominant religious majority. Although they do not necessarily represent a large proportion of Muslims, these groups are cleverly exploiting religious sentiment in relation to several socio-political issues. It is argued here that this engagement in so-called 'Muslim politics' has become the primary means of strengthening the dominant position of Islam, and that this threatens Indonesia's democratisation by infringing the rights of religious minorities. Moreover, as the case studies in this chapter will show, successive governments have failed not only to act impartially on religious issues as required by the constitution, but also to refrain from providing unnecessary concessions and privileges to the religious majority, thus threatening Indonesia's transition to democracy.

The following section provides a theoretical discussion of how Muslim politics has become a crucial factor negatively affecting the rights of religious minorities. This is followed in the subsequent section by three case studies, the first on regulation of the establishment of places of worship, the second on the anti-pornography bill and the third on the enactment of bylaws containing Islamic law (sharia) injunctions. These case studies illustrate how the rights of religious minorities are potentially or actually infringed as a result of Muslim politics. The fourth section of the chapter evaluates the increasingly important role played by the Indonesian Council of Ulama (MUI) in Muslim politics in the post-New Order era. The chapter concludes by presenting two strategies for ensuring the protection of minorities' rights.

MUSLIM POLITICS AND THE RIGHTS OF MINORITIES

Ghanea (2004) explores the relationship between Muslim politics and the human rights of religious minorities in Middle Eastern countries. Following Eickelman and Piscatori (1996),[2] she uses the term 'Muslim politics' to mean 'the symbolic capital and the shared ideas and practices of Muslims that [are often] mobilized to impact the human rights of minorities' (Ghanea 2004: 706–7). In other words, Muslim politics involves mobilisation of widespread emotional commitment to Islam for political purposes, and it provides a powerful means for religious actors and politicians to gain the support of Muslims across numerous political and ethnic divides for their own particular interests. What is seen as 'Muslim'

---

2 Eickelman and Piscatori (1996: 5) define 'Muslim politics' as the competition and contest over both interpretation of symbols and control of the institutions that produce and sustain them.

in such activity is the language employed to sustain the activity and the claim of its association with religion. As used in this chapter, therefore, the term 'Muslim politics' encompasses the various kinds of contemporary Islamist movements that attempt to advance the reach of Islam as a political project; efforts to establish a close relationship between Islam and the state; and the purely tactical use of religious language by otherwise non-religious parties.

Many of those involved in Muslim politics presume that their ways are authentically and rightly 'Muslim' whereas those of others are not (Ghanea 2004: 712). This presumption of religious superiority helps to spread the notion that non-Muslims have inferior status and limited rights, and that it is acceptable to treat non-Muslims differently because of their religious preferences. One consequence of Muslim politics, therefore, is to create inequality between citizens of different religious persuasions in various aspects of everyday life. This includes inequality before the law as well as unequal participation in political life, and it is often accompanied by a resort to tokenism (appointment of members of minorities to prominent positions) to obscure what is happening. As Ghanea notes, tokenism does not signify engagement with minorities and their acceptance into the mainstream, but rather clearly demonstrates their absence from it in any genuine sense. Tokenism is not based on full respect for human rights, and it does not accord minorities the same degree of dignity as the rest of the community. Under this approach, minorities lack the ability to contribute to the outcome of events and structures that influence their lives, whether in the legal, political or cultural sphere (Ghanea 2004: 723).

According to Ghanea, inequality comes into focus most at times of economic and political flux. This indicates either a fundamental discomfort with the presence of religious minorities, or a propensity to exploit them in order to provide distraction in times of severe social disruption, heightened political tension and periods involving serious societal disjuncture between liberals and conservatives. This exploitation may involve individuals, mobs or the government (Ghanea 2004: 714).

Such a scenario may be valid for present-day Indonesia. By invoking Islamic ideas and symbols, the proponents of Muslim politics are attempting to mobilise the symbolic capital of Islam in the public arena at the expense of religious minorities. Muslim politics is advocated not only by Muslim groups and Islamic institutions, parties and publishers, but also by regional bureaucracies and even secular political parties. While activists in Islamic groups seek to establish Muslim political dominance, politicians seek to enhance their prospects by identifying with the interests of Muslim voters. The temptation for politicians to appeal to the sentiments of the Islamic majority, and for governments to seek legitimacy by an appeal to Islam, has been very strong in the post-New Order era. And as Muslim politics has become an integral part of government policy, the state has become increasingly identified with the majority religion.

A key argument of those seeking to justify Muslim politics in Indonesia is the fact that Muslims are a large majority, and that Islam is the strongest unifying bond among people from diverse locations with different ethnic and language backgrounds. According to this self-serving view, Muslim interests must be prioritised over those of other religious faiths. But whereas a fundamental characteristic of democracy is that all citizens have equal rights in the decision-making process, for democracy to work well, this process must not enfeeble the legal standing or rights of minorities; democracy is not equivalent to majoritarian government (Beetham and Boyle 1995).

THREE CASE STUDIES

The Establishment and Regulation of Places of Worship

On 21 March 2006, the ministers of religion and home affairs, Maftuh Basyuni and Muhammad Ma'ruf, signed a revised joint ministerial regulation on the establishment of places of worship.[3] It replaced a 1969 decree that had been blamed for allowing mob action directed to the destruction or closure of a number of 'illegal' places of worship. In explanatory remarks delivered on 17 April 2006, Maftuh said that three basic considerations had underpinned the revised regulation.[4] First, an increasing number of places of worship were being built without appropriate procedures being followed, often leading to conflict between adherents of different religions. A clearer regulation was therefore needed, not to restrict religious freedom, but to ensure harmony between people of different religious persuasions. Second, amid much criticism of the continued failure of the state to protect religious freedom, the revision aimed to demonstrate the responsibility of the state for guaranteeing the right of all citizens to worship. Third, because religious communities should also be responsible for ensuring religious harmony, the regulation would require them to become more closely involved with each other through

---

3 Joint Regulation No. 9/2006 of the Minister of Religion and Joint Regulation No. 8/2006 of the Minister of Home Affairs on the Implementing Guidelines for Heads of Districts/Municipalities in the Maintenance of Religious Harmony, the Empowerment of Communication Forums for Religious Harmony and the Establishment of Places of Worship.

4 A copy of the minister's address is held by the author.

newly established Communication Forums for Religious Harmony. The aim was to improve relationships among religious groups.

The revised regulation consists of 10 chapters containing 30 articles. Several aspects are relevant to the discussion here. First, the regulation stipulates that a Communication Forum for Religious Harmony is to be formed in each district/municipality (*kabupaten/kota*) to help settle inter-religious disputes and to issue written recommendations that authorise, or disallow, the establishment of places of worship. Second, provincial and local government officials—specifically, the governor, district head or mayor, and head of the local office of religious affairs—are responsible for ensuring religious harmony in their areas. Third, the establishment of places of worship is to be based on the religious composition of the local population. To obtain a building permit, at least 90 residents of a religious community and 60 residents from another religious community must give their approval. Fourth, disputes concerning the establishment of places of worship should be settled by consultation (*musyawarah*) between residents if possible; failing that, the matter is to be brought to district officials for resolution.

The crucial articles of the regulation arguably favour the local religious majority; because Muslims constitute the majority in most districts, the regulation generally works against the interests of non-Muslims. In practice it is often very difficult for minorities to obtain building permits, not only because they may be unable to get approval from the required number of residents, but also because local officials tend to take the side of members of the religious majority who wish to refuse the request (*Suara Pembaruan*, 16 December 2005). The fact that district governments may delay, or even refuse, issuance of building permits for new places of worship to religious minorities with valid applications shows that these governments represent the religious majority rather than the people as a whole.

Thus Muslim politics plays a significant role in reinforcing the position of the religious majority. Politicians occupying leadership positions in a province or district are likely to side with the religious majority in exchange for its support in local elections. In addition, Muslim politics may be employed by certain Islamic groups as a means to awaken religious sentiment among ordinary Muslims residing in the area of a proposed new place of worship, provoking them to refuse the application. The typical justification for this is that the proposal is not in line with local ethno-religious identities, but the underlying reason is more likely to be fear of conversions away from Islam.

Some 42 members of the People's Representative Council (DPR) issued a memorandum protesting the regulation two days after it was signed, on the grounds that it contravened constitutional stipulations on religion and human rights and created difficulties by restricting the activities of religious groups, especially minorities.[5] Some moderate Muslim figures have voiced the same concerns. Hasyim Muzadi, chair of Indonesia's largest Muslim organisation, Nahdlatul Ulama (NU), argued that the revised regulation was more restrictive of religious minorities than its predecessor. In the eyes of Muhammadiyah intellectual Muslim Abdurrahman, the regulation was a 'time bomb' that might explode at any time, putting existing harmonious relations between believers of different faiths in danger (*Suara Pembaruan*, 26 October 2005). For Dawam Rahardjo, another leading Muslim intellectual, what was urgently needed was not a restrictive regulation, but a statute that offered religious liberty to all citizens (*Suara Pembaruan*, 15 October 2005).

But many other Muslim leaders shared the view of the minister of religion that the regulation was necessary to serve as a 'legal umbrella' to ensure religious harmony. They included Din Syamsuddin (chair of Muhammadiyah), Amidhan (chair of MUI), Ma'ruf Amin (MUI) and Jazuli Juwaini (Prosperity and Justice Party; PKS). They argued that there should be no policy of *laissez-faire* in relation to interaction between religions, but rather a mechanism to prevent the emergence of religious conflict (*Suara Karya*, 3 December 2005; *Republika*, 25 March 2006). President Susilo Bambang Yudhoyono (SBY) also appeared to support the revised regulation. In a meeting with a delegation of Muslim organisations led by the minister of religion some time before the regulation was signed, he reportedly said that the regulation was important not only for establishing religious harmony among believers of different faiths, but also for maintaining Indonesian unity. Enactment of the regulation has failed to guarantee religious harmony, however. Several days after it came into force an angry mob expelled Christians from a Pentecostal church in Bogor and then closed it. A similar attack took place in south Jakarta in March 2006, when a Bethel church community became the victim (Hosen 2006: 6).

The joint regulation is problematic for four reasons (Hosen 2006: 6–7). First, it fails to compensate for individual circumstances in order that the law may treat everyone equally; such an approach is essential to protect minorities and ensure religious liberty in a multicultural society. Second, it creates a long and complicated procedure for establishing places of worship. Third, it ignores smaller or 'unrecognised' religious groups, such as the Ahmadiyah, Shi'a Islam and non-mainstream Christian sects, implying that they will not be accommodated in the Communication Forums for Religious Harmony. Fourth, it is vague, because the requirement for

---

5   *Suara Pembaruan*, 24 March 2006; *Suara Merdeka*, 24 March 2006; *Republika*, 25 March 2006.

approval by 90 worshippers and 60 people of other faiths is arbitrary. What would happen if, for example, 1,000 people disapproved? Would a building permit be issued in the face of such huge opposition? As we have noted, the constitution guarantees freedom of worship to everyone. But unfortunately, the government perceives a difference between the right to worship and the right to establish places of worship. Its logic is inherently Islamic: Muslims may pray in any situation. But this ignores the importance for adherents of other religions to be able to pray in places built for that specific purpose.

The Anti-pornography Bill

The draft Anti-pornography Bill stemmed from an earlier draft prepared by the Ministry of Religious Affairs in the last years of the New Order. Following Soeharto's demise, MUI refined this draft and called for its promulgation by the legislature (*Media Indonesia*, 21 April 2005). In September 2005, a special legislative committee was set up to discuss the new draft. It was chaired by Balkan Kaplale, a legislator from SBY's secular Democratic Party (Partai Demokrat); its deputy chair was Yoyoh Yusroh, a legislator from the Islamically oriented PKS.

The bill originally covered a range of matters, including nudity, the female body, sex, erotic dance, pornographic materials and indecent activities (see Table 7.1 for examples). Its definition of pornography was unclear and open to multiple interpretations, however.[6] The definition included explicit photographs of anything—but mainly parts of the female anatomy—that might arouse sexual desire. This was discriminatory in so far as only female body parts were defined as sensual, thus demonising women as the root of all sexual evil. Indeed, as Suryakusuma and Lindsey (2006) have argued, 'The bill would criminalise much sexuality, force women to cover up almost completely, largely exclude them from public space, and tightly censor the arts and media'.

The bill immediately sparked vigorous debate. Its supporters argued that significant moral decay had resulted from the widespread availability of pornography, making an anti-pornography law a matter of urgency. Others contended that the regulation of pornography required careful consideration, since it raised the possibility of women being victimised and of discrimination against citizens based on their personal values. In addition, there were strong doubts about whether such a law would be effective in overcoming the alleged problem of moral decay,

---

6 The initial bill defined pornography as follows: 'Pornography is material in the media or on communication devices that is made to deliver sexual concepts in a way that is sexually exploitative, obscene and/or erotic'.

Table 7.1   Penal Sanctions in the Anti-pornography Bill

Type of Infringement	Penalty	
	Imprisonment (years)	Fine (Rp million)
Displaying genitals	1–5	50–250
Exposing buttocks in public	2–6	100–300
Displaying female breasts in public	1–5	50–250
Intentionally becoming naked in public	2–6	100–300
Kissing on the lips in public	1–5	50–250
Dancing erotically in public	2–10	100–500
Masturbating in public	2–10	100–500
Simulating masturbation in public	1–5	50–250
Having sex in public	2–10	100–500
Simulating having sex in public	1–5	50–250
Having sex with children	3–10	100–1,000
Organising sex shows	3–10	100–1,000
Organising sex parties	½–2	25–100
Watching sexually explicit performances	½–2	25–100
Providing funds or venues for indecent acts	1–5	50–250

Source: Adapted from 'Langgar Konstitusi, Langgar HAM?' [Violate Constitution, Violate Human Rights?], *Kompas*, 4 March 2006.

let alone eradicating rape, sexual harassment or loose sexual behaviour (*Kompas*, 25 February 2006).

Some people argued that a number of the bill's stipulations were a blatant call for the implementation of sharia. For example, in the definition of the 'sensual areas' of a woman's body that must be covered. R. Husna Mulya, coordinator of the Legal Reform Division of the National Commission on Women's Rights, noted that:

> the definition in the bill that mentions thighs, hips, the navel and part or the whole of the female breast as sensual areas that must not be exposed is a definition that refers to the understanding of women's *aurat* [those parts of the body that must be kept covered in public] in accordance with Islamic injunction.

For her, this kind of definition neglected the diversity of values embraced by the Indonesian people as a whole.[7] The extent to which pornography was identified and measured varied from one location to the next and from one community to another — and, indeed, Muslims themselves had never reached a consensus on the boundaries of 'pornography'.

The proponents of the bill denied that it was part of an Islamisation agenda, asserting that it supported the interests of society as a whole. The allegation nevertheless persisted that it was underpinned by the hegemonic passion of the majority over the minority: that it abandoned cultural plurality and attempted to impose the values of the religious majority on the entire population (Yudohusodo 2006). Concern about the bill therefore intensified as it became more apparent that the special committee was representing the interests of the religious majority only. According to committee chair Kaplale himself, the bill reflected the aspirations of the majority of Indonesians, with those who opposed it constituting a minority of no more than 10 per cent. In his words, 'In the final analysis, the strategy of the state is to side with the majority, so never underestimate [the majority]' (*Gatra*, 6 May 2006).

Clearly Muslim politics did play an important role in efforts to secure the passage of the anti-pornography bill, and its proponents generated strong support from a wide range of Islamic parties and organisations.[8] The bill became a means of furthering the interests of political parties. PKS, for example, accorded its enactment a high priority, clearly seeing it as an important way of winning the hearts of Muslim voters before the 2009 national elections (*Republika*, 30 January 2006; *Suara Pembaruan*, 23 February 2006).

Some secular parties also supported the bill, despite its Islamic symbolism. The appointment of a Democratic Party legislator and strong proponent of the bill as chair of the special committee suggested that the party saw this as an opportunity to boost its political standing and modify the image it had taken into the 2004 elections of being dominated by non-Muslim figures and having little concern for Muslim interests. The alliance between the Democratic Party and PKS in a joint attempt to have the anti-pornography legislation enacted can also be seen as a trade-off of Democratic Party support for the bill in return for increased PKS support in the DPR for the SBY government, including its unpopular policy of reducing fuel subsidies.

---

7 'RUU Anti Pornografi Dikhawatirkan Pintu Masuk Hukum Islam' [Fears Anti-pornography Bill Will Open Door to Islamic Law], available at <http://www.tempointeraktif.com/hg/nasional/2006/02/13/brk,20060213-73870,id.html> dated 13 February 2006, accessed 1 September 2006.
8 *Republika*, 6 May 2006, 22 May 2006; *Suara Karya*, 22 May 2006.

As a patron of the Democratic Party, the president clearly indicated his support for the bill after taking office. In early 2005, he warned the television media that he was disturbed by the images of women's navels that had been appearing on TV. In March 2005 he expressed his concern about moral decadence among Indonesians of all ages due to the wide-spread availability of pornography (Arivia 2005; *Kompas*, 29 March 2005). The anti-pornography bill was also supported by Golkar, the strongest party in the DPR. Both Jusuf Kalla, chair of Golkar and vice-president of Indonesia, and Agung Laksono, deputy chair of Golkar and speaker of the DPR, shared the view that Indonesia needed an anti-pornography law to deal with the problem of moral decay (*Suara Pembaruan*, 6 March 2006, 22 May 2006). In fact, the only major party that did not support the bill was the Indonesian Democratic Party of Struggle (PDI-P), the second largest party in parliament (*Media Indonesia*, 2 May 2006).

It was originally intended that the legislature would pass the bill in June 2006. This did not occur, however, in part because of a recognition of the bill's impact on minorities. For example, the bill threatened the cultural heritage and religious beliefs of Bali's predominantly Hindu population, who opposed it strongly. More generally, the bill was regarded as failing to reflect and represent Indonesia as an open, tolerant society with a profound respect for the unique social, cultural and religious values of its numerous ethnic and religious groups; it ignored the fact that Indonesia was a multicultural nation whose people had diverse attitudes to sensuality and sexuality. By enforcing a single interpretation based on the religious majority's understanding of what constituted pornographic materials and acts, the state would restrict individuals' freedom to celebrate their religious beliefs and cultural heritage. Indonesia's integrity as a nation would be put at risk, and pride in being Indonesian would decline as a consequence of majority hegemony and minority alienation.[9]

After lying dormant for several months the bill was reformulated in an attempt to accommodate many of the concerns of its opponents. In late November 2006, Kaplale said that the revised draft had been accepted by all factions in the DPR, and that it was scheduled to be discussed again with the government in early 2007. The title of the bill had now become either the 'Draft Law on Pornography' or the 'Draft Law on Pornography and Indecent Acts', leaving out the word 'Anti'.[10] The revised draft

---

9 'Agamawan dan Budayawan Bali Tolak RUU Pornografi' [Balinese Religious and Cultural Elite Rejects Anti-pornography Bill], available at <http://www.tempointeraktif.com/hg/nusa/bali/2006/02/11/brk,20060211-73813,id.html>, dated 11 February 2006, accessed 15 January 2007.

10 'RUU APP Jadi RUU PP, Siap Dibahas dengan Pemerintah' [Anti-pornography Bill becomes Pornography Bill, Ready for Discussion with Government],

contains only 36 articles, compared with 93 originally, although this big change in size does not necessarily extend to a change in content. Articles 14–21 on prohibitions (*larangan*) merely contain a summary of articles 4–33 in the original draft, albeit now with the main emphasis on the production, distribution and sale of pornography. What is significant is that many of the provisions mentioned in Table 7.1 have been removed, and that the bill now includes a definition of pornography on which a consensus among law makers has been achieved.[11] Whether the public fully understands and accepts this definition remains to be seen, however.

The Enactment of Sharia Bylaws

Boland (1982: 185) argued long ago that permitting the implementation of sharia in Aceh would create a precedent that other Islamic regions in Indonesia would be tempted to follow. And indeed, after post-Soeharto central governments allowed Aceh to implement sharia through a series of special autonomy laws, other provinces and districts did begin to imitate Aceh by introducing regional regulations (*perda*), decrees (*keputusan*), instructions (*instruksi*) and circulars (*surat edaran*) that contained Islamic injunctions (see Table 7.2 for details). These bylaws are concerned with three broad sets of issues: first, public order and social problems such as prostitution, consumption of alcohol and gambling; second, religious skills and obligations, such as reading the Qur'an, attending Friday prayers and paying the wealth tax (*zakat*); and third, religious symbolism, including Muslim dress.

This new development has generated heated debate among Indonesians, including members of the national legislature (*Seputar Indonesia*, 3 July 2006). The proponents of sharia-based regulations rely on at least three arguments. First, the majority of the Indonesian population is Muslim, and the Muslim kingdom antecedents of the state of Indonesia did implement sharia rules (Nurwahid 2006).[12] Second, sharia bylaws will not create problems as long as they are drafted openly and enacted by democratically elected provincial or district legislatures (Nurwahid

available at <http://www.detiknews.com/index.php/detikread/tahun/2006/bulan/11tgl/28/time/145>, dated 28 November 2006, accessed 28 November 2006.

11 Pornography is now defined as consisting of 'human works that deliberately exploit sexual objects by displaying them publicly and infringing society's moral values'.

12 In fact, the extent to which sharia was implemented in these kingdoms depended largely on the piety of their individual rulers. For further details, see Salim and Azra (2003).

2006). And third, Indonesia's legal–political system allows the implementation of sharia bylaws: under Laws No. 22/1999 and No. 32/2004 on regional government, it is legitimate for provincial and local governments to enact regulations that seek to overcome social problems and maintain public order (Indrayana 2005).

In relation to this last point, Indrayana (2005: 6) asserts that the bylaws were deliberately designed to avoid clashing with higher laws stipulating that regional governments have no authority to regulate on religious matters. To this end, the bylaws emphasise methods and measures to establish public order within the society, rather than appealing to Islamic sharia itself. This means that they cannot be annulled by the central government following executive review, as would be possible if a lower-level government regulation was considered to be in conflict with a higher-level law or the constitution.

Opponents of sharia bylaws are unconvinced by these arguments. For example, Todung Mulya Lubis, a high-profile lawyer and human rights activist, has set out three objections to sharia bylaws. First, they conflict with the constitutional guarantee of religious freedom for all citizens to practice their religion according to their own beliefs. Second, much of the content of the bylaws (on gambling, prostitution and alcohol consumption) is already covered by the penal code, so additional regional regulations are redundant. Third, even if introduced by democratically elected legislatures, the bylaws are unacceptable because they amount to non-democratic negation of minority rights by discriminating against non-Muslim citizens.[13]

It has been argued that the introduction of sharia bylaws is motivated by religious piety; indeed, several regions adopting them have a strong Darul Islam tradition.[14] It may also be motivated by political considerations, however. According to Ahmad Suaedy (2006a), executive director of the Wahid Institute, some bylaws clearly were issued merely to further the short-term political agendas of the incumbent governors or district heads—that is, to improve their chances of re-election. This view is supported by the research findings of the Institute for the Study of Islam and Society (LK3), a Banjarmasin-based NGO. It found that sharia was often utilised to enhance the good image of the government and increase public trust in the government and the legislature, and that the introduction

---

13 'Menguji Perda Syariat di Ranah Majemuk' [Examining Sharia Bylaws in a Pluralistic Society], available at <http://www.liputan6.com/view/8,127209,1, 0,1155356468.html>, dated 10 August 2006, accessed 12 August 2006.

14 Darul Islam (House of Islam) was a revolutionary Islamic movement that fought between 1948 and 1963 to make Indonesia an Islamic republic. Aceh, West Java and South Sulawesi were the main strongholds of this movement.

Table 7.2 Sharia Bylaws in Selected Districts and Municipalities

Province	District/ Municipality	Content of Regulation	Type and No. of Regulation[a]
Aceh	All	Incorporation of aspects of theology (*aqidah*), rituals (*ibadah*) and activities that glorify Islam (*syiar Islam*) into sharia bylaws	Qanun 11/2002
	All	[Prohibition on] liquor	Qanun 12/2003
	All	[Prohibition on] gambling	Qanun 13/2003
	All	[Prohibition on] close proximity between unmarried or unrelated couples (*khalwat*)	Qanun 14/2003
	All	Management of *zakat*	Qanun 7/2004
West Sumatra	All	Eradication of immoral acts (*maksiat*)	Perda 11/2001
	Padang	Requirement to wear Muslim dress	Mayoral Instruction 451.442/2005
	Padang	Requirement for ability to read the Qur'an	Perda 3/2003
	Solok	Requirement to wear Muslim dress	Perda 6/2002
	Solok	Requirement for students, brides and grooms to be able to read the Qur'an	Perda 10/2001
	Padang Pariaman	Eradication of immoral acts (*maksiat*)	Perda 2/2004
	W. Pasaman	Requirement to wear Muslim dress	Unidentified
South Sumatra	All	[Prohibition on] immoral acts (*maksiat*)	Perda 13/2002
	Palembang	Ban on prostitution	Perda 2/2004
Bengkulu	Bengkulu	Ban on prostitution	Perda 24/2005
		Enhancement of faith and religiosity	Mayoral Instruction 3/2004
Banten	Tangerang	Prohibition on sale and distribution of liquor	Perda 7/2005
	Tangerang	Prohibition on prostitution	Perda 8/2005
	Pandeglang	Requirement to wear Muslim dress at work on weekdays	Bupati Decree 25/2002
		Requirement that student uniforms include the headscarf	Bupati Decree 9/2004
		Requirement that incoming primary school students be able to recite the 30th chapter of the Qur'an	Bupati Decree 3/2005
West Java	Cianjur	Establishment of an institute to study and develop sharia	Bupati Decree 36/2001
		Movement to improve the moral behaviour of the government apparatus and society	Bupati Circular Letter 551/2717/ASSDA. I/9/2001
		Administration of *zakat*	Perda 7/2004
		Recommendation to wear Muslim dress at work on weekdays	Bupati Circular Letter 061.2/2896/org.

	Tasikmalaya	Requirement for students to dress modestly	Bupati Circular Letter 451/SE/04/Sos/2001
	Garut	Requirement for female civil servants to wear Muslim dress	Unidentified
		Improvement of moral behaviour	Perda 6/2000
East Java	Gresik	Prohibition on prostitution	Perda 7/2002
	Gresik	[Limitation on] distribution of liquor	Perda 15/2002
	Pasuruan	Ban on prostitution	Perda 10/2001
	Pamekasan	[Limitation on] distribution of liquor	Perda 18/2001
		Application of sharia	Bupati Circular Letter 450/2002
	Jember	Prohibition on prostitution	Perda 4/2001
South Sulawesi	All	Requirement for competency among Muslims in reading the Qur'an	Perda 4/2006
	Bulukumba	Requirement to wear Muslim dress	Perda 5/2003
		Prohibition on sale and distribution of liquor	Perda 3/2002
		On *zakat*, donations (*infak*) and charity (*sedekah*)	Perda 2/2003
		Requirement for students, brides and grooms to be able to read the Qur'an	Perda 6/2005
	Sinjai	Requirement to wear Muslim dress	Unidentified
	Gowa	Requirement to wear Muslim dress; increase in hours devoted to religious subjects in schools	Perda 7/2003
	Takalar	Requirement to wear Muslim dress	Unidentified
	Maros	Requirement for students and civil servants to be able to read the Qur'an	Perda 15/2005
		Requirement to wear Muslim dress	Perda 16/2005
		Administration of *zakat*	Perda 17/2005
	Enrekang	Requirement for females to wear Muslim dress and for students to be able to read the Qur'an	Perda 6/2005
South Kalimantan	All	Prohibition on liquor consumption	Perda 1/2000
	Banjarmasin	Observance of Friday as a day of religion	Perda 8/2005
		Requirement that students be able to recite the Qur'an	Perda 4/2004
	Banjarmasin	Respect for the month of Ramadan	Perda 4/2005
West Kalimantan	Sambas	Prohibition on prostitution and pornography	Perda 3/2004
	Sambas	Prohibition on gambling	Perda 4/2004
West Nusa Tenggara	E. Lombok	Administration of *zakat* for professional workers	Perda 9/2005
Gorontalo	Gorontalo	Prevention of immoral acts (*maksiat*)	Perda 10/2003

a   Bupati = District Head; Perda = Regional Regulation; Qanun refer exclusively to regional regulations produced by the Aceh legislature since 2002, whether or not they are connected to sharia.

of sharia bylaws was often an investment by district heads and political parties in achieving success in local elections (Indrayana 2005: 8).

Clearly Muslim politics has generated an 'Islamisation race' between Islamic and non-religious parties to win the support of Muslim voters. By supporting the introduction of sharia bylaws, secular parties such as Golkar hope to cultivate a public image of being friendly to Islam and Muslims, thus preserving their strong foothold among Muslim voters. Golkar's commitment to this strategy has been somewhat ambivalent, however. On the one hand, many of the district heads and mayors who promote and support sharia-inspired bylaws are active in Golkar.[15] On the other hand, both the deputy chair and chair of Golkar have expressed ambivalence about the bylaws: Agung Laksono seems undecided as to whether to support or oppose them[16] and Jusuf Kalla has made conflicting statements on the issue. In response to a demand from 56 legislators representing various factions that the sharia bylaws be annulled,[17] Kalla said that there was nothing to fear from the bylaws.[18] On another occasion, however, he was quoted as saying that he fully supported the stance of NU in 'opposing the sharia-inspired bylaws that have been enacted in several regions' (*Jakarta Post*, 29 July 2006). Golkar's ambivalent stance again demonstrates that the introduction of sharia through regional regulations is not motivated by religious piety alone, but also by political considerations.

The growing involvement in Muslim politics of non-religious parties with strong representation in regional legislatures has shifted the focus of debate from the choice between religious and secular legislation to the degree to which Islamic legislation should be applied. This shift of focus may have a significant effect on the rights of minorities. As Philip (1995: 146) has noted, the role of non-Muslims in Egypt as participants in the legislative process gradually diminished because of a similar shift of focus. As strong non-religious parties involve themselves more heavily

---

15 They include the mayors of Padang and Tangerang and some district heads in South Sulawesi.

16 'Agung Laksono: Perda Syariat Perlu Dikaji' [Agung Laksono: Sharia Bylaws Need to Be Examined], available at <http://www.detiknews.com/indeks. php/detik.read/tahun/2006/bulan/06/tgl/15/time/130503>, dated 15 June 2006, accessed 24 June 2006.

17 '56 Anggota DPR Minta Perda Syariat Islam Dicabut' [56 DPR Members Demand Annulment of Sharia Bylaws], available at <http://www.detiknews. com/indeks.php/detik.read/tahun/2006/bulan/06/tgl/13/time/165314>, dated 13 June 2006, accessed 24 June 2006.

18 'Kalla: Jangan Takut dengan Perda Syariat Islam' [Kalla: Don't Be Afraid of Sharia Bylaws], available at <http://www.detiknews.com/indeks.php/ detik.read/tahun/2006/bulan/06/tgl/15/time/173339>, dated 15 June 2006, accessed 24 June 2006.

in Muslim politics, non-Muslim minorities may lack the means to resist decisions or regulations that disadvantage them.

Since religious minorities do not identify with sharia bylaws, the introduction of such laws often causes them to feel like outsiders or half citizens, and to feel that their religious liberties are being violated. This is the case in districts where non-Muslim female students are obliged to comply with the Muslim dress code (*Jakarta Post*, 10 July 2006). Moreover, discriminatory regulations, produced by either the legislature or the bureaucracy, send the wrong message to non-state actors — that it is acceptable to discriminate against minorities.

MUSLIM POLITICS AND MUI

This section will focus on the attempts by MUI to strengthen the position of Muslims as the dominant religious majority in the post-New Order era.[19] In so doing, MUI has gradually taken over one of the roles played by the Ministry of Religious Affairs during the New Order period. Whereas the ministry was a strong fighter for an Islamic agenda under the New Order, MUI and the Islamic parties in the legislature — PKS in particular — are now actively pursuing that agenda. This is clearly a consequence of the change from autocracy to democracy, where non-state actors have greater access to, influence on and opportunity to participate in the decision-making process, including on religious affairs.

One of the functions of MUI is to issue legal opinions (fatwas) on socio-religious matters. Even though they are not binding, functioning more as a form of moral appeal, these fatwas have become politically important since the New Order drew to a close.[20] Since that time, MUI's fatwas have become a means to reinforce a homogenised Islamic identity in the Indonesian political context. They are cited as a reference for the sharia-derived decrees issued by local governments, and have even been seen as a legitimate excuse for attacking certain groups (*Jakarta Post*, 1 August 2005; Suaedy 2006b). For example, the violent mob actions against Ahmadiyah communities in West Java and West Nusa Tenggara in 2005 were allegedly based on an MUI fatwa.[21] More generally, MUI's

---

19 There are a number of studies that discuss MUI; see, for instance, Mudzhar (1993), Mufrodi (1994), Hosen (2004) and Ichwan (2005).

20 For a study of MUI's fatwas and politics, see Hosen (2003).

21 'Ahmadiyah Makin Terzalimi dengan Fatwa MUI' [Ahmadiyah Increasingly Tyrannised by MUI Fatwa], available at <http://detik.com/jkt1.detiknews. com/index.php/detik.read/tahun/2005/bulan/07/tgl/30/time/144657/ idnews/413047/idkanal/10>, dated 30 July 2005, accessed 15 January 2007; *Jakarta Post*, 1 August 2005.

fatwas have contributed to the strengthening of Islamic conservatism in the current political arena by mobilising Islamic ideas and symbols.

Ichwan (2005: 50) has noted two significant features of MUI in the post-New Order era. First, it began to distance itself from the government as it sought to align itself with Muslim aspirations. Second, it has been using an Islamic reformist strategy to bring Indonesia's Muslim communities closer to its definition of orthodoxy. The transformation of MUI into an independent Islamic institution leaning more towards the political aspirations of the Muslim majority began when it opened its membership to activists from groups with a radical Islamic agenda — such as the Liberation Party (Hizbut Tahrir), the Islamic Defenders Front (Front Pembela Islam) and the Council of Indonesian Mujahideen (Majelis Mujahidin Indonesia)[22] — with the aim of bridging the gap between radical and moderate Muslims (Ichwan 2005: 49). It is now seeking to transform itself from the state-sponsored organisation it had been during the Soeharto era to a social organisation embracing almost all Muslim organisations and Islamic groups, including those of radical orientation. As a result, the moderate view is being overwhelmed by the more extreme views of these newly included Islamic movements, which now have a strong influence over MUI fatwas (Suaedy 2006b). It is little wonder, then, that MUI has been active in each of the three areas discussed above.

In the case of the anti-pornography bill, MUI formed a special team consisting of various Muslim organisations and Islamic groups, including some of radical orientation, to push for its enactment (*Kompas*, 22 May 2006). In addition, in May 2006 it issued a fatwa banning pornographic material and actions, followed about two weeks later by a recommendation (*tausiyah*) advocating ratification of the bill (*Suara Islam*, 1–11 August 2006: 11; *Suara Karya*, 31 May 2006).

With regard to the sharia-driven bylaws, MUI issued a statement strongly supporting the enactment of the bylaws and recommending their extension to other territorial jurisdictions.[23] Ma'ruf Amin, chair of MUI's fatwa commission, defended the sharia bylaws, arguing that they were legitimate so long as they did not conflict with higher-level regu-

---

22 Hizbut Tahrir is the Indonesian branch of a party founded in Jerusalem in the 1950s with the central aim of reviving the caliphate. Front Pembela Islam (FPI) is an Islamic vigilante group formed in 1999 to combat immoral behaviour. Majelis Mujahidin Indonesia (MMI) was established in 2000 primarily to champion the enactment of sharia.

23 'MUI dan Ormas Islam Tolak Pencabutan Perda Syariah' [MUI and Islamic Mass Organisations Reject the Annulment of Sharia Bylaws], available at <http://www.tempointeraktif.com/hg/nasional/2006/06/21/brk, 20060621-79223,id.html>, dated 21 June 2006, accessed 24 June 2006; *Jawa Pos*, 22 June 2006.

lations, and claiming that there was a consensus on the need for them among local members of the community.[24]

MUI was also closely involved in drafting the joint ministerial regulation of the Ministry of Religion and Ministry of Home Affairs on the establishment of places of worship. It was active in defending the regulation from criticism based on human rights concerns, emphasising the importance of having a regulation to control the construction of places of worship and build religious harmony (*Suara Merdeka*, 24 March 2006).

MUI's fatwas, and its efforts to give Islam priority over other religions, have clearly favoured the Muslim majority at the expense of religious minorities. In July 2005 it issued a number of fatwas confirming that Ahmadiyah was a heretical sect and prohibiting religious pluralism, among other things.[25] In seeking to create a society that is less tolerant of religious diversity, MUI is ignoring the fact that diversity is to be found not only *among* religions, but also *within* Islam itself. This has inevitably led to tensions among the various religions as well as within the Muslim community (*Jakarta Post*, 1 August 2005).

CLOSING REMARKS

Muslim politics is an important feature of Indonesia's democratisation. The willingness of the religious majority to impose its religious views and values on the country's religious minorities may jeopardise the future of the Indonesian nation state. Close identification of the state with Islam will push religious minorities to the margins of the polity and reduce their participation in the political process. But democracy can be sustained only if people agree to live together in harmony.

Although the state ideology, Pancasila, is widely believed to reflect secular principles, it can be interpreted in many different ways. On 1 June 2006, in a speech marking the 61st anniversary of the birth of Pancasila, President Yudhoyono emphasised that the five guiding principles of Pancasila[26] offered a source of resolution for any kind of emerging socio-political problem. He said that the basic principle underlying religious observance and the relationship between people of different faiths was tolerance and mutual respect. Unfortunately, his speech made no explicit mention of the anti-pornography bill, the regulation on construc-

---

24 'Menguji Perda Syariat di Ranah Majemuk' [Examining Sharia Bylaws in a Pluralistic Society], available at <http://www.liputan6.com/view/8,127209,1, 0,1155356468.html>, dated 10 August 2006, accessed 12 August 2006.
25 For further details, see Gillespie (2007).
26 They are belief in Almighty God, humanitarianism, nationalism, democracy and social justice.

tion of places of worship and the promulgation of sharia bylaws. Instead, he left it to others to interpret his comments in light of the debate over those issues. His seemingly strong endorsement of Pancasila will amount to little without concrete action to bridge the gap between the political ideals of Pancasila and contemporary inter-religious realities.

Just before the president delivered his speech, Todung Mulya Lubis read out a 'Declaration of Indonesian-ness' (Maklumat Keindonesiaan) signed by 17 prominent Indonesians (*Kompas*, 6 June 2006). It argued strongly for the defence of Pancasila as an ideology that respects pluralism and separates religion and the state. The president's speech and the declaration differed in terms of their respective articulations of the relationship between Pancasila and religion. Even though the president's speech actually referred to the declaration, it seemed 'soft' and open to different interpretations because it avoided any explicit discussion of the conflict between religion and Pancasila. The declaration, on the other hand, clearly mentioned the distinction between the two, stating that: 'Indonesia does not regard Pancasila as religion, and Indonesia is not based on any religion'.

The declaration, rather than the president's speech, drew an immediate response from MUI. The Islamic daily *Republika* published an article by Ma'ruf Amin stating that Pancasila was not incompatible with religion; he added that the statement that religion should not dictate the truth was 'an attempt to disgrace religion and separate Pancasila from religion' (Amin 2006). Later, a collective declaration by MUI and other Muslim organisations emphasised their determination 'to guard and protect Pancasila from efforts to secularise it ..., to cause Pancasila to clash with religion, and to distance Pancasila from religion, particularly Islam'.[27] The whole episode is clearly indicative of the tight contest between those wanting to create a balance among religions in Indonesia and those wanting to reinforce Islam's position as the dominant religion.

What then can be done to support the rights of minorities? Separation of religion from politics is often suggested as the solution, and many see the lack of such separation in the constitution as contributing to the majority's declining tolerance of religious minorities. But promoting a secular framework as a 'quick fix' solution to this human rights challenge would not be easy; indeed, it would be very unlikely to succeed. The key issue is not whether the state will adopt constitutional secularity but rather whether it will enforce religious freedom and plural equality. In

---

27 'Pernyataan Bersama MUI-Ormas-ormas Islam' [Joint Declaration of MUI and Islamic Mass Organisations], available at <http://hizbut-tahrir.or.id/main.php?page=news&id=658&print=1>, dated 10 July 2006, accessed 12 July 2006.

this light, two alternative strategies to ensure the rights of minorities are important (Ghanea 2004: 724–6, 729).

First, the government's responsibility to protect religious minorities from discrimination by providing them with effective legal remedies must be emphasised, and clearly defined in the constitution. While this may sound straightforward, the constitution remains vague as an effective instrument for protecting religious liberty, despite having been amended four times, resulting in the failure of the government to prosecute perpetrators of religious discrimination (Salim 2006: 141–2). Although Indonesia has a new Constitutional Court whose functions include the defence of constitutionally stipulated human rights (see Chapter 10, this volume), its jurisdiction extends only to the examination of laws, and not to the examination of provincial and local government bylaws, which can be reviewed only by the Supreme Court. Until now, no judicial review case involving any sharia bylaw or sharia-derived statute has been brought before either the Supreme Court or the Constitutional Court. This may be because people are afraid of being considered intolerant of Islamic practices, possibly sparking resentment among Muslims, or because those affected by the regulations lack confidence in the impartiality of the courts.

Second, the great diversity of Islamic legal opinion and Islamic culture must be demonstrated, to crack the myth of homogenous Muslim religious practice towards non-Muslim minorities. Although there are many Islamic injunctions on how Muslims should treat non-Muslims, a doctrine of multicultural coexistence or plural equality between members of different faiths is beyond the scope of classical Islamic legal textbooks. It is imperative, therefore, that the precise implications of religious liberty and the rights of religious minorities be authoritatively discussed and settled within the Islamic tradition itself (An-Na'im 1987). In the absence of firm action by the government on emerging problems affecting religious minorities,[28] the big hope for the future in maintaining a pluralistic society in Indonesia lies, paradoxically, with a number of influential Muslim figures, including young Muslim intellectuals, female Muslim activists and, most importantly, NU—which has been a bastion of support for tolerance, democracy, religious freedom and the de-politicisation of religion.

To conclude, let me recall that both McVey (1983) and Wertheim (1986) argued that, during the New Order, Muslims actually saw themselves

---

28 The government apparently fears the reaction of Islamic hardliners, and of influential Islamic parties in the governing coalition, particularly PKS and the Crescent Moon and Star Party (PBB) (see Suaedy 2006a; 'Anti-porno Fight Tests Muslim Tolerance in Indonesia', *Reuter News*, 30 July 2006).

more as a minority because they perceived themselves as being badly treated by the state. This changed in the last years of the New Order period, and especially after Soeharto's departure, as Muslims became increasingly conscious of their majority status. Beetham and Boyle (1995) explain that, in democracies, minorities are often given three special political rights due to their minority status: the right to be represented proportionally in government; the right to veto statutes that threaten their major interests; and the right to regulate their own affairs separately and autonomously. Ironically, all these rights have been demanded from time to time by the Muslim majority in modern Indonesia, reflecting a minority mentality on its part. The 'majority with a minority mentality' continues to have a strong impact in the newly democratic Indonesia.

REFERENCES

Amin, Ma'ruf (2006), 'Mencegah Sekularisasi Pancasila' [Preventing the Secularisation of Pancasila], *Republika*, 14 June.
An-Na'im, A.A. (1987), 'Religious Minorities under Islamic Law and the Limits of Cultural Relativism', *Human Rights Quarterly*, 9: 1–18.
Arivia, G. (2005), 'SBY dan Pusar Perempuan' [SBY and Women's Navels], *Kompas*, 28 January.
Beetham, D. and K. Boyle (1995), *Introducing Democracy: 80 Questions and Answers*, Cambridge: UNESCO Publishing/Polity Press.
Bell, G.F. (2001), 'Minority Rights and Regionalism in Indonesia: Will Constitutional Recognition Lead to Disintegration or Discrimination?', *Singapore Journal of International and Comparative Law*, 5(2): 784–806.
Boland, B.J. (1982), *The Struggle of Islam in Modern Indonesia*, The Hague: Martinus Nijhoff.
Eickelman, D.F. and J. Piscatori (1996), *Muslim Politics*, Cambridge: Cambridge University Press.
Ghanea, N. (2004), 'Human Rights of Religious Minorities and of Women in the Middle East', *Human Rights Quarterly*, 26(3): 705–29.
Gillespie, P. (2007), 'Current Issues in Indonesian Islam: Analysis of Indonesian Ulama Fatwa No. 7 Opposing Pluralism, Liberalism and Secularism', *Journal of Islamic Studies*, 18(3) (forthcoming).
Hosen, N. (2003), 'Fatwas and Politics in Indonesia', pp. 168–80 in A. Salim and A. Azra (eds), *Sharia and Politics in Modern Indonesia*, Singapore: Institute of Southeast Asian Studies.
Hosen, N. (2004), 'Behind the Scenes: Fatwas of Majelis Ulama Indonesia (1975–1998)', *Journal of Islamic Studies*, 15(2): 147–79.
Hosen, N. (2006), 'Substantive Equality and Legal Pluralism in Indonesia: A Case Study of Joint Ministerial Decrees on the Construction of Worship Places', paper presented to the Commission on Folk Law and Legal Pluralism International Conference, Depok, 29 June – 2 July.
Ichwan, M.N. (2005), 'Ulama, State and Politics: Majelis Ulama Indonesia after Suharto', *Islamic Law and Society*, 12(1): 45–72.
Indrayana, D. (2005), 'Kompleksitas Peraturan Daerah Bernuansa Syariat: Perspektif Hukum Tata Negara' [The Complexity of Sharia-derived Bylaws:

A Constitutitonal Perspective], paper presented to the Seminar Kebijakan Publik dan Partisipasi Masyarakat di Era Otonomi Daerah: Studi Kasus Perda-perda Berdimensi Agama [Seminar on Public Policy and People's Participation in the Era of Regional Autonomy: A Case Study of Bylaws with Religious Dimensions], Banjarmasin, 1 October.

Lev, D. (1972), *The Islamic Court: A Study in the Political Bases of Legal Institutions*, Los Angeles CA: University of California Press.

McVey, R. (1983), 'Faith as an Outsider', pp. 199–225 in J.P. Piscatori (ed.), *Islam in the Political Process*, Cambridge: Cambridge University Press.

Mudzhar, A. (1993), *Fatwa-fatwa Majelis Ulama Indonesia: Sebuah Studi tentang Pemikiran Hukum Islam di Indonesia, 1975–1988* [The Fatwas of the Indonesian Council of Ulama: A Study of Islamic Legal Thought in Indonesia, 1975–1998], Jakarta: INIS.

Mufrodi, A. (1994), 'Peranan Ulama dalam Masa Orde Baru: Studi tentang Perkembangan Majelis Ulama Indonesia' [The Role of the Ulama in the New Order Era: A Study of the Development of the Indonesian Council of Ulama], PhD thesis, Jakarta: IAIN Syarif Hidayatullah Jakarta.

Nurwahid, H. (2006), 'Yang Tidak Suka Syariat Berlindung di Balik Pancasila' [Those Who Dislike Sharia Seek Protection behind Pancasila], *Tempo*, 19–25 June.

Philip, T. (1995), 'Copts and Other Minorities in the Development of the Egyptian Nation-State', pp. 131–50 in S. Shamir (ed.), *Egypt from Monarchy to Republic: A Reassessment of Revolution and Change*, Boulder CO: Westview Press.

Salim, A. (2006), 'Islamizing Indonesian Laws? Legal and Political Dissonance in Indonesian Sharia 1945–2005', PhD thesis, Melbourne: University of Melbourne.

Salim, A. and A. Azra (2003), 'Introduction: The State and Sharia in the Perspective of Indonesian Legal Politics', pp. 1–25 in A. Salim and A. Azra (eds), *Sharia and Politics in Modern Indonesia*, Singapore: Institute of Southeast Asian Studies.

Suaedy, A. (2006a), 'Perda Syariat Islam Tidak Menyelesaikan Masalah Sosial' [Sharia Bylaws Do Not Alleviate Social Problems], available at <http://www.wahidinstitute.org/indonesia/content/blogcategory/1/54/>, accessed 8 August 2006.

Suaedy, A. (2006b), 'MUI Mestinya Diswastanisasi' [MUI Must Be Privatised], *Indopos*, 17 June.

Suryakusuma, J. and T. Lindsey (2006), 'Indonesia's Powderkeg', *The Age*, 31 August, available at <http://www.theage.com.au/news/opinion/indonesias-powderkeg/2006/08/30/1156816965281.html>, accessed 19 January 2007.

van Bruinessen, M. (1995), 'State–Islam Relations in Contemporary Indonesia 1945–1990', pp. 96–114 in C. Van Dijk and A.H. de Groot (eds), *State and Islam*, Leiden: CNWS.

Wertheim, W.F. (1986), 'Indonesian Moslems under Sukarno and Suharto: Majority with Minority Mentality', pp. 15–36 in *Studies on Indonesian Islam*, Occasional Paper No. 19, Townsville: Centre for Southeast Asian Studies, James Cook University.

Yudohusodo, S. (2006), 'Negara dan Keragaman Budaya' [The State and Cultural Diversity], *Kompas*, 29 March.

8   CHILDREN, WELFARE AND PROTECTION: A NEW POLICY FRAMEWORK?

Sharon Bessell

INTRODUCTION

Over the past decade, Indonesia has faced a series of shocks—economic, social, political and humanitarian—that have adversely affected child welfare. The economic and social shocks resulting from the financial crisis of 1997–98 had deep effects that continue to be felt. The 2004 Aceh tsunami and the 2006 earthquake in Yogyakarta resulted in humanitarian crises in which children were especially vulnerable. Meanwhile, ongoing problems such as high infant mortality, low retention rates from primary to junior secondary school, and the issue of protection of children without parental or familial support have continued to challenge policy makers.

The transition to democracy, rarely considered for its impact on children, has also had a marked effect on child welfare and child protection. Greater commitment to human rights on the part of the national government, at least rhetorically, has seen the introduction of a range of new policies that have been influenced by international concepts of human rights. In line with this new direction, there has been a rethinking of approaches to child welfare and child protection, with the relevant policies giving serious consideration to children's human rights for the first time. There are, of course, strong contradictory trends in policy in Indonesia, particularly given the interplay (and occasional clash) of democratisation and decentralisation forces. While the national government has enacted several laws that align the policy agenda for children more closely with human rights principles, particularly those set down in the United Nations Convention on the Rights of the Child, policy and legislation at the local level is more conservative, and at times even hostile to the concept of rights-based policy for children.

While recognising the significance of local policy discourse for children's welfare and protection, I do not deal with these issues in this chapter. Rather, I aim to provide an assessment of the policy framework for children at the national level. Decentralisation has reshaped the social policy landscape in Indonesia and empowered local policy makers to an extent unimaginable a decade ago. Nevertheless, the national framework remains critical in providing an overarching framework for child welfare and protection.

THE POLICY FRAMEWORK FOR CHILD WELFARE

Law No. 4/1979 on Child Welfare

While education and child health were consistent features of the New Order's social policy agenda, the regime's child welfare policy was weak. Little attention was given to children's issues beyond a narrow focus on extending basic schooling and lowering the country's disturbingly high infant mortality rates. Child protection in particular received almost no attention from policy makers. Policy on juvenile justice, children in institutions or without family support, child abuse and child labour was either nonexistent or wholly inadequate. In 1979, designated the International Year of the Child by the United Nations, Indonesia passed its first piece of legislation designed specifically to promote the welfare of children. Law No. 4/1979 on Child Welfare applied to all persons under the age of 21 who had not been married. It was primarily concerned with 'the satisfaction of the child's basic needs' (article 1.1b).

Adopted almost three decades ago and still in force, the child welfare law is a product of the time in which it was drafted. As Iwaniec and Hill (2000: 250) point out, the 1990s represented a watershed for social policy on children around the world. There was a sharp departure from welfarist approaches focusing on neglect, destitution and anti-social behaviour among children — as in the child welfare law — to rhetorical concern about child protection and taking account of children's views. Before the 1990s, ideas about the human rights of children and their role as social actors rather than citizens in the making had little traction. Thus it is not surprising that these concepts are nowhere to be found in the child welfare law. The law does refer to the rights of the child, but those rights are carefully circumscribed and are limited to the provision of basic care and services necessary for child development. In line with New Order constructions of childhood (Bessell 1998), the emphasis is on the development of future citizens. This is articulated in the opening paragraph of the law, which states:

> Children are the potential successors of the nation's ideals, which were laid down by the former generation;
>
> In order that every child be able to bear the abovementioned responsibility, it is deemed necessary to obtain the best opportunities for them to grow and develop normally: spiritually, physically and socially.

To paraphrase Qvortrup (1994), the child welfare law responds to children as human 'becomings' rather than human beings. Lee (2001: 8) argues that within this construction of childhood, 'children's lives and activities *in the present* are still envisaged, in the main, as a preparation for the future'. Lee goes on to suggest that 'ideas of "socialization" and "development" … carry the sense that childhood is a journey towards a destination'. This approach is apparent in the child welfare law, which emphasises the growth and development of the child as a means to an end. To illustrate, article 2(2) states:

> The child shall be entitled to services for the development of his capabilities and social life, pursuant to the nation's culture and personality, for his development into a good and useful citizen.

In keeping with its interpretation of childhood as a journey to adulthood, the law adopts a deficit model of childhood. Children are presented as being vulnerable, incomplete and largely incompetent. As a consequence, the law does not address the inadequacies of services and policies for children who play an active role in society, the largest group of whom are children who work either within or outside the family. On the issue of child labour or children's work, the law is silent. It also ignores the complex issues surrounding the juvenile justice system and children in conflict with the law. To the extent that these issues are touched on, the emphasis is on the prevention of anti-social behaviour rather than the welfare and human rights of the individual child. Article 6 states:

1   Children experiencing a behavioural problem shall be entitled to services and guidance, with the aim of assisting them to overcome the constraints occurring during their period of growth and development.
2   The service and guidance mentioned in paragraph (1) shall also be granted to children declared guilty by a court of committing a legal offence.

The children identified by the law as being of particular concern are distinguished by their deficiencies. The accompanying explanatory notes state that the special services provided for in the law should focus on destitute children, neglected children, children experiencing behavioural problems, and physically and/or mentally handicapped children.

This has two important implications. First, a narrow welfarist approach displaces any consideration of child protection issues. As a consequence, measures to protect children from abuse, exploitation and discrimination are ignored. Second, little attention is paid to a broader range of policies and services designed to enhance the well-being of all children. For example, issues such as health and education find no place within the law, despite the government's stated prioritisation of them elsewhere. As a consequence, there has been little coordination among the various government sectors with responsibility for issues related to children.

Beyond the shortcomings discussed above, the law has several practical deficiencies. It is rather thin on detail, with much left to elaboration in government or presidential decrees. While mandating the state's responsibility to initiate, guide, aid and supervise child welfare activities, it provides little concrete guidance on the role of the state in supporting children, including the groups of children identified in the law as being in need of special assistance. This lack of precision leaves open the prospect of both inaction and interpretations of the law that could be detrimental to children. The child welfare law is so general in nature that it leaves scope for ad hoc policy making on a number of critical issues relating to the welfare of children. The removal of a child from a situation of parental neglect illustrates the point. Under the law parents bear the primary responsibility for child welfare (article 9). Should a parent fail to fulfil this responsibility, parental rights can be revoked and guardianship of the child transferred to another individual or to an agency. The relationship of this individual to the child is not addressed, nor is the nature of the agency. The law is also vague on the circumstances under which parental rights can be revoked, and fails to set out the process for revocation of parental rights.

Throughout the 1990s, disquiet grew among a range of organisations with an interest in child welfare. There was general consensus that although the child welfare law was the cornerstone of child welfare policy, it provided only a shaky foundation on which to build services and interventions.

Law No. 23/2002 on Child Protection

In 2002 the People's Representative Council (DPR) adopted Law No. 23/2002 on Child Protection. This law complements rather than replaces Law No. 4/1979 on Child Welfare, but is emerging as the key policy document on children's issues. The political environment in which the child protection law was drafted and adopted was very different from that in the late 1970s. In the early 2000s Indonesia was in the midst of a political transformation in which the often conflicting agendas of democratisation and decentralisation were reshaping the social, political and policy landscapes. Whereas concepts of human rights had once been rejected by the New Order regime, they were now squarely on the political agenda—if still contested. As a consequence, the child protection law adopted an approach that would have been unimaginable in 1979 when the child welfare law was promulgated.

Article 2 of the 2002 law states that the protection of children is to be based on three pillars: the national ideology of Indonesia (Pancasila); the constitution; and the United Nations Convention on the Rights of the Child. Pancasila makes no specific reference to children, but the constitution—following its amendment in 2002—does, in Chapter 10A, which outlines the human rights to which Indonesians are entitled. Under article 28B(2), 'each child has the right to a viable life, growth and development, and to protection from violence and discrimination'. Article 31 states that 'each citizen has the right to education', and obliges each citizen to attend primary school, the cost of which shall be borne by the government. Article 34 states that 'poor and abandoned children shall be cared for by the state'.

Democratic transformation has thus resulted in greater attention being placed on social issues and the well-being and rights of citizens. Moreover, unlike the constitution before the 2002 amendments, there is now recognition of children's rights. It is notable that article 31 on education casts primary school children as citizens, rather than *future* citizens. This is a marked departure from earlier representations of children, and can be interpreted as a change—at least rhetorically—in the value placed on children's present roles, value and contribution. The constitutional amendments reflect the fact that both international and non-government organisations concerned with children's issues—many of which emphasise the human rights of children—have had greater influence on the policy debate in Indonesia since 1998.

The language of rights adopted in the Constitution—particularly in articles 28B(2) and 31—is reinforced by the third pillar of the child protection law, the Convention on the Rights of the Child. Indonesia ratified the convention in 1990 but did not translate it into domestic law until 2002, when it was enshrined in the explicitly rights-based child protection law.

Notably, the child protection law moves away from the notion that children's value and entitlements to state support arise from their future status. Article 3 of the law exemplifies this shift:

> Child protection is intended to guarantee the fulfillment of children's rights to live, grow, develop and participate optimally in accordance with the status and dignity of human beings, and to be protected from violence and discrimination, so as to actualise Indonesian children of quality, high moral character, and in a state of well-being.

Article 5 states:

> Every child shall be entitled to possess a name to show his individual identity and status as a citizen.

What is striking in these articles when compared with the child welfare law is the representation of children as human beings rather than human 'becomings', and as citizens rather than citizens in the making. In this respect the child protection law reflects the constitution's portrayal of children as citizens — at least when it comes to the right to an education, as discussed above.

The child protection law addresses a number of issues omitted from the child welfare law. Notably, the processes by which a child may be placed in the care of an individual or agency other than his or her parent are set out with considerably greater precision (articles 33–41). Guidelines for the fostering and adoption of children are set out in articles 37–41, and have proven to be the most controversial of the law's provisions. After intense debate about the relationship between adoption and religion, parliament agreed that adoptive parents must be of the same religion as the child to be adopted (article 39(3)). If the religion of a child is unknown, his or her religion will 'be taken to be the same as that of the majority of inhabitants in the area in question' (article 39(5)).

While media attention and political debate has tended to focus on the relationship between adoption and religion, there are other issues worthy of attention. In particular, the law introduces the concept of the best interests of the child as a guiding principle in adoption cases. Although well established in policy on children in many countries, particularly in matters of adoption and custody, this principle is regularly criticised as being indeterminate, vague and open-ended (Parker 1994: 26). The question of who decides what is in a child's best interests, and based on what criteria, is often the subject of scrutiny and criticism (Bessell and Moore 2006). Parker (1994: 26) has noted that the principle of best interests can 'legitimate practices in some cultures which are regarded in other cultures as positively harmful to children'. Indeed, this is pertinent to the child protection law, which states that adoption must be carried out in the best interests of the child and 'be based upon local custom' (article 39(1)). The law does not establish a hierarchy between these two principles, which can collide. Nor does it determine the appropriate authority to arbitrate such disputes, although there is an implicit suggestion that they would be resolved through the courts.

In recognising the limitations and problems inherent in the best interests principle, Eekelaar (1994: 58) nevertheless finds grounds for optimism. He argues that the best interests principle is a 'mode for enhancing' children's well-being and rights if coupled with a respect for children's views and an acceptance of their right to self-determination. Notably, the right of children to express their views on matters affecting them, in line with their evolving capacities, is a guiding principle of the Convention on the Rights of the Child (article 12). The principle is also enshrined in articles 3 and 10 of the child protection law. Article 3 gives children the right to 'participate optimally in society'. Article 10 states:

> All children shall be entitled to speak and have their opinions listened to, and to receive, seek and impart information in accordance with their intellect and age for the sake of their personal development, in accordance with the norms of morality and propriety.

Clearly, the child protection law does not give children the unfettered right to say and do what they please. Rather, in line with the Convention on the Rights of the Child, it seeks to ensure that children's views are taken into account in decision-making processes, at both the societal and individual levels. This is to be done within a broader context of social and cultural norms. The law can be interpreted as seeking to ensure that democratic values of expression and representation are extended to all citizens regardless of age.

The foregoing discussion on adoption and the best interests principle shows that debate on the child protection law is likely to continue for some time to come. It also serves to demonstrate the greater complexity of the child protection law than the child welfare law. One significant consequence of that greater complexity has been to trigger public and policy debate and deeper thinking among policy makers and commentators on critical child welfare issues.

The child protection law rectifies many of the shortcomings and omissions of the child welfare law. For example, it entitles children who are in contact with the law to legal representation and support (article 64). Children are to be protected from violence, exploitation, abuse, neglect and injustice (article 13) in all areas of life, including within the home (article 13) and in school (article 54). Children are entitled to education (article 9), health care (article 8) and social security (also article 8), without discrimination. While the meaning of social security is not defined in the law, the 2004 social security law (discussed later in this chapter) can be seen as providing a partial explanation of children's entitlements. In line with the Convention on the Rights of the Child, the child protection law goes beyond the provision of social services, support and protection to what are often referred to as participatory rights. As noted above, children's rights to freedom of expression and conscience are to be exercised in accordance with 'intellect and age' (article 10). The precise meaning of intellect is not defined in the law, leaving a great deal to interpretation, but when taken together with the reference to age it can be understood as being similar to the concept of evolving capacities that underlies the Convention on the Rights of the Child.

The child protection law extends and strengthens considerably the foundation for child welfare, child protection and the promotion of children's human rights in Indonesia. In a marked shift reflecting the new political environment in which it was drafted and adopted, the law makes an explicit link between child welfare and the promotion of children's human rights. In some ways, the law raises more questions than it resolves; this is particularly evident with regard to adoption. Nor does it fully address the gamut of child protection issues; the issue of child labour and children's work, for example, is addressed only tangentially (Bessell 2006). Like other national laws in the context of decentralisation, the extent to which the child protection law will be implemented at the local level is — to put it mildly — questionable. While the national government sets the broad parameters for policy related to children, responsibility for implementation and the provision of services lies with local authorities. Adherence to the national child protection law is bound to vary markedly from one jurisdiction to another, depending on familiarity with and commitment to the law, and the availability of resources. Nevertheless, the law is an important development in policy discourse on child welfare in Indonesia.

Implementation of the Child Protection Law

Significantly, Law No. 23/2002 on Child Protection identifies legal sanctions for violations of its conditions. It also establishes a commission for the protection of children — an independent body charged with responsibility for improving the effectiveness of child protection. The commission's duties are identified as being:

1   to conduct socialisation of all laws and regulations involved in the field of child protection, collect data and information, receive community complaints, and conduct studies, monitoring, evaluation and supervision in respect of the protection of children's rights; and
2   to submit reports, advice, input and considerations to the president in respect of the protection of the rights of children.

The commission may raise issues and influence policy but has little hard power. The structure, procedures and — significantly — financing of the commission is to be established by presidential decree, raising the possibility that its independence may be compromised. Nevertheless, the establishment of the commission within the law is a significant step forward in putting children's issues on the public and political agendas.

At the national level, responsibility for the implementation of the child protection law ranges across a number of government agencies, and no single ministry is singled out within the law. Responsibility for specific sectoral issues — for example, health and education — will fall within the purview of the relevant line ministries. The Ministry of Social Affairs has responsibility for large parts of the law relating to child protection issues. Within the ministry, the Directorate for Social Services and Rehabilitation has primary responsibility for matters relating to children.

Responsibility for children's issues is not new to the Ministry of Social Affairs. During the New Order period, it had primary responsibility for guiding and supervising child welfare in accordance with the child welfare law. Often seen as ineffectual and dominated by political interests, the ministry was often criticised as failing to provide adequate services or support for children. In a dramatic measure, the Abdurrahman administration abolished the ministry in 1999, only to re-establish it a year later before it had been fully decommissioned. During that brief period of uncertainty, issues relating to child welfare were in something of a twilight zone. However, there are indications that, in its most recent incarnation, the ministry is taking child protection and children's human rights seriously. In early 2006, Dr Makmur Sunusi was appointed director-general of the Directorate for Social Services and Rehabilitation. Formerly the ministry's director for child welfare, Sunusi has a record of being proactive on issues of child protection and in the promotion of children's human rights. His appointment seems likely to elevate the priority accorded to child welfare and protection issues within the ministry.

The child protection law represents a clear shift in policy for children. But what are the practical implications? Before discussing two additional elements of the child welfare framework — universal basic education and social security — I will examine the implications of the new policy approach that the child protection law represents for a critically important child welfare issue: children without parental care.

Stepping Back from Institutionalisation: Children without Parental Care

An area currently being addressed by the Directorate for Social Services and Rehabilitation is the well-being and protection of children without parental care. The vulnerability of such children was highlighted dramatically in the aftermath of the 2004 tsunami, when there were reports that children who had been orphaned or separated from their parents were being abducted or abused. The reports received international media coverage and resulted in the government acting to prevent children being removed from the province of Aceh.[1] The veracity of the claims remains unclear, with the Ministry of Social Affairs and some NGOs suggesting that the number of children involved had been exaggerated.[2] The tragedy of Aceh did, however, place on the Indonesian policy agenda a broader issue that had long been neglected: the well-being, protection and human rights of children who are without parental care.

Historically, the government's response to children who have been orphaned, abandoned or removed from their homes due to abuse or neglect has been institutionalisation in children's foster homes (*panti sosial asuhan anak*) overseen by the Ministry of Social Affairs. In some cases the homes also house 'naughty children' (*anak nakal*) whose behaviour is considered too anti-social for them to remain with their parents; in some cases these children have been accused, or convicted, of committing (sometimes serious) crimes. The ministry provides funding, either directly or through provincial governments, to over 3,450 children's foster homes, which care for more than 127,000 children. The day-to-day operation of the homes, however, is carried out by non-government, community or religious organisations.

While responsibility for supervising the homes falls to the ministry, in practice little oversight has occurred. Many homes do not have licences and so are beyond the reach of ministry regulation. Decentralisation has made it even more difficult for the ministry to keep track of and regulate children's foster homes. In practice, the precise number of children's homes and children in homes is unknown, as is the quality of care provided.

Both officials from the Ministry of Social Affairs and representatives of NGOs believe that the number of children living in institutional arrangements has increased in recent years.[3] Ministry officials suggest that this may in part be due to a blurring of the lines between Islamic boarding schools (*pesantren*) and children's foster homes. *Pesantren* have long enjoyed widespread community support, and many parents send their children to such institutions to receive an education. Children's foster homes, in contrast, were once looked down on as places for the destitute and the neglected. In recent years, however, families who are unable to afford to pay for their children's schooling are more likely to send them to a children's home to ensure access to education. Because the homes' levels of funding are calculated according to the number of children in them, some have actively begun recruiting children from poor families,

---

1 See, for example, *Jakarta Post*, 2 January 2005, 3 January 2005, 4 January 2005.
2 Interviews conducted by the author, September 2006, Jakarta.
3 Interviews conducted by the author, September 2006, Jakarta.

largely on the promise of an education. Whether relationships between children and their families are maintained is a matter of speculation rather than evidence.

With increased attention now being focused on children's foster homes, three issues seem set to emerge as major concerns for child welfare and protection. First, the appropriateness of institutionalising children is being questioned, particularly at senior levels of the Ministry of Social Affairs; community-based care is emerging as the preferred model of caring for children without parental support. Second, the lack of regulation of many children's homes is a major problem, placing some of the nation's most vulnerable citizens beyond the reach of any form of state protection. Third, indications that parents are turning to children's homes when they are unable to afford to support their children or provide them with an education are a serious concern. Significantly, in the current policy environment, each of these issues is being couched in terms of human rights.

The Universal Basic Education Policy

The child welfare law and the child protection law represent two critical elements of Indonesia's child welfare framework. A third element is universal basic education. The provision of basic education to all children was first identified as a policy priority in Indonesia in the early 1970s. The New Order's first five-year development plan, Repelita I (1969–74), set the goals of expanding the education system, increasing the rates of primary school enrolment and increasing the rates of transition from primary to junior secondary school. In 1973 a large-scale infrastructure program designed to accommodate the targeted influx of pupils was established under a presidential instruction (Inpres). Enrolment rates increased steadily throughout the 1970s and into the early 1980s. In 1984 a policy of universal education (*wajib belajar*) was introduced under which all children would be required to complete six years of basic education. In 1994 the period of basic education was extended from six to nine years, with the policy to be implemented fully within 15 years, that is, by 2008.

The focus on basic education was driven largely by the need to enhance human resources rather than concern for child welfare. Jones (1994: 164) points out that Indonesia's universal education policies are 'entirely in accordance with the policy implications of rates of return studies, both in other countries and those few conducted in Indonesia'. According to these studies, investment in primary school education results in the highest returns to national development and investment in higher education the lowest. While questioning the value of rates of return studies, Jones (1994: 167) acknowledges their influence over Indonesian education policy.

One consequence of the emphasis on human resource development rather than child welfare has been the neglect of issues that have a significant impact on children's experience of school and, in some cases, contribute to them exiting the system. As a result, the experience of children at school has at best been a marginal concern in education policy and practice. A 2005 study of the attitudes and experiences of 813 Indonesian schoolchildren found that violent forms of punishment were a common feature of many children's school experience (Beazley et al. 2006). While the issue of violence in schools has received little attention in the past, it is notable that the child protection law (article 54) states that:

> Children attending school must be protected against violence from teachers, school managers and other schoolchildren both in the school in question and in other educational institutions.

Based on the experience of other countries in changing behaviour and attitudes towards corporal punishment, the actual abolition of violence in schools is likely to be some time coming. Nevertheless, the child protection law does set out a new policy approach to a serious child welfare issue that has been long ignored.

The child protection law states that every child is entitled to an education, including children living with a disability (article 51). Under the law, the government is required to provide a minimum of nine years of basic education for all children, without discrimination (article 49). Amendments to the Constitution in 2002 require the state to bear the costs of education, stating that both national and regional budgets should give priority to education. In practice, achieving the objective of nine years of basic education will require proactive strategies to target those children most at risk of dropping out of school prematurely, as well as the comparatively small percentage who never enrol, often due to disability or extreme disadvantage. Under the child protection law, the state, the government, the family and the parents are each identified as having a responsibility to provide 'the widest possible opportunities for a child to obtain an education' (article 49).

While the child protection law addresses education in a far more comprehensive manner than the child welfare law, Law No. 20/2003 on the National Education System is now the primary embodiment of education policy. While human resource development remains an important rationale for efforts to extend universal education to nine years, the well-being of individual children is given greater attention within the policy framework, including within the education law. The subtle but significant difference in language and intent is signalled in article 1, and continues throughout the document:

Education means a conscious and well-planned effort to create a learning environment and learning process in which learners will be able to develop their potential to acquire the spiritual and religious strength, self-control, personality, intelligence, morals, noble character and skills they need for themselves, for the community, for the nation and for the state.

While the education law fails to address issues of school violence and child protection, in conjunction with the child protection law it represents an important policy shift.

Implementation of the Universal Basic Education Policy

Indonesia achieved its target of universal primary education in 1988. Enrolments in junior secondary school have increased slowly, but efforts to extend universal education to nine years have not been successful. Using data from the National Socio-economic Survey (Susenas), Suryadarma, Suryahadi and Sumarto (2006: 1) calculated the net enrolment rate in junior secondary schools in 2004 to be 65 per cent — considerably short of the universal target and only 10 percentage points higher than in the mid-1990s. The authors conclude that the transition from primary to junior secondary school is the critical point for retention, with specific groups of children particularly at risk of dropping out at this point. The second Indonesian Family Life Survey found that cost was by far the main reason for children not continuing on to junior secondary school; 71 per cent of parents cited cost as the major factor in this decision (Suryadarma, Suryahadi and Sumarto 2006: 21). Susenas data show that among the poorest 20 per cent of households, the cost of education per student accounts for 10 per cent of total household expenditure at the primary school level, rising to 18.5 per cent at the junior secondary level and 28.4 per cent at the senior secondary level (Bappenas 2005). Suryadarma, Suryahadi and Sumarto (2006) shed light on the other factors that come into play in determining a child's chances of continuing on to junior secondary school. They are:

1 a child's ability, as measured by performance in the primary school national final examination;
2 gender, with girls less likely to continue;
3 religion, with children from Muslim families having a slightly lower probability of continuing;
4 proximity to and availability of a school, indicating that infrastructure is an important issue;
5 community variables, with greater opportunities for employment in a community impacting negatively on the likelihood of a child continuing on to junior secondary school.

The authors' findings have important implications for the implementation of Indonesia's universal education policy. As they conclude:

> the government should start refocusing its spending and scholarship programs to target those who go missing from the education system after finishing primary school (Suryadarma, Suryahadi and Sumarto 2006: 29).

At present, the major scheme to assist students from poor families to stay in school is the School Operation Assistance (BOS) program, introduced at the beginning of the 2005/06 school year. It is financed through funds that have become available as a result of the large reduction in oil subsidies in 2005, and is intended to compensate the poor for the increases in fuel prices flowing from this policy adjustment. One of the objectives of the BOS program is to reduce the expense of schooling at the primary and junior secondary levels. It differs from its predecessor, the Special Assistance for Students (BKM) program, in providing funds to schools rather than directly to poor households. An appraisal of the program undertaken by the SMERU Research Institute in February–March 2006 found that BOS funds tended to be used to subsidise schools' operational costs, including teachers' salaries, teaching activities and the purchase of stationery and textbooks (SMERU 2006: 7–8). Only 22.6 per cent of students from poor households received special assistance, usually in small amounts (SMERU 2006: 9).

Notably, however, 22 of the 43 schools surveyed had eliminated school fees, thus making education more affordable for all children. The SMERU study concluded that although the BOS program had the potential to increase access to schooling among children from poor families, this objective had yet to be 'explicitly formulated in the objectives of the program, nor is it emphasized in the socialization activities' (SMERU 2006: 12). Nevertheless, it did provide the basis for a concerted effort to keep children in school, by removing tuition fees for all students and targeting assistance to those known to be most at risk of dropping out. Such a combination of universal access without the barrier of fees and carefully targeted support for at-risk groups could be expected to contribute significantly to increased retention rates.

One area where the BOS program has yet to achieve current educational objectives is in encouraging wider community involvement in decision making. Article 25 of the education law established school committees consisting of teachers, parents and community representatives to ensure that decisions on planning, implementation, monitoring and evaluation of school programs were taken jointly by the school and the community. The goal was to institutionalise more democratic decision-making processes in schools and enhance community commitment to education. The SMERU appraisal found, however, that principals continued to make all decisions about the allocation of BOS funds in the majority of schools surveyed. Thus, closing the gap between reality and the more democratic ideal remains a challenge.

It is clear that the objective of nine years of formal schooling for all children will not be achieved by 2008. Nevertheless, the expansion of universal education remains a policy priority. Scholarship programs and efforts to enhance community involvement in, and commitment to, education are examples of the ongoing policy focus on education. However, the low quality of education and issues around punishment and violence in schools have yet to be adequately addressed. To date the important linkages between these issues and low retention rates have not been recognised. Greater coordination between those sections of government responsible for education and those responsible for the implementation of both the 2002 child protection law and Indonesia's commitments under the Convention on the Rights of the Child could result in greater recognition of the multiple factors contributing to low retention rates. This would create the conditions for more coordinated and holistic policy approaches to achieving universal education – and potentially better outcomes.

Law No. 40/2004 on the National Social Security System

The child welfare law, the child protection law and the universal basic education policy constitute critical elements of the policy framework for children in Indonesia. A fourth policy that is potentially important in shaping child welfare is Law No. 40/2004 on the National Social Security System. As noted earlier, this law can be seen as providing some context for the vague reference to social security in article 8 of the child protection law.

The social security law came into effect in October 2004, and aims to extend social security coverage progressively to all Indonesian citizens over the next decade. Influenced by the approach advocated by the International Labour Organization, this law represents social security as a right. It provides for the development of five social security schemes: health insurance; work injury insurance; self-funded retirement savings (whereby accumulated contributions are eventually repaid); old age, disability, widow/widower and child pensions; and death benefits. Under the child pension scheme, children will receive 40–60 per cent of the minimum wage upon the death of one or both parents. Under section 41 of the law, this pension will continue until the child marries, commences full-time employment or reaches the age of 23 years, whichever comes first. Thus, the scheme guarantees some financial support for children who are orphaned. The disability and work injury insurance schemes will provide families facing an internal crisis with some small degree of financial security.

The social security system is built on the principle of mutual assistance (*gotong royong*) — in this instance essentially a euphemism for cross-subsidisation from wealthier and low-risk sections of the population to economically disadvantaged and high-risk groups (Arifianto 2004: 9). Under the law, employers must enrol their employees in the scheme, while the government is required to provide social assistance to the indigent and those unable to support themselves, the vast majority of whom do not have formal sector employment.

The health insurance component of these arrangements represents a marked change in the government's commitment to publicly funded health care. Government spending on health care has been relatively low, at around 0.6 per cent of GDP between 1996 and 2000 (Arifianto 2004: 21; Stalker 2000). This is lower than in neighbouring countries, and lower than the average of 2.2 per cent for all developing counties (Stalker 2000). While the contribution rates to be paid by formal sector workers and employers have yet to be decided, it has been suggested that they will be significant (see Arifianto 2006). Arifianto (2004: 21) argues that 'it is questionable as to whether Indonesian workers who work in the formal sector could fully subsidize health insurance for informal sector workers [who comprise] two-thirds of Indonesian workers'.

The social security law represents an ambitious overhaul of social policy. The financing and sustainability of the system present major challenges, not least because of the large proportion of the population engaged in the informal sector. Recognising the challenges, the government plans to introduce the new system in phases. The elucidation of the law states:

> Although membership is mandatory for all citizens, implementation will take place in accordance with the economic capacity of the people and the government as well as the feasibility of the program. The first stage will start with workers in the formal sector, in parallel with voluntary membership of informal sector workers, including farmers, fishermen and the self-employed.

Prospects for Implementation of the Social Security Law

Of the many obstacles to success of the new system, three are particularly pressing. First, the cross-subsidy from the roughly one-third of workers who work in the formal sector to the two-thirds who work in the informal sector raises crucial — and largely unanswered — questions about the financing and sustainability of the new system. It is pertinent to note here that around 40 per cent of the current members of the existing social security scheme for formal sector workers (Jamsostek) do not pay regular contributions (Angelini and Hirose 2004: 27). The likelihood of the new system being able to overcome these problems seems remote. Second, it seems probable that individuals on low or insecure incomes will be unable to afford to contribute to the scheme, especially given the proposed high levels of health scheme contributions. Compulsory contributions may place an impossible burden on some families, forcing them to make difficult decisions about spending and consumption. Thus, while the system may bring longer-term benefits, its short and medium-term effects may be deleterious, especially in the areas of education (a large cost burden on poor families) and preventative health care. Third, there is an urgent need to resolve uncertainties around management, transparency and corruption. Serious failings in the corporate governance of Jamsostek have not been resolved, raising concerns about whether the new scheme will be properly managed. Its administration will be an enormously complex task, and the current capacity of the bureaucracy to respond is at best questionable.

CHILD WELFARE AND PROTECTION IN THE 21ST CENTURY: A SHIFT TO CHILDREN'S RIGHTS?

The policy framework for children in Indonesia is unrecognisable from that which existed 10 years ago. There has been a move away from a welfarist approach whereby children were viewed as passive recipients of services and future citizens, to an explicitly rights-based approach in the form of the child protection law. Following international trends (see Hallett and Prout 2003), the law — despite some shortcomings — places children at the centre of child welfare and protection measures, and requires consideration of children's views in decision making. This has provided an opportunity to rethink social policy for children in a way that genuinely meets their interests. The aim of child welfare policy has been reformulated — at least in the rhetoric of the child protection law — as a question of how the state can realise its duty to children, rather than how children can be utilised in the quest for development.

That social policy for children has been radically reformed is unquestionable. There has been a clear shift towards children's rights. In practice, however, the vexed question of how to implement the promises of the new framework remains. Programs such as the BOS scheme show the government's commitment to achieving universal basic education, but the goal of extending this to nine years remains a major challenge. To achieve its stated targets for education, the government will need to combine universally accessible services with carefully targeted programs to reach the children most at risk. Similarly, carefully targeted and conditional payments to poor families may be a necessary incentive to discourage them from sending their children to foster homes. Providing avenues through which children can express their views on the issues that affect them will require major changes to the way decisions on child welfare and child protection are made—at both the individual and general levels—and in the way services are provided.

The 2004 social security law is likely to have only a limited impact on children. In a best case scenario, the obstacles identified above would all be overcome and the new system would provide greater security for all Indonesian citizens, including in situations of personal crisis (such as the work-related injury or death of an income provider). In a less positive, but perhaps more realistic, scenario, the costs visited on individuals in the form of compulsory contributions would have an adverse effect on children's well-being and protection. Thus, the social security law introduces several unknowns into Indonesia's child welfare mix.

Nevertheless, as a result of democratisation and greater consideration of human rights, a stronger policy framework for child protection and welfare is now in place. Despite the considerable challenges in implementing this new framework, there is an opportunity to develop services and interventions that are genuinely in the best interests of the child.

REFERENCES

Angelini, J. and K. Hirose (2004), *Extension of Social Security Coverage for the Informal Economy in Indonesia: Surveys in the Urban and Rural Informal Economy*, Manila: International Labour Organization Subregional Office for South-east Asia and the Pacific.

Arifianto, A. (2004), 'Social Security Reform in Indonesia: An Analysis of the National Social Security Bill (RUU Jamsosnas)', Jakarta: SMERU Research Institute.

Arifianto, A. (2006), 'The New Indonesian Social Security Law: A Curse or a Blessing for Indonesians?', *ASEAN Economic Bulletin*, 23(1): 57–74.

Bappenas (Badan Perencanaan Pembangunan Nasional) (2005), 'Strategi Nasional Penanggulangan Kemiskinan' [National Poverty Eradication Strategy], Jakarta: Bappenas Poverty Reduction Committee.

Beazley, H., S. Bessell, J. Ennew and R. Waterson (2006), *What Children Say: Results of Comparative Research on the Physical and Emotional Punishment of Children in Southeast Asia and the Pacific, 2005*, Bangkok: Save the Children Sweden.

Bessell, S. (1998), 'The Politics of Children's Work in Indonesia: Child Labour in Domestic and Global Contexts', PhD dissertation, Melbourne: Monash University.

Bessell, S. (2006), 'Children, Work and Citizenship: A Framework for Policy Development and Analysis', paper presented to the Asia Pacific Childhoods Conference, Singapore: National University of Singapore, 17–20 July.

Bessell, S. and T. Moore (2006), 'Children, Human Rights and Participation: Bridging the Gap between Assumptions and Research', paper presented to the GovNet Conference, Canberra: Australian National University.

Eekelaar, J. (1994), 'The Interests of the Child and the Child's Wishes: The Role of Dynamic Self-determinism', pp. 42–61 in P. Alston (ed.), *The Best Interests of the Child: Reconciling Culture and Human Rights*, Oxford: Oxford University Press.

Hallett, C. and A. Prout (eds) (2003), *Hearing the Voices of Children: Social Policy for a New Century*, London: Routledge.

Iwaniec, D. and M. Hill (2000), 'Law, Policy, Practice and Research in Child and Family Social Work', pp. 249–64 in D. Iwaniec and M. Hill (eds), *Child Welfare Policy and Practice: Issues and Lessons Emerging from Current Research*, London: Jessica Kingsley Publishers.

Jones, G. (1994), 'Labour Force and Education', pp. 145–78 in H. Hill (ed.), *Indonesia's New Order: The Dynamics of Socio-economic Transformation*, Sydney: Allen & Unwin.

Lee, N. (2001), *Childhood and Society: Growing Up in an Age of Uncertainty*, Buckingham: Open University Press.

Parker, S. (1994), 'The Best Interests of the Child: Principles and Problems', pp. 26–41 in P. Alston (ed.), *The Best Interests of the Child: Reconciling Culture and Human Rights*, Oxford: Oxford University Press.

Poerwanto, S., M. Stevenson and N. de Klerk (2003) 'Infant Mortality and Family Welfare: Policy Implications for Indonesia', *Journal of Epidemial Community Health*, 57: 493–8.

Qvortrup, J. (1994), 'Introduction', pp. 1–23 in M. Bardy, J. Qvortrup, G. Sgritta and H. Wintersberger (eds), *Childhood Matters: Social Theory, Practice and Politics*, Avebury: Aldershot.

SMERU (2006), 'The Implementation of the School Operational Assistance (BOS) Program 2005', *SMERU Newsletter*, No. 19, July–September, SMERU Research Institute, Jakarta, available at <http://www.smeru.or.id/newslet/2006/News19.pdf>.

Stalker, P. (2000), *Beyond Krismon: The Social Legacy of Indonesia's Financial Crisis*, Florence: UNICEF Innocenti Publications.

Suryadarma, D., A. Suryahadi and S. Sumarto (2006), *Causes of Low Secondary School Enrollment in Indonesia*, Jakarta: SMERU Research Institute.

PART III

The Institutions of Government

9   THE CIVIL SERVICE: TOWARDS
EFFICIENCY, EFFECTIVENESS
AND HONESTY

Staffan Synnerstrom

INTRODUCTION

In this chapter I outline what civil service reform needs to address and
what it should achieve, as well as how it should be implemented to
secure progress and sustainable outcomes. The chapter sets out a strategic framework for civil service reform and the objectives to be achieved
under such a framework. It is written from a civil service policy-making
perspective, focusing on technical solutions based on sound international
practices.

I argue that there are two key paths to improved performance:
increased transparency and strengthened accountability. I identify two
prerequisites for a sustainable improvement in civil service performance
and elaborate seven immediate and long-term objectives. All the objectives are important and need to be addressed simultaneously, although
they will take varying lengths of time to be achieved. Finally, I argue
that successful civil service reform requires a gradual approach, targeting selected key institutions in the early stages. This can be expanded to
other targets later as reform gains momentum and good practices can be
replicated.

The political dimensions attached to any reform related to the public
sector workforce are barely touched on in this chapter, although these will
be of utmost importance for decision makers if they decide on a comprehensive program of civil service reform. Clearly political considerations
are not always favourable to achieving technical or rational objectives.

Background

The legacy of the authoritarian New Order regime can be characterised briefly as non-transparent processes, underfunded institutions, an inadequately skilled public workforce, and institutionalised corruption reflecting a self-serving and opaque administration. Today, however, Indonesian public institutions are expected to secure democracy, support a market economy and provide good governance. Experience from other countries shows that such a transformation of public institutions needs time, strong commitment, persistent effort and determined leadership. These requirements were not met in Indonesia during the first six years of post-Soeharto government. It was not until President Susilo Bambang Yudhoyono took office in late 2004 that there were indications of a strong commitment to reforms, albeit with some doubt as to the capacity of the government to see them through (see, for example, Basri and Patunru 2006: 316).

Crucial to progress towards deepened democracy in Indonesia is civil service reform. A broad consensus on the necessity for this has gradually emerged. A large number of civil service reforms are being implemented at all levels of government, mostly with the support of multilateral or bilateral funding institutions. The sustainability of many of those interventions can be questioned, however, as long as a strategic framework for civil service reform is lacking and as long as fundamental features of the civil service system continue to provide distorted performance incentives. In spite of the president's ambitions, there has been very little action from the leaders and institutions that should spearhead reform.

Civil service reform is often presented as simply a matter of reforming human resource management practices. This is important, but it is not enough. Civil service reform must be both broader and deeper than that, while at the same time selective. It must target features of the civil service that preserve old behaviour in defiance of new legislation and the new democratic system of government. It must also target the way public institutions are structured, operate and are financed, in addition to human resource management practices and the distorted incentives facing individual civil servants.

The Indonesian Civil Service

In December 2005 there were 3.6 million civil servants, excluding the military and the police. This is a relatively modest number considering that Indonesia has about 220 million inhabitants. Approximately 2.5 million civil servants, most of them teachers and health care workers, are posted to regional governments. Civil servants belong to one national civil service. Law No. 43/1999 on the Civil Service defines two types of civil service position: 'structural' and 'functional'. A structural position is a management position within a hierarchy of 17 ranks divided into four echelons. A functional position is a non-management position involving a specialised activity, and is occupied by an individual with particular expertise. While functional positions are common in the health and education sectors (doctors, nurses, teachers), core administrative institutions are dominated by structural positions. Structural positions are considered more attractive than functional ones, as they provide better prospects in relation to career advancement, remuneration and other conditions.

Indonesia has what, in a comparative context, would be called a career civil service system, in which civil servants are recruited when they are young on the basis of entry examination results and level of education. Promotion through the ranks is based on seniority and completion of training. Lateral entry into the ranks from outside is not possible. Civil servants are allocated to positions through management decisions, not through competition among applicants. Indonesia's civil service differs from those of many other countries in having a highly militaristic nature. Like soldiers, civil servants are recruited after sitting tests in major national recruitment drives; many of the administration's institutions and processes are referred to by militaristic acronyms rather than by their names or logical abbreviations of their names. This practice represents a legacy of more than three decades of strong military influence.

In addition to the 3.6 million civil servants, an unrecorded number of auxiliary personnel, commonly referred to as 'honorarium staff', are contracted under the general labour law. They occupy a range of positions that the civil service regulations cannot accommodate. The World Bank (1999) estimated several years ago that as many as 1 million individuals may be contracted under this scheme. The number is still uncertain, but may have increased considerably following the advent of regional autonomy in 2001, and the ensuing creation of many new regional governments. Recent programs to hire assistant teachers would have swelled the numbers even more. Honorarium staff are mostly poorly paid — sometimes even below official minimum wage levels — and are excluded from most of the other benefits available to civil servants.

PREREQUISITES FOR A SUSTAINABLE IMPROVEMENT IN PERFORMANCE

Taking Command of the Administration and the Reform Process

In new democracies there is often a disconnect between the new democratic leadership and the administration it inherits, as the latter tends to live its own life guided by the old paradigms — doing business as usual. Indonesia is no exception to this rule. While a new democratic leadership knows what it wants, it may not always have the necessary tools or resources available to achieve it. The democratic leadership needs to take command of the inherited administration and, with the help of democratic forces in society, compel it to change—because it will not change without such pressure. Taking command of the administration also implies the replacement of key officials to break resistance to reform and gain a foothold in an otherwise self-sustaining administration.

Civil service management at the central government level in Indonesia is divided between several institutions. This set-up has so far proven incapable of delivering reforms. A body with the capacity to push for, coordinate and follow up on reforms needs to be established, with the ultimate aim of restructuring the current set-up. This body needs to be close to the president and have his clear backing. A unit in the president's office, tasked with designing, promoting, implementing and monitoring reforms in his name, and enabling him to take command of the reform process, is thus a prerequisite for progress. While responsibility for implementation would lie with the heads of the respective institutions, such a unit would provide the president with the tools and methodologies required to formulate changes and follow up on progress.[1]

Improving Budgeting and Strengthening Accountability

The traditional Indonesian separation of policy making from budgeting, and the practice of splitting the budget into 'development' and 'routine' components, has led to at least three serious shortcomings. First, policy change, performance standard setting, expenditure caps and so on are attempted through administrative regulations without links to the budget. Because the budget is the only meaningful tool for implementing such measures, these attempts mostly fail, or have unpredictable and random outcomes. Second, formula-driven institutional budgets result in underfunding for most institutions and regional governments, and excessive funding for a few, most obviously in the case of local government budgets. Third, the overall size of the budget is out of the control of the Ministry of Finance because institutional budgets are determined by fixed formulae, and because decisions implying budget impositions and financial liabilities are taken administratively and separated from the budget process.

Implementation of Law No. 17/2003 on State Finance is the key to improved budgeting and strengthened accountability. The law consoli-

---

1 Presidential Decree No. 17/2006 established a Presidential Work Unit on Program and Reform Management with a mission and mandate similar to this. At the time of writing the unit had not yet become operational, however.

dates a budget previously split into routine and development parts; introduces an integrated budget and planning process guided by a medium-term expenditure framework (MTEF); and envisages performance-based evaluation of budgetary outcomes. It also stipulates financial reporting in accordance with new, common standards for public sector accounting. In comparable fashion, Law No. 1/2004 on State Treasury strengthens this aspect of government operations. It stipulates provisions for budget management and financial planning, as well as debt and property management; and it envisions a single consolidated treasury account for the whole government administration. Double-entry bookkeeping is already the norm, and accrual accounting is to be introduced in the years to come.

Thus, Indonesia already has in place an adequate basic legal framework for public expenditure management in accordance with sound international practice, promoting transparency and accountability at all levels of the state. But although the general principles of public expenditure management and the concept of an MTEF as the basis for performance-based budgeting are contained in the elucidation of the law on state finance, they are not detailed in its provisions. The current budget process is thus still based on one-year planning rather than the three- to five-year horizon required by the MTEF. Also, the procedure for executive–legislature consultations for MTEF-guided budgeting and planning is not regulated in the law. Thus, although the law on state finance is a major step forward, it still requires further elaboration to make the principles and new mechanisms effective. Full implementation of the new standards and procedures may take several years, due to the magnitude and complexity of the task of reforming the whole public-expenditure management system, and to the lack of capacity at different levels of government to tackle this adequately.

In addition, implementation of the law on state finance has sometimes been obstructed by vested interests that have taken advantage of the general lack of understanding of how crucial the law is for improved governance. For example, in its very last days when it was clearly nothing more than a caretaker government, the Megawati government succeeded in having Law No. 25/2004 on National Planning passed. The intention seems to have been to retain the status quo and protect the existence of the National Development Planning Agency (Bappenas). There are no links between the budgeting and planning processes in the law on national planning, as it basically reflects the old system. The government will eventually have to decide whether the law on state finance should prevail, or if the retrograde law on national planning should be allowed to continue to delay the introduction of a modern planning and budgeting process characterised by increased transparency and strengthened accountability.

KEY OBJECTIVES IN CIVIL SERVICE REFORM

Making Management More Productive

Today three bodies—the State Ministry for Administrative Reform (MenPAN), the National Civil Service Agency (BKN) and the Institute of National Administration (LAN)—share responsibility for public administration and civil service issues. Regional governments are also subject to regulations issued by the Ministry of Home Affairs and the line ministries, as well as to regional regulations, all of which can be related to civil service management issues. This fragmentation partly explains the lack of any meaningful, centrally initiated reform, in spite of the clear need for it. The three civil service agencies have further failed to adapt their operations sufficiently to regional autonomy.

It would probably be more effective to have a single central institution taking responsibility for central civil service functions in a decentralised administration. These functions might include formulating general civil service policies and legislation, monitoring civil service management, providing an appeal function, managing the database of civil servants, accrediting training programs, and providing advisory services to line ministries, government agencies and regional governments. It would be better if the other functions that these institutions now have were made part of the budget process, devolved to the organisations that employ civil servants, or abolished. The central civil service authority would need to work closely with the Ministry of Finance (as paymaster) in any policy development, rather than making administrative decisions without appropriate concern for their budgetary implications, as happens today.

It is extremely important that Indonesia retains a central, competent and adequate civil service management authority, as it needs to have a national civil service to support the concept of the unitary state. Basic processes and quality standards should be uniform throughout the country to minimise the extent to which ethnic, religious, political or other extraneous considerations influence recruitment and promotion. Such tendencies exist locally, and need to be countered strongly.

Improving Organisational Structure and Staff Allocation

Currently, the organisational structures of civil service institutions are required to be compatible with models provided by MenPAN. These models are mainly concerned with symmetry, such that each unit has similar numbers of subunits at each level; they show little concern for the kinds of operations or workloads of particular institutions, and certainly no concern for cost efficiency. Staff resources are not allocated according to operational needs but—as in the army—through a superficial and mechanistic procedure to ensure that each organisational unit has a certain number of structural positions at each level. The resulting establishment plans (*formasi*) must be such that if, for example, a unit is headed by an echelon I official, there need to be at least four echelon II, 16 echelon III and 64 echelon IV officials. Including functional civil servants and auxiliary staff, any unit headed by an echelon I official will end up with over 600 people, regardless of the task, and regardless of the workload of that unit. This mechanistic and inflexible way of allocating staff is wasteful.

Although local governments are free in principle to organise their business as they see fit, in practice they encounter several constraints. One is that their *formasi* must be approved by MenPAN, whose main concern is symmetry rather than efficiency. Another is a decree by the Ministry of Home Affairs defining the number of organisational units that a local government should have. A third, and contradictory, element is the pressure from line ministries for local governments to establish specialised units (*dinas*) to deal with their respective issues. As the portfolios of the line ministries are determined by central political considerations rather than local communities' need for services, such pressures are counterproductive, and obstruct local governments' ambitions to rationalise and improve services through innovative organisational solutions. They are directly wasteful when local governments are pressured to set up *dinas* for functions that are not relevant to their localities (USAID 2006).

Good international practice requires that staff allocations at all levels of government should be based on real needs related to the tasks and workload of the organisation in question. The administrative authority of MenPAN and BKN to approve staff allocations is not compatible with the need to determine staff allocations as part of the budget process. The law on state finance provides that budgets for civil servants' salaries and other costs will be allocated in accordance with need—as guided by budget indicators and performance standards—and not based on formula-driven calculations. With a new budget system in place, staff resources would be allocated more efficiently than in the current system, where staffing and budgeting remain separate exercises.

Professionalisation

The opposite of a career system like Indonesia's is a position-based system, where civil servants are recruited to professionally classified positions in open competition, and where selection is based on specific professional requirements. Lateral entry into the civil service is possible at all levels. Careers (and pay) in position-based systems are based more on the responsibilities and complexity of the job and on the incumbent's professional qualifications and performance than on seniority. Training focuses on technical, functional and managerial skills. Civil service systems based on professional classification promote professionalism, transparency and accountability, and are able to ensure supply of the various skills needed in a modern and complex government administration.

The Indonesian civil service operated with some 2,000 professionally classified jobs up until 1968, when the professional positions were replaced by the current military-style structure of 17 ranks divided into four echelons complemented by functional positions. It is now time to replace the inefficient system established under Soeharto with one based on professional skills and focused on performance. Without professional classification of positions and meaningful job descriptions, it is impossible to define adequate pay, select candidates on merit or measure performance. Failure to professionalise the civil service will mean that young people with professional ambitions and high motivation will remain outside it, so that it will continue to be filled by those who view a civil service career as attractive because it offers job security, a pension guarantee and the possibility of taking part in rent-sharing activities.

Civil service reform is therefore about fundamentally transforming the current military-style civil service, largely lacking professional classification and performance focus, into a body built on professional skills in which performance is monitored and accountability enforced. This does not necessarily mean that Indonesia needs to totally abolish its career system, but it certainly means that it needs to reform it fundamentally. Job evaluation, job classification and grading schemes need to be developed and implemented. Functional reviews or 'staff inspections' to determine optimal organisational structures and staff allocations are required for each institution or regional government. Reform would imply a much stronger focus on functional positions, a considerable reduction in the number of structural positions, and a unification of career advancement possibilities and incentives between the two groups. A similar development can be seen in Germany, where the number of officials (*Beamte*) is steadily declining and the number of employees (*Angestaellte*) is correspondingly increasing.

As a consequence of introducing professionally classified jobs, specific selection criteria would be used to ensure that candidates with the right educational and professional backgrounds were selected. Competition and transparency in the selection process would further guarantee the selection of the best candidates and prevent the buying and selling of positions. A right of appeal should be part of the process.

At present, honorarium staff are applying strong pressure on the government to improve their employment situation by making them civil servants, and they seem to be receiving a positive response to their requests. The employment conditions of most honorarium staff do need to be improved, but this should be done by improving the working conditions related to their current status rather than accepting them into the civil service ranks. The latter would be highly counterproductive, as it would increase the number of unskilled staff holding unclassified positions without proper job descriptions, and add to the already considerable levels of overstaffing at the institutional level. More importantly, it would lead to an increased budgetary burden without any process of budgetary review.

'One size fits all' is not the appropriate approach when it comes to professional qualifications and performance standards for civil servants. Most countries have a number of corps within their civil services: one for accountants and auditors, one for prosecutors, one for academic university staff, one for customs officials, one for school teachers, one for doctors and so on. Indonesia might do well to follow this tradition, replacing its current single corps with several corps, each with its own professional standards for qualifications and performance developed by the relevant professional association in cooperation with the responsible line ministry. The employer, whether a central agency, university or regional government, would be responsible for the recruitment and management of its civil servants within the general policy and legal framework provided by the central civil service authority, and in accordance with the professional qualifications and performance standards developed for the corps.

In a professional civil service, the training system would have to be fundamentally different from that in the current system. The prevailing training for those holding structural positions is generally obsolete in today's democratic environment. Training should instead be geared towards acquiring technical, functional and managerial skills. Several other changes also need to be made, the most important one being to make training demand driven and related to identified needs. Training should thus be financed through the relevant institution's budget, and represent part of its overall performance improvement strategy. It should not be supply driven, and certainly should not be financed by the institution supplying the training.

Making Remuneration Transparent and Fair

Civil Servants in General

It is frequently claimed that Indonesian civil servants are less well paid than their counterparts in the private sector. Over the past decade, however, the take-home pay of civil servants has increased at rates well above those in sectors dominated by private activity. In 2003 the avere

age take-home pay of government employees was 250 per cent higher than average earnings in the agricultural sector, 100 per cent higher than in wholesale and retail trade, 75 per cent higher than in manufacturing, and even 10 per cent higher than in the finance, real estate and insurance sectors (Steedman and Kenward 2005). In addition, many civil servants receive free housing, free transport to and from the office, and free medical care for their families. To make meaningful comparisons with private sector remuneration levels, the monetary value of such fringe benefits should be included as part of total remuneration, since private sector employees have to cover most of these costs themselves.

In addition to their basic salaries, civil servants receive a range of supplementary allowances. Some of these (such as payments for attending meetings) border on the absurd, since they amount to payments simply for doing one's job. These additional allowances make civil servants' overall remuneration non-transparent, and certainly make their take-home pay considerably higher than the published basic pay levels would indicate. The problem seems to be, not the overall level of remuneration for civil servants, but its composition, with civil servants receiving a published basic salary funded from the budget plus a plethora of non-transparent allowances funded from budgetary or off-budget funds. Aside from this, the frequently observed need for pay reform focuses on the current failure to link pay to performance, and on the fact that civil servants are paid in accordance with their rank—no matter what they do—rather than in accordance with the difficulty and responsibilities of the job.

It is not possible to effectively reform a salary system when a large part of take-home pay is made up of non-transparent components that are discretionary and arbitrarily distributed, and where the source of funding may not be known. To make any progress towards creating a salary system that remunerates civil servants for what they do and how well they do it, the first step is to replace the current system providing basic pay and numerous allowances with a system providing a single, transparent payment funded from the budget. For most civil servants, such a salary would be considerably higher than their current basic pay, but not necessarily higher than their current overall remuneration. The Anti-Corruption Commission, the Aceh–Nias Rehabilitation and Recovery Agency and Gadjah Mada University (one of seven autonomous state universities) are examples of institutions that have taken the first step in salary reform, by introducing transparent, single-component pay for key staff. Several regional governments have undertaken similar reforms to increase transparency and improve performance.

To achieve success and sustainability, salary reform of this kind would need to be complemented by a reformed budget process in which funds to cover the new salaries would be provided in full from the budget.

Such a change would lead to increased pension liabilities for the state, since pension entitlements are related to basic salaries. This would need to be balanced by corresponding reforms to the civil servants' pension scheme, as discussed below.

Top Officials

Published pay levels for top officials, such as *pejabat negara*[2] and echelon I officials, suggest that they would lead modest lifestyles if they lived entirely on their salaries. In reality, however, many of them appear to enjoy lifestyles that their colleagues in Singapore — who receive the highest published salaries of civil servants anywhere in the world — could not afford (Hood, Peters and Lee 2003). In addition to the same entitlements as lower-level civil servants, top officials receive substantial fringe benefits. Many of them also receive extra perks by virtue of appointment as commissioners of state-owned enterprises, or from other earning opportunities in the private sector.[3] Finally, there are large amounts of off-budget funds available in most of Indonesia's public institutions, a proportion of which is no doubt skimmed off for private purposes. Thus, as in some other countries in the region, the remuneration structure for top officials can be compared to an iceberg, with only a small portion of total remuneration — the modest basic salary — visible, and with by far the greater portion comprised of additional hidden components, both legitimate and, in some cases, illicit (Hood, Peters and Lee 2003).

Determining an appropriate level of remuneration for top officials is beyond the scope of this discussion, but making all elements of remuneration transparent and consolidating them into a single salary payment, as proposed for other civil servants, would be helpful, not least because this would make it possible to judge what would be politically acceptable in terms of pay levels for the highest office holders, and the lifestyles these would imply.

Handling Redundancies Productively

In any public institution taking part in reforms like those proposed here, significant staff redundancies may occur. When the 'pyramids' are replaced by an organisation with positions classified in accordance with

---

2 *Pejabat negara* is the term for the highest state officials outside the civil service ranks, such as ministers, commissioners and members of parliament.

3 Although *pejabat negara* may no longer accept commissioner assignments, other top officials may still do so.

operational needs, a large number of structural, and possibly other, positions will need to be abolished. It is also likely that many civil servants currently employed will not qualify for the new, professionally classified jobs. The current system has been incapable of providing institutions with adequate numbers of sufficiently skilled staff, or of making sure that the right people are in the right places. The reforms outlined here will therefore threaten the well-being of large numbers of civil servants whose interests have been well served by the current system. Any challenge to the system will lead to resistance and obstruction unless the negative effects are handled in a constructive manner, providing sufficiently attractive terms of separation for those who become redundant.

Already, several regional governments that have attempted to streamline their organisations after estimating their real staffing requirements have ended up in a cul-de-sac, as no policies, mechanisms or funds have been available to resolve the attendant redundancy problems. Similarly, central ministries that have lost functions following the introduction of regional autonomy have failed to downsize their organisations correspondingly. A good example is provided by several ministries' inspectorates-general, which no longer have any mandate to audit local government operations, yet are generally still the same size as before regional autonomy.

With this in mind, and even though the aggregate civil servant to population ratio is quite low, redundancies at the institutional level may be significant. Therefore, any reform initiative needs to encompass policies, mechanisms and funds that will make it possible to terminate the employment of civil servants and remove them from the institutional salary budget. The ultimate responsibility for defining redundancy policies and providing the necessary funds in a national civil service will have to rest with the central government, while the execution of such policies will need to take place locally, at the institutional level. Having said that, some local governments have the capacity to finance their own schemes to take care of redundant civil servants, provided they are given the freedom to do so.

The redundancy issue provides a clear example of the conflict between political and technical considerations, mentioned earlier. While redundancy is easy to define technically, and while there are mechanisms available to deal with it in a productive way, it may turn out to be politically difficult to actually make use of these mechanisms. The government has two roles in relation to employment. One is to act as the regulator of the economy in general and the labour market in particular, and in this role its objective should be to stimulate employment growth. The other is as the country's largest single employer. In this role it should be concerned about cost efficiency, performance and the quality of its output of services — not about the unemployment rate. In Indonesia, as in many other countries, these two roles are not clearly separated, and the public sector therefore tends to be seen as a mechanism for reducing unemployment, making it politically difficult to address redundancy effectively.

A 'zero-growth' policy is often seen as the only politically feasible way to address redundancy, as it does not challenge any vested interests. An administratively imposed zero-growth policy is not the answer to redundancy, however. Such a policy applied for more than three years or so has both unpredictable and highly predictable effects. The unpredictable effect arises because vacancies occur randomly in institutions and areas of expertise, as they are mainly a consequence of the age structure of the workforce. The predictable effect is that in any given government institution subject to a zero-growth policy for some time, there will eventually be a lack of people in low and middle-level positions. Moreover, a zero-growth policy will not have any impact on the quality of the workforce or on its performance, as it is a totally passive instrument for solving problems that require selective and proactive policies.

There are instead two kinds of scheme that could be used to manage redundancy: a retrenchment scheme providing financial support to help redundant civil servants find new jobs in the private sector appropriate to their skills and experience, or to start a business of their own; and an early retirement scheme providing them with a topped-up pension until the normal retirement age, then to be replaced by the normal pension. In relation to the latter option, civil servants who retired early would not lose too much in comparison to what they would earn if they continued their employment. Considering the age structure of the civil service population, it is likely that this would be the more attractive option. Moreover, given that as many as 36 per cent of current civil servants are over 45 years old, and perhaps around 20 per cent over 50 years old, an early retirement scheme targeting civil servants over 50 years of age would make a significant contribution to dealing with the redundancy problem.

Such a scheme could be financed by transferring funds from the budgets of the institutions or local governments in question. Additional funds, as required, might be provided as loans from international funding agencies such as the Asian Development Bank (ADB) or the World Bank. If it was a one-time effort, the duration of the scheme and the corresponding need for financing would be around six years, with a gradual reduction of outlays as early retirees reached the normal retirement age. In practice, however, such a scheme would probably need to remain in place for a longer period of time.

The fact that many civil servants receive unknown allowances financed from unknown sources could be a serious obstacle to willing participation in an early retirement scheme. Without compensation for the loss of such remuneration, the attraction of an early retirement package for individual civil servants would fall. Once again this underlines the importance of replacing the current diverse composition of take-home pay with a single salary funded by the budget.

Securing Civil Servants' Pensions and Making Budget Savings

In any reform that changes salary conditions for civil servants, the effects on the pension system are usually the most difficult ones to handle, because of the huge and long-term commitments that pension liabilities imply. In an administration ruled by law, it is not possible to reduce compensation levels retroactively, nor is it feasible from the budgetary point of view to improve them retroactively. The solution to this problem lies in transitional arrangements under which civil servants above a certain age remain on the old scheme while younger civil servants become subject to the reformed scheme. In Indonesia, the level of basic pay may have to continue to provide the basis for pension entitlements for most civil servants, even if they receive a higher consolidated salary following reform. That way, retroactive additional costs for the state would be avoided.

The Indonesian civil service pension scheme is a defined benefit scheme but is poorly financed relative to its benefit provisions. In 2000, it was already estimated to have a negative cash flow (that is, an excess of payouts over contributions) of some Rp 13.5 trillion, or $1.4 billion at the end-of-year exchange rate (ADB 2002). This underfunding is mainly explained by the fact that only the employees — and not their government employer — have contributed to the scheme. The government handles its liabilities as pay-as-you-go obligations, financing pension payments from the yearly budget as they occur rather than pre-financing them. As a result, the government's share of total civil service pension payments was already as high as 75 per cent in 2000. The underfunding of the civil service pension scheme is clearly at least as great today, while the magnitude of the pension liability remains unknown.

There may have been good reasons to handle the pension liabilities on a pay-as-you-go basis during the financial crisis, but circumstances have changed. It is time for the government to build for the future, by introducing a modernised and more cost-efficient pension scheme for its civil servants to complement the other kinds of reform outlined above. The long-term solution is to replace the pay-as-you-go defined benefit scheme with a pre-financed defined contribution scheme. Under such a scheme, the pension liability of the state would be known at all times, because the state guarantees accumulated contributions, not the size of the benefit eventually to be paid out. Moreover, it would make movement between the public, private and other sectors possible, as employees would be able to transfer their pre-financed entitlements from one scheme to another, making lateral entry into, and exit from, the civil service feasible for all.

Such far-reaching changes to the pension system cannot be introduced overnight. Comprehensive studies and simulations need to be made to assess the actuarial effects and budget implications. Transitional arrangements are essential to make pension reform financially sustainable and avoid retroactive costs. Once again, budget reform will be required. In the current budget system, institutions and local governments that carry no responsibility for financing the pensions of their employees are able to increase the state's financial liability by obtaining administrative approval for an expansion of their workforces. The possibility of administrative decisions outside the control of the Ministry of Finance resulting in an increase in the financial liabilities of the state should be ended as a matter of urgency.

Finally, the pre-financed scheme needs to be built on transparency and accountability, and to include effective anti-corruption mechanisms. The prospect of very large amounts of pension funds accumulating in an environment characterised by a corrupt bureaucracy and legal system poses major risks. These will need to be sufficiently mitigated before such a scheme is introduced.

Preventing Corruption through Administrative Reform

General anti-corruption laws and institutions aim to punish perpetrators, but they do not address the roots of corruption or necessarily do away with the prevailing 'corruption culture'. The eradication of corruption is a more complex and demanding process than detecting and prosecuting perpetrators. To be fully effective, Indonesia's fight against corruption requires that fundamental elements of the governance system be addressed, as well as the behaviour of individuals operating within or in contact with it. Increased transparency and strengthened accountability are essential to minimise corruption, as are improved public expenditure management and civil service reform, as outlined above.

In Indonesia, most public institutions are underfunded, and therefore finance a significant proportion of their operations from revenues that are not recorded in the budget. Off-budget funds are raised to cover legitimate expenses such as electricity, transport, communications and other necessities, but also for illicit purposes such as rent sharing among staff. Rents solicited or collected by civil servants often go into office 'kitties' rather than a particular individual's pocket, eventually to be distributed among staff by a higher-ranking 'patron'. This ensures that corruption is systemic—that all in the pyramid participate—making it difficult to expose and eradicate. The undoubtedly large scale of off-budget funding highlights the need for comprehensive budget reform, such that all revenues are recorded in the budget and all financial transactions are accounted for appropriately.

In spite of the establishment of genuine democracy in Indonesia, and the introduction of new laws and institutional arrangements similar to those found in more highly developed and largely non-corrupt states, corruption continues to prevail. The process is little changed, and is facilitated by lack of transparency and weak accountability: business as usual. Citizens and businesses have to pay bribes and illicit fees for most things when dealing with the administration. Parents have to pay to be able to keep their children in school. Traffic regulations and the institutions that enforce them are used to collect rents rather than actually enforce the regulations. Even public institutions have to make illicit payments to get certain things approved by some other public authority. For example, to get its accounts replenished in accordance with the approved budget, an institution may have to hand over a portion of the funds to the authority controlling their release. The fact that the allocation of positions to an organisation (*formasi*, as described above) is determined administratively rather than being imposed by the budget turns quests for such administrative approvals into rent-seeking games.

When corruption is endemic, everything is for sale. In Indonesia, most civil service positions are for sale, rather than being acquired in open competition based on merit. The practice of selling civil service jobs goes hand in hand with corruption more generally—from one perspective, the investment needed to obtain a position needs to be recovered; from another, the likelihood of access to lucrative opportunities for self-enrichment makes such an investment worthwhile. The practice of selling positions should be a particularly high-priority target of reform. In turn, this will require a combination of professional classification of jobs and increased transparency and accountability in the selection and appointment process.

Misuse of funds in public procurement results in poor public sector investments: the materials or services provided may be of substandard quality, or not supplied in the correct quantity. Practices of collusion carried over from the New Order regime still give a strong and inappropriate role to middlemen in the public procurement process. Interest-based associations distribute contracts among their members based on criteria other than those stipulated in the procurement regulations. Contractors are caught in a prevailing system of collusion in which they are obliged to share contract revenues with middlemen and government officials if they are to have any chance of obtaining government contracts.

The World Bank has now begun to enforce accountability on government recipients of aid by requesting the government to repay funds that have been used corruptly. In turn, the government will need to enforce accountability on officials, middlemen and contractors. If the ADB and other funding agencies also begin to enforce government accountability in Indonesia, rather than dissipating their energy by investigating and blacklisting small contractors and individuals who are merely trying to survive within a corrupt system, the government will have to accept its responsibility in this regard for all foreign-assisted projects.

IMPLEMENTATION STRATEGY

Aiming for Some Quick Wins

While fundamental reform of government administration is bound to take some time, improved performance could be achieved quickly and selectively within the existing system through increased transparency and enforced accountability. One way of doing this would be to set delivery targets for selected services, and persuade agency heads to commit to them in published agreements with the president. A special unit would help the president monitor progress, as proposed earlier. Performance in relation to pre-defined delivery targets would be published on the internet so that any interested person could check on it. Showcase success stories could be used to strengthen reform momentum through the power of good example.

For instance, the government could select a major infrastructure project as a showcase for corruption-free project management and procurement, using integrity pacts, increased transparency, procurement agents, good management and enforced accountability to achieve these ends. Through transparency, reinforced by the use of information and communication technology, it would be possible to make comparisons with other projects in respect of deadlines, efficiency in financial management and procurement and, as a consequence, the quality of the construction outputs. The mechanisms required are available and successful examples from other countries do exist, so it would mainly be a matter of political determination to establish such a showcase in Indonesia.

At the time of writing, the minister of finance was introducing several reforms related to civil service management and improved performance of civil servants within the ministry. Job evaluation and grading of jobs are to be undertaken; functional positions are to replace structural positions; and organisational structures and staffing are to be determined by operational needs. The minister is also contemplating appointing a commission to advise her on appropriate pay levels for *pejabat negara*. As suggested previously, providing this commission thinks in terms of setting a single and transparent salary for each position, the new salary scheme for *pejabat negara* (though not its actual salary levels) could serve as a model for civil service salaries in general. The minister of trade is undertaking similar reforms in her ministry, with the support of the Partnership for Governance Reform.[4] The manner in which reforms are attempted in these two ministries, and the progress made, should serve as good examples to guide civil service reform in a wider context.

Several regional governments have already achieved radical reform in the way they operate and are staffed. A few of them could be used to demonstrate to the public, central government policy makers and regional government officials what can be achieved if there is sufficient determination. Selecting a few local government showcases would also highlight the need to reform the civil service regulatory framework to make these local achievements sustainable.

Pursuing a Comprehensive Civil Service Reform Agenda

A successful reform strategy must identify the risks that need to be managed. It must also be built on certain strategic choices. I turn now to a discussion of the issues to be taken into account when pursuing medium and long-term civil service reform in Indonesia.

It is unlikely that civil service institutions in Indonesia will be able and willing to reform themselves. Such a process requires political pressure, management determination, adequate guidance, effective coordination and continual follow-up. In this regard, I argue that an arrangement like a supporting unit within the president's office is a prerequisite for significant progress. Success will depend on effective two-way communication mechanisms, stakeholder participation, adequate design and excellent leadership with strong political backing. Much can be gained from experiences both within and outside Indonesia, especially with respect to the implementation of sound practices.

Considering the magnitude and complexity of the Indonesian administration and the issues at stake, a selective approach to reform is needed. Civil service reform cannot be achieved overnight; it will more likely take several years, and require transitional solutions in which old and new features and schemes coexist. I have argued that a few national institutions

---

4 The Partnership for Governance Reform is a multi-stakeholder association dedicated to supporting governance reform initiatives in Indonesia. It works with both state institutions and civil society organisations to advance the national reform agenda.

and local governments should be selected on the basis of their reform-minded leadership and potential to show real progress, and given full support in their efforts to pioneer the reform process. Other institutions and local governments whose progress is likely to be slow should be dealt with later, after reforms in other areas have gained momentum and begun to demonstrate their success. The practices that have been proven to work can then be replicated elsewhere with greater confidence.

REFERENCES

ADB (Asian Development Bank) (2002), 'Report and Recommendation of the President to the Board of Directors on a Proposed Cluster, First Loan and Technical Assistance Grant to the Republic of Indonesia for the Financial Governance and Social Security Reform Program', RRP: INO 33399, Manila: Asian Development Bank, November, available at <http://www.asian-devbank.org/Documents/RRPs/INO/rrp-ino-33399.pdf>.

Basri, M.C. and A.A. Patunru (2006), 'Survey of Recent Developments', *Bulletin of Indonesian Economic Studies*, 42(3): 295–319.

Hood, C. and B.G. Peters with G.O.M. Lee (2003), *Reward for High Public Office: Asian and Pacific Rim States*, London: Routledge Research in Comparative Politics.

Steedman, D.W. and L.R. Kenward (2005), 'Civil Service Reforms at the Regional Level: Opportunities and Constraints', working paper, Washington DC: World Bank.

USAID (United States Agency for International Development) (2006), 'Decentralization 2006: Stock Taking on Indonesia's Recent Decentralization Reforms', report prepared by the USAID Democratic Reform Support Program for the Donor Working Group on Decentralization, August, available at <http://pdf.usaid.gov/pdf_docs/PNADH312.pdf>.

World Bank (1999), 'Indonesia: Public Spending in a Time of Change', Washington DC: East Asia and the Pacific Region, Poverty Reduction and Economic Management Sector Unit, World Bank, April.

10 THE CONSTITUTIONAL COURT'S DECISION IN THE DISPUTE BETWEEN THE SUPREME COURT AND THE JUDICIAL COMMISSION: BANISHING JUDICIAL ACCOUNTABILITY?

Simon Butt

This chapter discusses Indonesia's main recent judicial reforms, particularly those that appear to have been designed to increase judicial independence and judicial accountability, and the teetering balance that had been struck at the time of writing. I will focus on three institutions — the Constitutional Court (Mahkamah Konstitusi), the Supreme Court (Mahkamah Agung) and the Judicial Commission (Komisi Yudisial) — and the dispute in which they were involved for much of 2006.

The United Nations' basic principles on the independence of the judiciary (UN 1985) require governments to provide conditions that enable judges to decide cases impartially, that is, 'without any restrictions, improper influences, inducements, pressures, threats or interferences, direct or indirect, from any quarter or for any reason' (article 2). Judicial independence requires that 'the term of office of judges, their independence, security, adequate remuneration, conditions of service, pensions and the age of retirement ... be adequately secured by law' (article 11). The principles also require that judges be immune from civil suits for 'improper acts or omissions in the exercise of their judicial functions' and that their decisions not be 'subject to revision' (article 16). Moreover, judicial independence permits judges to be removed from office before their term has expired only for conduct that is inconsistent with their role as a judge (such as a serious criminal conviction) or that indicates that they are incapable of continuing in office (such as incompetence or illness) (article 18; see also Volcansek 1996: 9).

Judicial independence is often justified on the basis that an impartial third party is necessary to resolve disputes between individuals, entities and governments that they cannot resolve themselves (Shapiro 1981: 1, 7). If judges are not independent, then the public is unlikely to have confidence in the courts, and such confidence is essential to a legal system that depends for its effectiveness on voluntary compliance with judicial decisions (Holland and Gray 2000: 117). Moreover, many scholars accept that judicial independence is crucial to a functioning democracy, the rule of law and human rights protection. Hirschl notes the 'growing acceptance and enforcement of the idea that democracy is not the same thing as majority rule' and that minorities must be protected by a bill of rights, enforced by judges 'removed from the pressures of partisan politics' (Hirschl 2004: 1–2; see also Ginsburg 2003: 2, 96). He adds that 'by its very nature' democracy requires a set of

> procedural governing rules and decision-making processes to which all political actors are required to adhere. The persistence and stability of such a system in turn requires at least a semiautonomous, supposedly apolitical judiciary to serve as an impartial umpire in disputes concerning the scope and nature of the fundamental rules of the political game. ... Moreover, the transition to and consolidation of democracy entails the establishment of some form of separation of powers between the major branches of government and between the central and provincial or regional legislatures (Hirschl 2004: 31–2).

Perversely, however, judicial independence is often criticised as being an anomaly in a functioning democracy. Judges in many countries hold significant power — sometimes even more power than legislators. For example, because judges interpret and apply the laws of democratically elected parliaments, they often have the final say on the way a law will operate in practice. In many countries, judges are permitted to create law — a function that some democratic theorists argue is more properly done by democratically elected legislatures. Moreover, many constitutional and supreme courts around the globe have powers of judicial review, often enabling their judges to invalidate the laws or actions of democratically elected officials. Yet, in most countries outside the United States, judges are not directly elected by citizens. Rather, they are appointed by parliament or, in many civil law countries, by government departments. Of course, many of these parliaments or governments are themselves democratically elected, but this is no guarantee that the judges they appoint will reflect the views of their constituents for the duration of their judicial terms.

In this context, some commentators argue that judicial independence provides too much protection for judges, because judges often use it to insulate themselves from criticism of their decisions, performance or actions. To ensure that public confidence in the judiciary is maintained, critics argue that the competence and impartiality of judges must be checked periodically. Without accountability mechanisms, judicial corruption and impropriety are more likely (Dakolias and Thachuk 2000: 354).

Striking an appropriate balance between judicial independence and judicial accountability can be difficult, and is a matter of significant academic debate.[1] Countries around the world achieve the balance differently. In most countries, judges are granted statutory or constitutional judicial independence. However, in most states of the United States they are held publicly accountable through elections; and in many European countries, judicial commissions have been established with varying responsibilities, some of which include assisting with judicial appointments and promotions and supervising judicial performance. In most countries, judges who are proven to have been involved in corruption or the commission of a crime, or who are ill, can be censured or removed (Wallace 1998: 344), but countries differ on whether parliament should take action (perhaps more justifiable from an accountability standpoint) or whether the judiciary should control the process (perhaps more justifiable from a judicial independence perspective) (Volcansek 1996). Many of the world's judges are subject to appraisal and criticism by the media, civil society and academics, and most of their decisions are reviewable through the appeals process (Dakolias and Thachuk 2000: 363, 380).

Balancing judicial independence and accountability is more difficult in countries in which the judiciary is widely perceived to be, or is in fact, largely incompetent, corrupt or both. If strong levels of independence limit the action that can be taken to investigate and sanction errant judges, then will the courts use their independence as a 'shield' to allow themselves to run rampant? In such circumstances, should accountability be prioritised until judicial competence and prestige are sufficiently high and corruption less prevalent? Or should judicial independence be prioritised over accountability? That is, will the judiciary be utterly ineffective without adequate levels of judicial independence, particularly in disputes between citizens and government (Wallace 1998: 343–4)? If the judiciary is susceptible to outside influences — whether from the government, private parties or another source — will this not reduce its com-

---

1 See, for example, Volume 61(3) of *Law and Contemporary Problems* (1998) and Volume 28(1) of *University of Arkansas at Little Rock Law Review* (2005) on judicial independence and accountability.

munity support and respect, causing parties to avoid the courts for fear of biased decisions? In particular, will the judiciary's credibility plummet if the executive or legislature uses 'investigations as retaliation for unpopular decisions or to exert subtle pressure on judges through hints or threats of investigation' (Wallace 1998: 344)?

This chapter explores the balance between judicial independence and judicial accountability that has been struck in Indonesia—virtually unilaterally by the Constitutional Court. After discussing the Constitutional Court, the Supreme Court and the Judicial Commission, it will explain the dispute that arose between the Judicial Commission and the Supreme Court in 2006 over the extent to which the former could legitimately investigate the latter's judges for alleged impropriety. The Judicial Commission, clearly concerned to increase levels of judicial accountability in Indonesia, had attempted to call several Supreme Court judges to account for their actions. These judges refused to comply with this request, setting in motion public hostilities between the two institutions. Eventually, in March 2006, the Supreme Court asked the Constitutional Court to rule on the dispute. The Constitutional Court's decision, handed down in August 2006, will be discussed and analysed below.

THE CONSTITUTIONAL COURT, THE SUPREME COURT AND THE JUDICIAL COMMISSION

The Constitutional Court

Indonesia's judicial system has undergone significant legislative reform since 2003. In that year the national parliament established a constitutional court,[2] as required by the November 2001 third amendment to the constitution.

Clearly this was a very significant judicial reform. The Constitutional Court is the first court in Indonesia's history with the jurisdiction to assess whether legislation conforms with the constitution. The court therefore has a prominent human rights function, given that the newly amended constitution contains an impressively extensive bill of rights—a list of human rights that the state must protect.

The court also has the power to settle disputes between state institutions and over electoral returns, and to decide on parliamentary impeachment motions against the president and vice-president.[3] The

---

2 Law No. 24/2003 on the Constitutional Court.
3 Articles 24C(1) and 24C(2) of the constitution; articles 10(1) and 10(2) of Law No. 24/2003 on the Constitutional Court.

court is therefore an important institutional feature of Indonesia's new constitutional 'separation of powers', which replaces the executive-heavy 'sharing of powers' put in place by the pre-amended constitution. The Constitutional Court's judicial review power provides a check on the legislature; its impeachment power provides a check on the executive; and its decisions on electoral results help ensure the integrity of the democratic process.

In its first three years of operation, the Constitutional Court has shown impressive levels of independence and has exhibited competence far higher than that of other Indonesian courts. It is beyond the scope of this chapter to discuss the court's performance in detail. However, several of its decisions deserve brief treatment here.[4]

First, the Constitutional Court has indicated that the prime reference point for its decisions is the constitution, not government or legislative preferences. In a series of cases, a majority of the court's judges have held that article 50 of the constitutional court law contradicts the constitution. This is significant, because the constitutional court law is the very statute that established the court and that deals with its composition and procedures. Article 50 attempted to prevent the Constitutional Court from reviewing the constitutionality of statutes enacted before the first amendment to the constitution in 1999. The court found this provision to be unconstitutional because the constitution does not impose any such restriction.[5] The Constitutional Court has therefore reviewed several statutes enacted well before 1999.

Second, in a 2003 case, the Constitutional Court invalidated legislation that would have prohibited former members of the Indonesian Communist Party or other prohibited organisations, or people involved in the 1965 coup, from being nominated for candidature in local, regional and national elections.[6] According to the court, this legislation breached the constitutional right of Indonesians to participate in government and to be free from discrimination.[7]

---

4 The following discussion draws on Butt (2006).
5 Constitutional Court Decision No. 004/2003, reviewing Law No. 14/1985 on the Supreme Court (the *Mahkamah Konstitusi Law case No. 1*); Constitutional Court Decision No. 013/2003, reviewing Law No. 16/2003 (the *Bali Bombing case*); Constitutional Court Decision No. 066/2004, reviewing Law No. 1/1987 on Kadin and Law No. 24/2003 on the Constitutional Court (the *Kadin Law case*).
6 Constitutional Court Decision No. 011-017/2003, reviewing Law No. 12/2003 on General Elections for Members of the DPR, DPD and DPRD (the *PKI case*).
7 In particular, the legislation was said to breach article 27(1) of the constitution, which gives citizens the right to equal treatment before the law; and article 28I(2), which provides the right to be free from discriminatory treatment.

Third, the Constitutional Court has upheld the constitutional right of citizens to be free from prosecution under retrospective laws.[8] Controversially, in 2003 a majority of the Constitutional Court invalidated a statute that would have permitted the investigation and prosecution of those involved in the 2002 Bali bombings using an anti-terrorism law that had been enacted after the bombings took place (Butt and Hansell 2004; Clarke 2003). The court was strongly criticised for being soft on terrorism, but undeniably the majority's concern to uphold the text of the constitution in the face of domestic and international pressure indicates its strong levels of independence, matched with sound legal reasoning.

Fourth, the Constitutional Court has imposed obligations on the state that the court has discovered are implicit, rather than explicitly expressed, in the constitution. The court has primarily used two provisions as a basis to imply these obligations. The first is the preamble to the constitution, which states that the government is 'to protect all Indonesians and their native land, to further public welfare and the intellectual life of the people, and to contribute to the world order of freedom, peace and social justice'. The second is article 1(3), which states that Indonesia is a 'law state' (*negara hukum*). From these provisions, the Constitutional Court has implied apparently broad state obligations, including the obligation to protect citizens from corruption,[9] to protect the domestic broadcasting industry from foreign domination[10] and to provide for a fair trial, access to justice and legal aid.[11]

The Supreme Court

In 2004, the Indonesian national parliament replaced or revised many of the country's judiciary laws, including the statute covering the exercise of judicial power generally,[12] and the statutes relating to the Supreme Court[13] and to Indonesia's general and administrative courts.[14] The new statutes introduced a number of reforms, perhaps the most important

---

8 This right is contained in article 28I(1).
9 Constitutional Court Decision No. 006/2003, reviewing Law No. 30/2002 on the Corruption Eradication Commission (the *KPK Law case*).
10 Constitutional Court Decision No. 005/2003, reviewing Law No. 32/2002 on Broadcasting (the *Broadcasting Law case*).
11 See, for example, Constitutional Court Decision No. 006/2004, reviewing Law No. 18/2003 on Advocates (the *Advocates Law case No. 2*).
12 Law No. 4/2004 on Judicial Power.
13 Law No. 5/2004, which amended Law No. 14/1985 on the Supreme Court.
14 Law No. 8/2004, which amended Law No. 2/1986 on the General Courts; Law No. 9/2004, which amended Law No. 5/1986 on the Administrative Courts.

of them being to bring the administration, organisation and finances of these courts under Supreme Court control – the so-called 'one-roof' (*satu atap*) reforms. For most courts, these tasks were previously carried out by the Justice Department.[15] This kind of government-controlled administrative structure is commonly employed by countries adhering to a civil law tradition. However, proponents of legal reform during the Soeharto period often claimed that the Justice Department was misusing its managerial and administrative control over the judiciary to ensure that the courts delivered decisions that favoured the government and its officials. Legal reformists had therefore been pushing for *satu atap* for decades (see, for example, Lev 1978).

The *satu atap* reforms appear to have achieved one of their intended purposes: improved judicial independence from government. Allegations of government interference in cases before the courts were very common during the Soekarno and Soeharto periods, but are now encountered much more rarely.

Other aspects of the reforms appear to have been less successful, however. In 2003 the Supreme Court composed a four-volume 'blueprint' for Indonesian judicial reform – directed particularly towards its own reform – in collaboration with the Institute for an Independent Judiciary (LeIP), a respected Jakarta legal NGO (Supreme Court 2003). The blueprint aimed to provide a step-by-step strategy for the Supreme Court to take over the court-related functions of the Justice Department, and made many sensible suggestions, such as how the Supreme Court should tackle its new responsibilities to train, appoint and promote judges.

But the magnitude of the required administrative, structural and managerial reforms seems to have been underestimated, particularly given the budgetary constraints within which the Supreme Court must operate. The Soeharto regime's deliberate subjugation of the judiciary as an institution, and judges as individuals, by intruding into cases and judicial administration, and by failing to ensure reasonable levels of judicial competence and integrity, has dramatically reduced the capacity of the judiciary to manage itself, implement change or, indeed, carry out its core adjudicative tasks. As a result, at the time of writing very little of the blueprint had been put into practice, and progress appeared to have stalled.

Meanwhile, the Supreme Court and the courts below it continue to suffer from a raft of significant problems that have brought the judicial system to the brink of complete dysfunction. One problem is corrup-

---

15 The Department of Religion handled these functions for the religious courts and the Department of Defence and Security handled them for the military courts.

tion.[16] Commentators have described courtrooms as 'auction houses', where the highest bidder wins the case (Lindsey 2001). Aspandi (2002: 145) claims that some trials are conducted in a farcical manner, often because a bribed judge must somehow direct the trial towards a predetermined outcome. He notes also that some lawyers have complained of being 'ambushed' by decisions that do not reflect the evidence adduced and legal arguments presented in the case, blaming their opponents for bribing the presiding judges (Aspandi 2002: 140). According to one lawyer, illicit payments determine judicial decisions so regularly that the 'law' is almost entirely irrelevant:

> I no longer feel it's important to read law books, no longer important to prepare an argument based on precedents. That kind of thing is no longer important. It's more important that I know whether my client has enough money to pay the judge (Pemberton 1999: 202).

A second serious problem is the judiciary's generally low level of competence. Under Soeharto's New Order regime, judicial standards were deliberately sabotaged, with very low budgets provided for orientation training and continuing education for judges, and for other necessary expenditures.[17] The bureaucratic promotion systems put in place emphasised seniority and loyalty over achievements, knowledge and ability, ensuring that judges in positions of relative power would be very likely to obey instructions from the government. An unfortunate legacy of the Soeharto period was therefore more than an entire generation of judges with only rudimentary legal and judicial skills (Pompe 2002, cited in World Bank 2003: 89). Despite the *satu atap* reforms, and the corresponding shift of responsibility for judicial education from the government to the Supreme Court, very little has been done to remedy this neglect.

Third, enforcement of judicial decisions in Indonesia is often difficult and sometimes impossible. Even litigants who obtain a decision untainted by corruption or incompetence may find it of little practical benefit. If a losing party in a civil suit fails to comply with a judicial decision, the winning party must usually file a further application to compel the losing party to comply. Only if this order is ignored will a court seize property to pay any compensation required by the decision (Butt 2007). However, this process too is significantly flawed: the court

---

16 See, for example, Asia Watch (1988: 170), Indonesian Corruption Watch (2001), Aspandi (2002) and World Bank (2003).

17 Pompe cites recent reports estimating that only 30 per cent of the judiciary's institutional needs, including electricity, phone use, postage, paper and cost of transfers, are met by the national budget (Pompe 2002, cited in World Bank 2003: 89). It has been said that this forces courts to engage in corruption simply to meet expenses and pay staff (Asia Watch 1988: 170).

can indefinitely delay the hearing of the application, or the execution of the decision itself, for any reason. The phenomenon of the 'magic letter' (*surat sakti*) has compounded the problem. Often accompanied by accusations of corruption against those who issue them—usually senior judges—these letters strongly urge lower courts to delay the execution of particular decisions (Butt 2007).

The Judicial Commission

A judicial commission law was enacted in 2004.[18] In 2005 the Judicial Commission was established, as required by the third round of amendments to Indonesia's constitution, introduced in 2001. The Judicial Commission is an independent institution made up of seven members drawn from the ranks of former judges, legal practitioners, legal academics and community members.[19] Its two main functions are to advise the People's Representative Council (DPR) on Supreme Court appointments and to supervise the performance and behaviour of judges as part of its function to 'uphold the honour and dignity, and to ensure the [good] behaviour, of judges'.[20] The commission receives community complaints about judges and investigates suspected breaches of proper judicial behaviour.[21]

Significantly, the Judicial Commission's powers are limited. If it determines that a judge has acted inappropriately, it cannot itself impose a sanction, such as a reprimand, suspension or dismissal, upon the errant judge; it can only send its findings, including a proposed sanction, to the Supreme Court or Constitutional Court for further action.[22] The Judicial Commission's efficacy therefore depends heavily on its relationships with the Supreme Court and the Constitutional Court—specifically, the willingness and ability of those courts to act on the commission's proposals and recommendations.

The Judicial Commission has indicated a strong desire to perform its functions with some vigour. In its first year it received 820 complaints and reports about judicial conduct (*Jakarta Post*, 29 August 2006), called 74 judges to account for their actions and recommended Supreme Court action against 18 judges (*Hukumonline*,[23] 3 August 2006). At the

---

18 Law No. 22/2004 on the Judicial Commission.
19 Articles 6(1) and 6(3) of Law No. 22/2004 on the Judicial Commission.
20 Article 24B(1) of the constitution; articles 13–20 of Law No. 22/2004 on the Judicial Commission.
21 Article 22(1) of Law No. 22/2004 on the Judicial Commission.
22 Article 23 of Law No. 22/2004 on the Judicial Commission.
23 *Hukumonline* (Lawonline) is a specialist online news service focusing on issues of interest to the Indonesian legal community (see <www.hukum online.com>).

time of writing, however, the commission appeared still to be finding its feet, and to be having difficulty attracting support from other institutions — particularly the Supreme Court. Although the Supreme Court has accepted some of the Judicial Commission's recommendations for Supreme Court appointments (*Hukumonline*, 4 August 2006), it has not accepted *any* of its recommendations relating to judicial impropriety or misconduct (*Hukumonline*, 3 August 2006). The commission's attempts to 'compel' the Supreme Court to act — particularly against its own judges — have resulted in great controversy, as will be discussed below. The net result is that the Judicial Commission has not been able to make any tangible improvement to address the problems plaguing the Supreme Court and the lower courts.

THE DISPUTE BETWEEN THE JUDICIAL COMMISSION AND THE SUPREME COURT

Background

The public 'war' between the Judicial Commission and the Supreme Court is said to have begun when Bagir Manan, the Supreme Court chief justice, rejected a Judicial Commission request that the Supreme Court investigate several of its own judges, including himself, for alleged corruption in cases they had handled. The chief justice stated that he had already provided explanations on the cases concerned to the Anti-Corruption Commission (KPK), so the Judicial Commission did not need to make its own enquiries (*Hukumonline*, 15 March 2006, 8 June 2006). Tension between the court and the commission had been brewing even before this; the Supreme Court had rejected several Judicial Commission recommendations to take action against particular judges in several earlier cases as well (*Hukumonline*, 29 June 2006).

The members of the Judicial Commission then visited President Susilo Bambang Yudhoyono, accompanied by Justice Minister Hamid Awaluddin. They are said to have asked the president to issue an interim law (*perpu*)[24] requiring the reselection or rigorous performance assessment of all 49 Supreme Court justices as the first stage of a comprehensive overhaul of the entire judiciary (*Hukumonline*, 15 March 2006). The call for the reselection was leaked to the media, as was a list of allegedly 'problematic' or corrupt judges, leading to media attacks on the judici-

---

24 Article 22 of the constitution permits the president to issue government regulations in lieu of legislation (*perpu*), which have authority equivalent to a statute. They are relatively rare, and must be ratified by the DPR in its following sitting to remain valid.

ary (*Hukumonline*, 15 March 2006). In response, several Supreme Court judges reported the chair of the Judicial Commission, Busyro Muqoddas, to the police for defamation (*Hukumonline*, 15 March 2006).

Finally, 31 Supreme Court judges lodged an application with the Constitutional Court seeking a review of the constitutionality of the provisions of the judicial commission law covering the commission's supervision of Supreme Court judges. It is to this case, and the Constitutional Court's decision – Constitutional Court Decision No. 005/PUU-IV/2006 (henceforth SC vs JC 2006) – that I now turn.

The Constitutional Court Decision

In their application to the Constitutional Court, the Supreme Court judges argued that the Judicial Commission lacked constitutional jurisdiction to monitor their performance. They pointed to article 24B(1) of the constitution, which sets out the Judicial Commission's jurisdiction:

> The Judicial Commission is independent and can propose judges for appointment to the Supreme Court, and has other powers within the framework of maintaining and upholding the honour, dignity and behaviour of *judges* [emphasis added].

The judges put forward two main arguments. First, they argued that the word 'judges' did not encompass Supreme Court and Constitutional Court judges; rather, it referred only to first-instance and appeal judges (SC vs JC 2006: 159). According to the applicants, this interpretation brought the constitutionality of several provisions of the judicial commission law into question. In particular, they argued that article 1(5) of the law defined 'judges' as 'Supreme Court judges and judges in all courts under the Supreme Court and Constitutional Court', thereby unconstitutionally expanding the meaning of 'judges' contained in article 24B(1) of the constitution, and providing the Judicial Commission with greater powers than the constitution permitted (SC vs JC 2006: 159). The judges therefore asked the Constitutional Court to invalidate all provisions of the judicial commission law allowing the Judicial Commission to supervise Constitutional Court judges and suggest punishments for them.[25]

Second, the applicants argued that the Judicial Commission's supervision of Supreme Court judges – in particular its attempt to call several Supreme Court judges to account for their decisions in controversial cases – constituted 'interference' with the independence guaranteed to the Supreme Court by article 24(1) of the constitution (SC vs JC 2006: 154, 160). Further, the Supreme Court judges argued that, because the Judicial

---

25 These provisions included articles 21, 22(1e), 23(2), 23(3), 24(1), 25(3) and 25(4).

Commission was the Supreme Court's partner in supervising the lower courts, it was not appropriate for the Judicial Commission to supervise the Supreme Court (SC vs JC 2006: 160).

Judicial Commission Supervision of Constitutional Court Judges

The Constitutional Court turned first to a matter that appeared unrelated to the Supreme Court's application: the Judicial Commission's jurisdiction to monitor the Constitutional Court itself. The court found that the definition of 'judge' contained in article 1(5) of the judicial commission law did not include Constitutional Court judges, and therefore that the Judicial Commission lacked authority to investigate Constitutional Court judges (SC vs JC 2006: 176).

The court put forward several arguments to support this conclusion, only four of which will be critiqued here for reasons of space. First, the Constitutional Court emphasised that, unlike most other judges in Indonesia, Constitutional Court judges were not 'career judges' and should therefore not fall under the supervision of the Judicial Commission (SC vs JC 2006: 174). Unfortunately the court did not explain this argument in any detail, nor did it clarify the relevance of the distinction between career and non-career judges.

For those unfamiliar with the Indonesian judicial career structure, some explanation is necessary. Like judges in many countries with a civil law tradition, most Indonesian judges begin their careers soon after they complete university, and make their way up the judicial ranks through promotions and transfers. For so-called career judges, the Supreme Court is the pinnacle of career progression. Although three Constitutional Court judges worked as judges before appointment to the Constitutional Court, the remaining six were former academics or parliamentarians. All Constitutional Court judges are appointed for a maximum of five years.

The Constitutional Court did not provide a legal basis for differentiating between career and non-career judges. In fact, there appears to be no reason to make such a distinction, given that all judges — whether career or non-career — are provided with judicial independence, perform a crucial adjudicative function and arguably require only minimum levels of accountability.

Perhaps the thrust of the court's argument was that if the Judicial Commission's supervisory function was mainly intended to provide information to the Supreme Court about matters relevant to career judges — appointments, promotions and so forth — then the commission should monitor only career judges. On this view, there would be no need to supervise Constitutional Court judges, who are appointed only once and are not promoted. However, a stronger counterargument is that the judicial commission law, as noted above, allows the Judicial Commission also to suggest punishments for errant 'judges'. Given that all judges — including Constitutional Court judges — can be sanctioned or dismissed for misconduct before their terms have expired or they have reached retirement age, providing such supervisory powers to the Judicial Commission would appear to have some benefit.

Furthermore, the Constitutional Court appears to have neglected to consider its argument in the context of the increasing number of ad hoc judges employed in Indonesia. In the last several years, a number of Indonesian courts — such as the human rights, anti-corruption and labour courts — have employed non-career judges with legal experience or specialised knowledge to preside over particular cases alongside career judges. Given that ad hoc judges, like Constitutional Court judges, are clearly not career judges, would the Judicial Commission be precluded from supervising their performance too?

Second, the Constitutional Court noted that the Judicial Commission had a say in the appointment only of Supreme Court judges — not of Constitutional Court judges. Why then, the court asked, should the Judicial Commission have a say in the supervision of Constitutional Court judges (SC vs JC 2006: 174)? Again, this argument does not withstand scrutiny. The Judicial Commission only *proposes* Supreme Court candidates to the DPR; it does not have the final say in their appointment. Also, it does not necessarily follow that the body that appoints judges should ultimately be responsible for ensuring that they perform their functions properly. Two separate institutions can, quite legitimately, perform these functions separately. Indeed, to ensure the impartiality of political judicial appointees, it might in fact be preferable for supervision to be performed by a body that is not involved in their appointment.

Third, the Constitutional Court noted that a mechanism already existed to monitor Constitutional Court judges and process alleged improprieties before the judicial commission law was enacted and the Judicial Commission established: an Honour Council under article 23 of the constitutional court law (SC vs JC 2006: 199). However, the mere pre-existence of such a mechanism does not constitute a particularly strong argument. By enacting the judicial commission law, the DPR could well have intended implicitly to replace Honour Council with Judicial Commission investigations.

The Constitutional Court's strongest argument for excluding itself from Judicial Commission supervision appears to have been that this might compromise the court's ability to impartially adjudicate disputes between state institutions — particularly if the Judicial Commission was one of the parties to the dispute, as in this case (SC vs JC 2006: 175-6, 199). The court noted that if the Judicial Commission could supervise the Constitutional Court, then the latter's credibility and legitimacy to adjudicate a case involving the Judicial Commission would be questionable. It argued that the independence of the Constitutional Court might be compromised, either in fact or in perception, if a decision against the Judicial Commission resulted in an adverse evaluation by the commission (SC vs JC 2006: 199). The court's apparent concern to uphold judicial independence at all costs is analysed below.

Judicial Commission Supervision of Supreme Court Judges

In its discussion of whether the Judicial Commission could monitor and investigate Supreme Court and other non-Constitutional Court judges, the Constitutional Court rejected the Supreme Court judges' argument that the 'judges' referred to in article 24B(1) of the constitution did not encompass Supreme Court judges. The Constitutional Court refused to invalidate article 1(5) of the judicial commission law to the extent that it applied to Supreme Court judges (SC vs JC 2006: 199).

The Constitutional Court accepted that article 24B(1) could be broken into two separate clauses. The first referred to the recruitment of 'Supreme Court Judges' (*Hakim Agung*); the second referred to the Judicial Commission's powers to maintain and uphold the honour, dignity and behaviour of 'judges' (*hakim*). Because the first clause referred specifically to *Hakim Agung* (capitalised), the Constitutional Court found that *hakim* (not capitalised) in the second clause was intended to apply to judges in general — including those of the Supreme Court (SC vs JC 2006: 177).

The Constitutional Court argued also that the Supreme Court should not be removed from supervision simply because it was at the pinnacle of the judicial hierarchy. It pointed out that Supreme Court judges were members of the Indonesian Judges' Association (Ikatan Hakim Indonesia) and had not disputed their status as mere 'judges' within that organisation (SC vs JC 2006: 178).

Almost in passing, the Constitutional Court mentioned that judicial accountability needed to go hand in hand with judicial independence, the necessity for which was universally recognised (SC vs JC 2006: 178). However, as will be discussed below, the court did not discuss judicial accountability in detail, or explain the appropriate balance that should be struck between independence and accountability.

What Supervision Can the Judicial Commission Perform?

Despite holding that Supreme Court judges are 'judges' within the meaning of article 1(5) of the judicial commission law, the Constitutional Court decided that the provisions in the law authorising the Judicial Commission to supervise Supreme Court judges were unconstitutional, for two reasons.

The first was judicial independence. Although the Constitutional Court certainly did not prohibit the Judicial Commission entirely from supervising the Supreme Court, it stated that the Supreme Court's constitutional judicial independence prevented the Judicial Commission from supervising the Supreme Court's exercise of judicial power (SC vs JC 2006: 181). Unfortunately, the Constitutional Court did not define 'exercise of judicial power'; presumably this would include judicial processes and decisions.

The second was that, according to the Constitutional Court, the judicial commission law caused legal uncertainty – in particular by failing to provide details on how the Judicial Commission should supervise Supreme Court judges. For example, it did not cover fundamental issues such as how honour and dignity were to be assessed, or what constituted reviewable behaviour (SC vs JC 2006: 193, 200). Were judicial standards to be measured by reference to a code of conduct or ethics? If so, which code (SC vs JC 2006: 187)? The Constitutional Court noted that this not only made the Judicial Commission's function unclear, but could confuse judges about what they could and could not do ethically, which might in turn affect the way they decided cases (SC vs JC 2006: 190).

Indeed, the Constitutional Court stressed that, at least in part due to this uncertainty, the Judicial Commission had interpreted the judicial commission law improperly so as to allow it to review judicial behaviour through a review of judicial decisions. The court declared that it was a universal norm of all legal systems that

> [evaluating] judicial decisions for the purposes of supervision outside the mechanisms of procedural law conflicts with the principle of *res judicata pro veritatem habetur*, which means that what is decided by judges must be considered correct (*de inhoud van het vonnis geld als waard*). Therefore, if a judicial decision is thought to contain an error, the supervision – through an evaluation of, or correction to, the decision – must be performed through legal avenues in accordance with the applicable procedural law. This principle does not reduce the rights of citizens, particularly legal experts, to evaluate a judicial decision … in an academic forum or media, such as a seminar or a commentary in a law review (SC vs JC 2006: 188-9).

In other words, even though assessing the technical–judicial skills of judges by reading judicial decisions might assist the Judicial Commission to identify a breach of a code of conduct or ethics (SC vs JC 2006: 190, 193), reviewing judicial decisions might place unjustifiable pressure on the judges, thereby breaching judicial independence (SC vs JC 2006: 193). Only the courts could review judicial decisions, and then only through the appeals process – not by evaluating and directly interfering with decisions or by influencing judges (SC vs JC 2006: 190).

Hopes Dashed of a Return to **Eksaminasi?**

In the mid to late 1960s, the Supreme Court developed a system of super-vision of judicial competence (*eksaminasi*) under which the superior of each judge periodically examined three criminal and three civil decisions handed down by that judge.[26] Some of the decisions examined were those that attracted public attention; others were chosen by the judges being examined (Pompe 1996: 222). Feedback was provided to the judges, and the results of the examination used to determine whether they should be promoted (Pompe 1996: 222; Supreme Court 2003: 107). However, *eksaminasi* was abandoned in the 1970s under then Justice Minister Seno Adji, and a system evolved in which judicial career advancement depended not on ability but rather on connections with Justice Department or Supreme Court officials (Pompe 1996: 222; Aspandi 2002: 75). Ever since, many Indonesian judges are said to have used judicial independence as a defence against allegations of corruption or incompetence, or in the face of calls for increased accountability (Aspandi 2002: 101). In response to the problems plaguing the Indonesian judiciary discussed above, some, including the Supreme Court itself (Supreme Court 2003: 117), have called for the reintroduction of the *eksaminasi* system of judicial supervi-sion, or a variation of it.[27]

The *eksaminasi* system has several obvious flaws. First, it presumes that the superior of the judge being examined has a higher level of knowledge or experience than that judge. Given Indonesia's standards of judicial education and competence, seniority and experience are no guarantee of greater legal knowledge or understanding, particularly in modern areas of law such as intellectual property, information technol-ogy and complex commercial transactions. Second, most trials in Indo-nesia are presided over by a panel of three judges. Although all three are in theory responsible for the content of the decision, in practice it may have been reached through negotiation and compromise. Therefore, the final written decision may not accurately reflect the precise analysis or decision favoured personally by the judge under review. Third, courts in many civil law countries—including Indonesia—do not always disclose all the relevant facts of a case, or the competing arguments raised, in their

---

26 See Supreme Court Memo (*Surat Edaran*) No. 1/1967 on Examinations, Monthly Reports and Appeals Lists; Pompe (1996: 222); DJBPUPTUN (1997: 45–6); Aspandi (2002: 80, 127).

27 For example, Bismar Siregar, a former Supreme Court judge, claimed that if *eksaminasi* was reinstated, then 'we will not have the strange decisions we get now' (cited in DJBPUPTUN 1997: 45–6).

decisions. Without reference to the broader context in which the decision was made, a reviewing judge may find it difficult to assess the decision effectively. Fourth, the process may be open to manipulation; that is, within the culture of judicial corruption in Indonesia, it may quickly become possible to buy and sell the favourable *eksaminasi* required for a promotion.

Now, perhaps the greatest impediment to the reintroduction of *eksaminasi* — or a modified version that addresses some of the flaws identified in the previous paragraph — is the Constitutional Court's decision in the case discussed above. It seems quite clear from the decision that the Constitutional Court is likely to declare invalid any statutory scheme under which judicial decisions are formally reviewed outside the formal judicial appeals framework — even if that system is run exclusively by judges. The Constitutional Court would probably hold that such a system could potentially interfere with the independence of judges, because it might make judges decide a case in a way they think will be most acceptable to their superiors, rather than according to their own conviction about the relevant facts and law.

In theory, the alternative proposed by the Constitutional Court — the formal appeals system — may appear to address the need for judicial independence while also ensuring that judges make sound decisions. In practice, however, the appeals system is not a reliable means of supervision, for several reasons. First, the Supreme Court blueprint itself acknowledges that the appeals process does not, in fact, impose real accountability upon errant lower court judges (Supreme Court 2003: 90). Although some judges may be shamed by having their decision overturned by a higher court, they are unlikely to suffer any more tangible consequences, such as having a promotion postponed.

Second, although lower court judges may receive some form of feedback through the appeals process, its value is likely to be limited. Many appeals court decisions that overturn first-instance court decisions do not contain extensive explanations of the reasons for doing so. It is therefore possible that the lower court judge may be left wondering why his or her decision was overturned.

Third, the appeals process will not 'catch' decisions that are not appealed (Supreme Court 2003: 90).

Finally, the Supreme Court blueprint itself notes that the appeals approach may suffer from one of the flaws in the *eksaminasi* system noted above: it presumes that judges at the higher levels of the judicature are more capable than those at the lower levels, when this may not necessarily be so (Supreme Court 2003: 90). Unfortunately, it also presumes that appeals court decisions are not regularly distorted by corruption.

CONCLUDING REMARKS

The Constitutional Court's decision has been poorly received by the media and legal observers alike.[28] Most commentators have focused on the apparent effect of the decision, that is, to keep the Supreme Court and lower courts virtually immune from punishment for corruption or incompetence (*Hukumonline*, 27 August 2006). In particular, the Constitutional Court has drawn criticism for unilaterally prohibiting the Judicial Commission from supervising its own judges. When viewed alongside another recent decision of the court that appears to make corruption investigations and prosecutions more difficult (*Jakarta Post*, 4 September 2006; *Hukumonline*, 26 July 2006), this decision has been seen by some as evidence of the court's 'soft' stance on corruption (*Hukumonline*, 27 August 2006; *Jakarta Post*, 25 August 2006).

In my opinion this view is rather overstated, and ignores the Constitutional Court's legitimate position, supported by some (albeit probably inadequate) reasoning, that judicial independence should, at this stage in Indonesia's judicial reform process, be prioritised over judicial accountability. In choosing this balance, the court emphasised the importance of judicial independence to a functioning state, legal system and judiciary. It stated that judicial independence was a crucial aspect of *negara hukum* and of the separation of powers, which the Constitutional Court described as the 'soul' of the constitution (SC vs JC 2006: 169). Judicial independence was, according to the court, indispensable to the protection of citizens' human rights and their right to a fair trial (SC vs JC 2006: 172, 182–3).

The Constitutional Court certainly did not completely ignore the need for judicial accountability. It was strongly critical of the Supreme Court for failing to impose sufficient accountability mechanisms of its own to ensure that its judges remained free from impropriety. Recognising that judicial corruption was one of the biggest problems facing the Supreme Court (SC vs JC 2006: 192), the Constitutional Court stated:

> It is hoped that the Supreme Court increases supervision, particularly through opening itself more to respond to criticism, hopes and suggestions from various quarters. Judges must define the principle of judicial independence as ... an obligation to create free courts (fair trials), which is a prerequisite for the rule of law. Therefore, within the principle of judicial independence, there is an obligation on judges to free themselves from persuasion, pressure, force, threats or fear of retribution [from] particular government, political

---

28 See, for example, *Jakarta Post*, 25 August 2006, 28 August 2006, 29 August 2006, 4 September 2006; *Hukumonline*, 24 August 2006, 27 August 2006, 31 August 2006, 1 September 2006.

or economic interests, other political forces or particular groups; and [from accepting] recompense or the promise of recompense ... or an advantage — financial or otherwise; and not to misuse the principle of judicial independence as a means to hide from supervision (SC vs JC 2006: 201–2).

Stating that accountability mechanisms must be devised carefully so that they do not affect the conduct, and outcome, of trials, the court continued:

> These days ... [community faith in] judicial decisions is in a dismal state. But, even though the faith remaining is low, it must not disappear altogether, rendering the intent to maintain the honour, dignity and behaviour of judges counterproductive and eventually causing legal chaos (SC vs JC 2006: 172–3).

In other words, the Constitutional Court appears to have taken the view that, if further intrusions are made into judicial independence — even through the supervision of judges — then the already low confidence of Indonesians in the judicial system will fall even further.

However, in addition to the questionable arguments referred to earlier, the Constitutional Court's decision contained a number of shortcomings that significantly undermine the veracity of what might otherwise have been a legitimate stance on judicial independence and judicial accountability. First, the Constitutional Court failed to discuss comprehensively the difficulties of striking a balance between judicial independence and judicial accountability for corruption and incompetence that it could point to in the face of criticism. Regrettably, the court did not adequately consider the consequences of providing very high levels of judicial independence in countries such as Indonesia that have strong traditions of abuse of judicial power and low levels of competence.

Second, the Constitutional Court did not consider the argument that the constitution's provision of judicial independence carries with it a corresponding need for judges to have adequate levels of competence and integrity. If judges did not need to be competent and honest, then how could the Supreme Court and other courts effectively perform their function as a check on the exercise of government power?

Third, the court also failed to consider a previous decision in which it had hinted that the state had an obligation to protect the people from corruption, to assist it to define the boundaries of judicial independence.[29] If it had applied this apparent obligation to the case, the court may have found that the state was justified in adopting more 'intrusive' accountability mechanisms aimed at reducing corruption.

---

29 Constitutional Court Decision No. 006/2003, reviewing Law No. 30/2002 on the Corruption Eradication Commission (the *KPK Law case*).

Finally, the Constitutional Court could have questioned whether the Judicial Commission's investigations did, in fact, constitute interference. The Supreme Court is able to ignore the Judicial Commission's protestations; like most ombudsmen, the commission has powers of recommendation only. If the commission cannot compel the Supreme Court to act, then how can it be said to be undermining judicial independence? It may well be that conducting an investigation into a judge's behaviour or decision in itself constitutes illegitimate pressure, as may the media frenzy that surrounds allegations of judicial impropriety. However, because the Constitutional Court did not define 'interference', these questions remain unanswered.

The Constitutional Court's decision places Indonesia's parliament in a difficult position. Some commentators, such as Kuok (2006), Susanti (2006), and Panjaitan (2006), have emphasised that the decision highlights inadequacies in Indonesia's judiciary laws, particularly their lack of harmonisation, certainty and detail on judicial supervision. They argue that the decision has the advantage of placing pressure on the national parliament to amend these laws, and therefore provides a starting point for further judicial reform. However, this optimism presumes that the national parliament will respond to the decision in a timely fashion, even though the parliament has never enacted a statute or amendment in response to any Constitutional Court decision. Moreover, the court has provided very little guidance as to what amendments the Constitutional Court would find constitutionally acceptable in future legislation. The potential constitutional scope of the Judicial Commission's supervisory powers therefore remains almost as unclear as the judicial commission law itself.

REFERENCES

Asia Watch (1988), *Human Rights Concerns in Indonesia and East Timor*, Washington DC: Asia Watch Committee.

Aspandi, A. (2002), *Menggugat Sistem Hukum Peradilan Indonesia Yang Penuh Ketidakpastian* [Challenging a Legal System Full of Uncertainty], Surabaya: LeKSHI and Lutfansah.

Butt, S. (2006), 'Indonesia's Constitutional Court: A Reform Over-achiever?', *Inside Indonesia*, 87(July–September): 10–11.

Butt, S. (2007), 'The Supreme Court and *Surat Sakti* in Indonesia', in T. Lindsey (ed.), *Indonesia: Law and Society*, 2nd edition, Sydney: Federation Press (forthcoming).

Butt, S. and D. Hansell (2004), 'The Masykur Abdul Kadir Case: Indonesian Constitutional Court Decision No. 013/PUU-I/2003', *Australian Journal of Asian Law*, 6(2): 176–96.

Clarke, R. (2003), 'Retrospectivity and the Constitutional Validity of the Bali Bombing and East Timor Trials', *Australian Journal of Asian Law*, 5(2): 2–32.

Dakolias, M. and K. Thachuk (2000), 'Attacking Corruption in the Judiciary: A Critical Process in Judicial Reform', *Wisconsin International Law Journal*, 18: 353–406.

DJBPUPTUN (Direktur Jenderal Badan Peradilan Umum dan Peradilan Tata Usaha Negara) (1997), 'Pembinaan Karier dan Prestasi Hakim Dalam Rangka Meningkatkan Martabat dan Wibawa Hukum' [Judicial Career Development and Achievements in the Framework of Increasing the Dignity and Authority of the Law], paper presented to a DJBPUPTUN panel discussion on judicial career development, Jakarta, July.

Ginsburg, T. (2003), *Judicial Review in New Democracies: Constitutional Courts in Asian Cases*, New York NY: Cambridge University Press.

Hirschl, R. (2004), *Towards Juristocracy: The Origins and Consequences of the New Constitutionalism*, Cambridge MA: Harvard University Press.

Holland, R. and C. Gray (2000), 'Judicial Discipline: Independence with Accountability', *Widener Law Symposium Journal*, 5: 117–40.

Indonesian Corruption Watch (2001), 'Menyingkap Tabir Mafia Peradilan (Hasil Monitoring Peradilan ICW), Dipersiapkan untuk Penelitian Pola-pola Korupsi pada Proses Beracara di Peradilan Umum' [Lifting the Curtain on the Court Mafia (Findings from ICW's Court Monitoring), prepared for Research into the Patterns of Corruption Appearing in the General Courts], Jakarta.

Kuok, H. (2006), '"Impeachment" Hakim, Muskilkah?' ['Impeachment' of Judges, Impossible?], *Kompas*, 25 August.

Lev, D.S. (1978), 'Judicial Authority and the Struggle for an Indonesian Rechsstaat', *Law and Society Review*, 13: 37–71.

Lindsey, T. (2001), 'Abdurrahman, the Supreme Court and Corruption: Viruses, Transplants and the Body Politic in Indonesia', pp. 43–67 in D. Kingsbury and A. Budiman (eds), *Indonesia: The Uncertain Transition*, Adelaide: Crawford House Publishing.

Panjaitan, T. (2006), 'Sekali Lagi tentang Putusan MK' [Once Again about the Constitutional Court Decision], *Suara Pembaruan*, 15 September.

Pemberton, J. (1999), 'Open Secrets: Conversations with a Javanese Lawyer, and a Comment', pp. 193–209 in V.L. Rafael (ed.), *Figures of Criminality in Indonesia, the Philippines, and Colonial Vietnam*, Ithaca NY: Cornell University Southeast Asia Program.

Pompe, S. (1996), *The Indonesian Supreme Court: Fifty Years of Judicial Development*, Leiden: Faculty of Law, Leiden University.

Pompe, S. (2002), 'Court Corruption in Indonesia: An Anatomy of Institutional Degradation and Strategy for Recovery', draft report, Washington DC: World Bank June.

Shapiro, M. (1981), *Courts: A Comparative and Political Analysis*, Chicago IL: University of Chicago Press.

Supreme Court (2003), *Policy Paper on Judicial Personnel Management Reform*, Jakarta: Supreme Court of Indonesia.

Susanti, B. (2006), 'Benang Kusut Lembaga Peradilan' [The Tangled Thread of Judicial Institutions], *Kompas*, 29 August.

Volcansek, M. (1996), *Judicial Misconduct: A Cross-national Comparison*, Gainesville FL: University Press of Florida.

Wallace, C. (1998), 'Resolving Judicial Corruption while Preserving Judicial Independence: Comparative Perspectives', *California Western International Law Journal*, 28: 341–51.

World Bank (2003), 'Combating Corruption in Indonesia: Enhancing Accountability for Development', Washington DC: East Asia Poverty Reduction and
Economic Management Unit, World Bank, 20 October.

UN (United Nations) (1985), 'United Nations Basic Principles on the Independence of the Judiciary', Office of the High Commissioner for Human Rights,
available at <http://www.unhchr.ch/html/menu3/b/h_comp50.htm>.

INDEX

INDONESIA UPDATE SERIES

Indonesia Assessment 1988 (Regional Development)
edited by Hal Hill and Jamie Mackie

Indonesia Assessment 1990 (Ownership)
edited by Hal Hill and Terry Hull

Indonesia Assessment 1991 (Education)
edited by Hal Hill

Indonesia Assessment 1992 (Political Perspectives)
edited by Harold Crouch

Indonesia Assessment 1993 (Labour)
edited by Chris Manning and Joan Hardjono

Finance as a Key Sector in Indonesia's Development (1994)
edited by Ross McLeod

Development in Eastern Indonesia (1995)
edited by Colin Barlow and Joan Hardjono

Population and Human Resources (1996)
edited by Gavin W. Jones and Terence H. Hull

Indonesia's Technological Challenge (1997)
edited by Hal Hill and Thee Kian Wie

Post-Soeharto Indonesia: Renewal or Chaos? (1998)
edited by Geoff Forrester

Indonesia in Transition: Social Aspects of Reformasi and Crisis (1999)
edited by Chris Manning and Peter van Diermen

Indonesia Today: Challenges of History (2000)
edited by Grayson J. Lloyd and Shannon L. Smith

Women in Indonesia: Gender, Equity and Development (2001)
edited by Kathryn Robinson and Sharon Bessell

*Local Power and Politics in Indonesia:
Decentralisation and Democratisation* (2002)
edited by Edward Aspinall and Greg Fealy

Business in Indonesia: New Challenges, Old Problems (2003)
edited by M. Chatib Basri and Pierre van der Eng

The Politics and Economics of Indonesia's Natural Resources (2004)
edited by Budy P. Resosudarmo

Different Societies, Shared Futures: Australia, Indonesia and the Region (2005)
edited by John Monfries

Indonesia: Democracy and the Promise of Good Governance (2006)
edited by Ross H. McLeod and Andrew MacIntyre

.